THE ED HUME GARDENING BOOK

Darlene:
Wishing you
all the best!
Ed Hume
4/25/87

THE ED HUME GARDENING BOOK

By ED HUME

HARPER & ROW · PUBLISHERS · NEW YORK

Cambridge   Philadelphia   San Francisco   London   Mexico City   São Paulo   Sydney

1817

FIRST EDITION

Designer: Margaret M. Wagner

Library of Congress Cataloging in Publication Data

Hume, Ed.
The Ed Hume Gardening book.

(Harper colophon books; CN/1028)
Includes index.
1. Gardening.   I. Title.   II. Title: Gardening book.
SB453.H845M   1983   635′.0974   82-48231
ISBN 0-06-091028-3 (pbk.)

83 84 85 86 87 10 9 8 7 6 5 4 3 2 1

Contents

What You Really Need to Know About Gardening But Probably Have Never Been Told

The object of this book is to give you ideas of some of the easiest and most efficient year-round gardening methods.

As you begin gardening, you are going to find that there are probably at least twelve different ways to accomplish any one particular gardening project. Your goal should be to successfully complete any gardening task in the simplest way possible. Once you have succeeded at this, don't listen to anyone. There's always someone standing around the corner who will tell you that you can't do it that way. Baloney! As long as you are having success, don't listen to anyone unless he or she can offer you a simpler way to achieve the same success.

We often make things difficult when it comes to gardening, but you are going to find that gardening is not difficult at all. It is simply a matter of using common sense, taking time to properly prepare the soil, planting at the correct time, and growing crops suited to the climatic conditions of your region.

I don't care how long you have been gardening, there will be times when you have tremendous successes, and times when there are failures, too. Sometimes Mother Nature plays tricks on us, and at other times we do some foolish things without realizing what the result will be. For example, some people assume that if a tablespoon of a product to a gallon of water will do a good job of fertilizing a plant, two tablespoons will do an even better job. That's not the case,

and in fact it will often burn the plant fatally. Another prime example is that we are often fooled by the weather. It's not unusual to have exceptionally nice weather in February or early March, generally followed by a cold snap. If we are fooled by this early good weather and go about planting some of our warm-weather vegetable and annual crops, we stand a good chance of losing them because it is simply too early to plant.

It is always fun to experiment with gardening by trying to grow a few things that don't normally do well in your region, but it is also important to protect yourself by growing those types and varieties of plants that have proven dependable in your region. Children love to plant watermelons, cantaloupes, and other crops that particularly appeal to them. Unfortunately, some of these warm-weather, long-season crops do not do well in your region and the results are apt to be very disappointing. It doesn't hurt to occasionally try them, however. If you select varieties that mature quickly and plant them in a sunny, bright, warm spot, there's a chance they'll make it.

When you buy a plant to include in your garden, it is important to know that it has certain planting limitations. Find out if it grows best in full sun, partial sun and shade, or full shade. Also examine the plant. Every plant has a front side and a back side, and it's important that you get full advantage of a plant by positioning it properly with the bushy, compact, attractive side of the plant forward. The begonia is a perfect example:

Always plant begonias with the point of the leaf forward, because that's the way the flowers face. You must also know whether the plant is eventually going to grow 2 feet, 10 feet, or 150 feet tall. I remember a couple saying that they had purchased three gray-foliage plants a few years ago. They believed the plants would grow to a height of only 2 to 2½ feet under a picture window that was approximately 2 feet off the ground, but found they continually had to prune these plants to keep them down to that height. On inspection it was discovered that the plants were actually trees that would grow over 70 feet tall! Needless to say, the plants had to be moved. Had the couple asked before trying to do it on their own, they would have found many suitable plants that would have accomplished what they were trying to do.

Speaking of advice, where do you go when you have a gardening problem? You should start by taking a sample of the affected leaves, branches, or, if it's a houseplant, the entire plant, to your local reliable garden center clerk, certified nurseryman, or to a local master gardening clinic. They are going to ask you the who-what-when-where-and-why, so be ready to provide information on how you cared for the plant, where it's growing, the type of soil, drainage, and any other special information they should know in order to properly diagnose the problem. Telephoning to ask a question is of little or no value to you; instead, take a sample and get an on-the-spot diagnosis. Phoning to ask about the problem would be like calling the doctor and saying, "I have a headache. What's wrong?"

If you are beginning to landscape a new home, you will find there are several ways to seek landscaping help. One of the ways discussed in this book is to observe what others have done; add your personal touch, and you will usually end up with a beautiful landscape setting. Landscape architects can provide you with a professional plan geared to your family's needs, and they will include the trees and shrubs that will enhance the beauty of your home and provide the family area you desire. Some landscape architects offer a consultation service, which usually costs less than a full-fledged plan. The on-the-spot consultation will provide you with information on how to landscape or relandscape your home without the cost of drawing up a finished plan. Landscape designers provide detailed landscape designs similar to those provided by landscape architects; however, landscape designers are not licensed and are not required to have the detailed knowledge of the landscape architect regarding landscape construction and plant material.

Many landscape contractors provide a landscaping service. This generally includes all forms of construction, placement of plants, and in some cases includes designing as well. Local nurseries and garden centers sometimes provide one or more of these services. If you want to do it on your own, one of the best ways to go about it is to simply snap a picture of a problem area, take it to your local nursery or garden center on a weekday at a time when they are not too busy, and ask for their suggestions. That way you will find out what particular plants are best for that area, yet you will be in a position to make the final choice.

It can become really frustrating when you can't find a specific plant that you want to include in your garden. Maybe it's a plant that grandma, your parents, or your neighbor has and you want to include it in your garden because it's just what you have always wanted. If repeated calls or vis-

its to local nurseries have resulted in disappointment, why not ask them if they can obtain the plant for you? It's impossible for nurseries and garden centers to stock all of the various types of annuals, perennials, and shrubs that grow here, but they may be able to order a specific plant if you ask them. If they can't, ask them if they know where you can get it. It's that simple.

Throughout this book you may find a few gardening terms that you do not understand. Please refer to the glossary in the back of the book, where I have tried to define these terms for you.

Thank-You's

It's quite a challenge and takes many people to edit, type, proof, and put together a gardening book. First, my special thanks go to Harper & Row for having confidence and encouraging me to write this book, and then for all their assistance in putting it into its final form.

My wife, Myrna, and our oldest son, Jeff, have spent countless hours proofreading and reediting my writings. They both have bent over backward to help get thoughts and ideas into their final form.

Janice Mears and Sandra Thwing enthusiastically researched my writings and suggested many gardening topics they, as first-time gardeners, would like to know something about. Their efforts are greatly appreciated.

Cindy Campen and Karen Holden have spent endless hours typing, retyping, and editing copy. The clever artistic drawings are by Janet Ellison, and the photography and cover are by David Hood. To all of these people, I say, "Thank you," a million times over.

A special thank-you goes out to you too! I really appreciate the support you have shown for my television and radio programs and my newspaper articles for the past couple of decades. This book is written for you, with hopes it will make your gardening a little more enjoyable and successful, and your harvest more bountiful. Thank you!

SPRING

Spring is the time when all thoughts turn to love: love and gardening. With the end of winter weather, all gardeners feel the urge to get their hands dirty. This urge is easily satisfied, as there are many projects that can be accomplished now.

Before Old Man Frost departs for the year, you can get a head start on spring by starting seeds indoors. Many varieties of vegetables, perennials, and annuals are easy to start inside. Later, they can be planted in the garden for good eating and year-round color.

Spring is definitely the best time of year to get your hands dirty. How better to do that than by planting? Besides vegetables, perennials, and annuals, you can plant a new lawn, fruit trees, herbs, berries, summer-flowering bulbs, and many types of trees and shrubs. Some of your plants can be used in hanging baskets, and others in St. Valentine's Day arrangements, or May baskets.

Spring is also the time for some pruning. Roses and many evergreens do best when pruned at this time of year.

Don't forget to include the children in your spring gardening. There are many projects they can do, with a little help. This time of year is especially exciting for them.

Remember to do basic spring maintenance. This includes taking care of your lawn and houseplants. Lawns need special care and feeding now. Houseplants may need repotting. These may not be glamorous jobs, but they are well worth spending a little time on.

When the weather turns nice, get out there in the garden and have fun.

Starting Your Seeds Indoors

You can get a jump on the spring gardening season by starting seeds of many vegetables and annuals indoors during the months of March and early April. The result of indoor seeding is about a sixty-day head start on the season, because the plants become established while the soil and weather outside are still unfavorable for planting directly into the garden.

One of the biggest mistakes made by gardeners in the Pacific Northwest is to sow seeds outside too early. Extra-nice weather early in the season fools one into thinking spring has arrived. All too often, cooler weather returns to rot the seeds in the ground or kill the seedling plants when they are young and tender. By starting the seeds indoors, damage from late frost, too much rain, or improper soil conditions can be avoided.

Another problem sometimes encountered as a result of early sowing of seeds is the tendency of some plants to bolt. This means they produce foliage, flower, and go to seed without ever producing a crop. Radishes and some other root crops are among the vegetables susceptible to this. Some of the vegetables that can be started indoors include cabbage, cauliflower, broccoli, lettuce, onions, and tomatoes. All of the annual, perennial, and biennial flowers can also be started this way.

Seeds can be started in practically any room of the house. However, the utility room, basement, and kitchen are the most popular places to start them. Select a spot where they will get as much indirect light as possible. Room temperatures should range between 60 and 70 degrees in order to establish a good, strong, and sturdy growth of your seedling starter plants. If possible, choose a spot where the seedlings will receive some bottom heat, such as on top of the water heater, refrigerator, or dryer. These are ideal spots for starting seeds.

Several types of containers can be used to start seeds indoors. Wooden or plastic flats are often used but are not required. You can substitute clay or plastic pots, cut-off milk cartons, cottage cheese containers, saucers, eggshells, or almost anything deep enough to give the new plants room to become established. The most important concern is that the container chosen be thoroughly cleaned before you use it. A stiff brush and hot water are best to clean clay or plastic pots. Wooden containers should be brushed, cleaned, then protected with an all-purpose insecticide, fungicide spray, or dust. Pots can also be disinfected by soaking them in undiluted chlorine bleach. You will find it easiest to start large seeds—such as peas, beans, corn, cucumbers, pumpkin, and squash—in individual containers. The small to medium-size seeds are easy to simply broadcast in flats, trays, or pots.

Several types of mediums are suitable for starting seeds. Soil from the garden, commercial seed-starting mixes, sand, peat moss, vermiculite, sponge rock, and other soilless mediums are excellent. Be sure to sterilize soil from the garden so there will be no chance of carrying over weed seeds, soil insects, or diseases. This can be accomplished by baking the soil in the oven for two hours at 170 to 180 degrees. Another method is to pour boiling water over the soil, then let it dry out before use.

Sow seeds sparingly, lightly covering with soil. Early indoor seeding will give you a 30- to 60-day jump on the spring gardening season.

As you fill the containers with soil, there are a few things you should keep in mind. First of all, be sure to leave ¼ to ½ inch of space below the rim of the container to provide room for watering the plants without having soil wash over the rim.

Avoid puddling, or the seeds will come to the surface and then settle all together. It is a good practice to moisten the soil thoroughly, then allow the excess water to run off prior to seeding. The soil needs to be kept moist, but should not be allowed to remain too wet.

Now you are ready to sow the seeds. It is easy to sow tiny seeds by the broadcast method. Medium and large seeds can be planted in shallow furrows about ¼ inch deep. Be sure to read the back of each seed packet for specific instructions about the particular type of seed you are starting. Most types of seeds should be covered with a fine layer of the seedling medium. However, some seeds germinate better if they are completely exposed to the light. In our greenhouse I cover newly seeded containers with newspaper until the first seedlings appear, at which time it is removed completely. Some seeds germinate quite rapidly, so check their progress each day. Moisture needs to be checked daily too.

The first few days after sowing are very critical. There is sometimes a tendency to overwater, which could be fatal; it could rot the seeds or encourage damp-off disease. Watch watering very closely. When possible it is best to use room temperature water so you do not shock the young plants with cold tap water.

As the young seeds begin to germinate, it is important to occasionally turn the container in which they are growing so that the seedlings do not become spindly or lopsided as they reach for light. If you give them a one-quarter to one-half turn once every two to three days, the seedlings should grow upright.

When the seedlings have developed one or two sets of true leaves, it is time for thinning and transplanting them into individual pots, flats, or trays. Space plants 2 or 3 inches apart, giving them enough room to develop healthy root systems and bushy top growth.

The young seedling plants can be lightly fertilized about ten days to two weeks after they have been separated or repotted. Be sure to use a non-burning weak solution of fertilizer. Generally, an all-purpose liquid fertilizer is used for this feeding.

Tall or leggy growth should simply be pinched back to encourage bushiness and a sturdier growth habit. Insufficient light, too much water, and temperatures that are too warm can cause your seedlings to develop straggly growth, so avoid these conditions.

Wait until weather conditions are favorable before planting any seedling starter plants outdoors. Most of the seedling plants that you start indoors should not be planted outdoors until all danger of frost has passed. This is usually not until May. So if you want to get a head start on the growing season, early spring is an excellent time to start many annuals, perennials, biennials, and vegetables from seed indoors.

Vegetable Gardening

It is hard to beat the fresh flavor of vegetables grown in your own garden, and springtime is when you should be giving special attention to preparing the soil and planting some of the early vegetable crops. Although some crops can be planted as early as March, the main ones are best planted during May. Here are some of the things you should be doing in the vegetable garden at this time.

First of all, take time to properly prepare the soil. Cultivate to a depth of 8 to 12 inches, mixing in ample amounts of peat moss, compost, and processed manure. The actual quantities of soil additives needed will depend on your soil. When in doubt as to what it needs, have it tested; or test it yourself with an amateur soil test kit. Then you will know exactly what to add to get it into top condition.

An all-purpose garden fertilizer should also be mixed in at planting time. 5-10-10 or a vegetable garden fertilizer is generally used for this purpose. Follow application directions on the label.

RAISED BED AND WIDE ROW GARDENING

Once the soil is prepared, you can either plant at ground level or make raised beds in your vegetable garden. One advantage of using raised beds is that you can get your vegetable gardening off to an early start. Elevating the soil dries it out much more quickly, soil temperatures are warmer, vegetable crops have deeper topsoil in which to grow, and the vegetables reach maturity faster than they do on level ground. Because of our marine climate here in the Northwest, it is important that the soil dry out rapidly. This permits the home gardener to plant much earlier. Also, if your soil tends to be clayish or hardpan and remains soggy until late into the season, the raised bed method of vegetable gardening will help. Whenever you raise the soil in the vegetable garden, rainwater drains into the aisles or walkways between your rows.

It is estimated that soil temperature is between eight to thirteen degrees warmer in a raised bed than on flat ground. This is an especially important factor here in the Pacific Northwest, where we tend to have cool evenings. These few degrees of added warmth will increase seed germination and accelerate early growth. At night, retained heat will protect the young plants from shock due to cold temperatures and allow you to plant earlier in the season than you could on flat ground.

Moreover, if you use the flat bed method in your vegetable garden, the soil in the walkways is generally wasted. By raising the beds, you are able to utilize the prepared soil you would normally be walking on, thus making your topsoil much deeper. Therefore, you will find it much easier to grow deep-rooted crops like carrots, turnips, parsnips, and beets.

It is really quite simple to make a raised vegetable garden area. It can be done either by hand or by tiller. If you use a tiller, simply attach a hiller-furrower attachment to your tiller. This attachment pushes the soil to both sides, raising the topsoil several inches higher and providing you with a raised vegetable garden bed.

If you do this job by hand, you can easily shovel the soil from the walkways and spread it over your raised beds; or you can use a rake, pulling the soil in from the sides. Be sure to rake the raised bed area level so that water does not collect in the low spots. Remember, it is the puddles or standing water in your vegetable garden that keep the soil cool and moist, thus delaying planting time. If the vegetable garden area is raised and leveled properly, the soil will be workable much sooner.

Raised beds can also be enclosed in wood. For example, in my own garden my raised beds are enclosed by 2-by-10's. The beds are 5 feet wide and 20 feet long. I have made mine this way because I find it convenient for me. They are 5 feet wide because I find it easy to reach across this distance from each side for watering, weeding, and harvesting. It is especially practical in our garden because we are so short on space. However, you can make a wide row any width you desire. I understand that the national average is approximately 21 inches.

Another method of gardening is wide row vegetable gardening. This is an especially good method to use for producing an abundant quantity of vegetables in a limited space. Rather than planting in single rows, rows are grouped together, reducing the amount of walking room between rows. In addition to saving space, it saves time, increases yield, and makes harvesting easier.

Here is an example of how much space this conserves. In one wide row bed 2 feet long, I can plant the equivalent of a 48-foot single row of garden carrots. Put another way, a bed 4 feet wide and 20 feet long seeded with carrots is the equivalent of 480 feet of carrots planted in a single row. Wide row planting also means I can expect to harvest up to six times as much produce per foot.

I find that this method of gardening saves me a lot of time, and it is important that I use my time to my best advantage. Watering time is cut down because the lower foliage tends to shade the entire area and reduce evaporation. Because the crops are planted closer together, they tend to crowd out weeds. Fertilizer is conserved, too, because all of the prepared soil is utilized.

Using the wide row method, more than one

row of a particular crop is planted. For example, instead of planting a single row of bush beans, two are planted close together. To make the wide row even wider, plant three, four, five, or more rows close together. Spacing of plants in the rows will depend entirely on the crops grown. Directions on the backs of the seed packets will specify how close together a particular crop should be spaced.

WHEN AND HOW TO PLANT

Pacific Northwest vegetable gardening is divided into two regions: the western slope and the eastern slope. The western slope encompasses the areas west of the Cascade Mountains in western Washington, Oregon, and British Columbia. The eastern slope includes areas east of the Cascade Mountains in Washington, Oregon, British Columbia, Idaho, and Montana. The types and varieties of vegetables grown vary considerably between these two geographical regions. The warmer coastal marine climate of the western slope provides for earlier planting dates, but the cool summer weather necessitates the planting of early-ripening vegetable crops. Although the colder winter weather delays spring planting on the eastern slope, the warmer summer days provide an ideal climate for a broader range of vegetable crops, including watermelons and cantaloupes.

Local conditions must be considered before deciding when to plant your vegetables.

Sometimes there is a tendency to plant vegetable crops too early. It is very important that all of the types of vegetables be planted at the correct planting time. Among the first ones to be planted are the perennial vegetables like artichokes, asparagus, horseradish, and rhubarb. These can usually be planted sometime in February or March. Garden peas, potatoes, and the onion family are the next to be planted. These are followed closely by many other leaf and root crops. Corn and beans are planted in late April or early May, followed by warm-weather crops like vining plants and tomatoes.

The biggest advantage of growing perennials is that they need to be planted only once; they come back year after year to provide a harvestable crop. However, in many cases they should be dug and divided every three to four years. This benefits you because it is a source of new plants.

Rhubarb. One of the most popular perennial vegetables. In fact, more rhubarb is grown in the Puyallup Valley than in any part of the western hemisphere. This immediately tells us that it is an excellent crop for this region. It is relatively easy to grow. About five plants will feed a family of five. It does take considerable space in the garden; spacing should be 24 to 30 inches apart. It is an attractive choice for the ornamental garden as well, because of its large bold leaves. It will do best in soil that is moist but never overwet. Plants getting maximum sunlight will bear best, but location is not a major concern.

Asparagus. Can be planted in individual rows or in the wide row. In fact, this is one plant that can even be included in the landscape because the attractive ferny foliage makes a nice addition to other landscape plantings. Whether planted in rows or in wide beds or in the landscape, space the asparagus about 5 to 9 inches apart. It is estimated that approximately twelve roots are needed to supply the needs of one person. Two-year-old rootstocks are available at most garden outlets. Few if any stocks should be harvested the first year. Asparagus will grow fast in well-drained soil in a spot where the plants will not be disturbed. The best time to fertilize them is in the fall with organic animal manure or with a 5-10-10 garden fertilizer. West of the Cascades, plant them only 2 inches deep.

Horseradish. Grows exceptionally well in the Pacific Northwest. The main concern in planting is that it be placed where its roots can be kept under control; it is a prolific grower. The number of plants grown will depend upon how popular this vegetable is with your family. It grow best in soil that is fertile and well drained.

Globe and Jerusalem artichokes. Globe artichokes are grown for their edible flower heads. Their attractive leaves and ornamental flowers mix very well with flowers and shrubs, making them an excellent choice for the landscaped areas of your garden. Jerusalem artichokes are grown for the tasty white tubers that develop in the soil. This robust grower needs to be placed where the roots can be confined so they will not take over the garden. Both varieties of artichokes can be placed in the garden in March and grow best in soil that has been treated with well-rotted cow or other farm animal manure. Sandy loam-type soil is ideal, but the plants are not fussy about this as long as drainage is good. Plant in a bright sunny part of the garden.

Garden peas. February and March are the months for planting garden peas. However, if soil conditions are not favorable, planting can be delayed into April or May if necessary. Garden peas can be planted in V-shaped furrows or in wide rows. Climbing garden peas are generally planted in individual or double rows, while bush peas are planted in the wide row. Soak the seeds overnight in water and sow the next day, covering them with about an inch of soil. For best air circulation and light exposure, the climbing or tall peas should be planted in a north-south direction. When planting bush peas in the wide row, sow the seeds about 2 inches apart in all directions and about ten rows wide.

Onions. As soon as the soil is workable, you can also plant your onion sets, shallots, and garlic. Like the peas, they can be planted in individual rows or in wide rows. Plant them 1 or 2 inches deep, spacing the sets 3 or 4 inches apart. They can be set slightly closer if you want to pull some of them for early green bunching onions. Onion seeds can be started indoors in March. However, green onion plants should not be planted out until all danger of frost has passed later in the spring.

Potatoes. Another crop that can be planted when the peas and onions are planted. Plant only certified seed potatoes available at garden and feed outlets or the new potatoes from seeds that can be started indoors. Quarter the potatoes and allow them to callous after being cut. Potatoes are often grown in clumps or rows. Plant three or four of the seed potato quarters per hill if grown in clumps. Allow approximately 24 to 30 inches between rows if grown in rows.

Root crops. In April after the garden peas, potatoes, and onions have been planted, it is time to plant many of the other root crops. Carrots, beets, radishes, parsnips, turnips, and rutabagas are among these. Relatively easy to grow, the root crops will need a little special attention to produce at their best.

To succeed with root crops, it is important to pay attention to weather conditions, timing, and soil preparation. Sometimes there is a tendency to plant too early, before conditions are favorable. When this occurs, vegetable root crops will often bypass the development of the crop and instead produce foliage and go to seed. This is a process commonly called "bolting." The use of high-nitrogen fertilizers also causes rank foliage growth instead of root development and causes the crop to bolt. To overcome these conditions, delay planting until the weather is warm enough for the particular crop you are seed-

ing, and avoid the use of high-nitrogen fertilizers just prior to or at planting time.

Vegetable root crops can be grown in individually spaced rows, or in the wide row, or by the intensified method of gardening. However you grow them, be sure they are thinned so that they have sufficient space to develop properly.

Radishes. One of the easiest and quickest root vegetables to grow in the Northwest region. Seed them approximately 1 inch apart in all directions. If grown in rows, space the rows 12 inches apart. You will keep radishes coming all summer long by reseeding at two-week intervals.

Beets. Seed directly into the garden between early April and August. Allow approximately 2 to 3 inches' spacing in rows 12 to 18 inches apart. If you want a continual crop, reseed every two to three weeks. Allow about 2 inches between plants if grown in rows; space the rows 12 to 15 inches apart. They need a bright sunny area and good drainage in order to grow and produce at their best.

Other root crops. Turnips, parsnips, and rutabagas are also popular vegetable root crops. They should be thinned to about 4 inches apart. When grown in rows, space the rows 12 to 18 inches apart.

Beans and corn. May is the month to begin your serious vegetable gardening; and two favorites, beans and corn, can be planted this month. Success with these two vegetables depends upon your selecting the right variety, choosing the right planting spot, and properly preparing the soil. Summer care is equally important.

Both beans and corn are warm-weather crops and should not be seeded into the garden until weather conditions are favorable. In other words, do not seed beans or corn until all danger of frost has passed. Cold soil and cool weather are not to their liking and are apt to check the germination of the seeds.

Since both beans and corn are tall-growing crops, it is important to plant them in a location where they will not shade your other vegetable crops. If possible, run the rows in a north-south direction for best sunlight exposure and good air circulation. Of course, bush beans are lower-growing and can be placed among the vegetables that grow about the same height.

Sow the seeds of both of these vegetables approximately 1 to 1½ inches deep. In a large vegetable garden, the rows are generally spaced 30 to 36 inches apart. In limited space, they can be grown much closer together. In fact, bush beans can be grown in the wide row: Simply seed a bed of beans, usually 18 to 24 inches in width; then space young seedlings 3 to 4 inches apart in all directions.

Corn and pole beans will also need to be thinned, and it is generally recommended that corn be thinned to about 12 inches apart when it is 2 to 3 inches high. Pole beans grown in rows should be thinned to about 6 inches apart. Beans grown in a hill should be thinned to three to five of the strongest plants.

Special attention should be given to the cultivation of both beans and corn. Since weeds rob valuable nutrients from the plants and also serve as hosts to many insects and diseases, it is important that they be pulled and destroyed. Both of these crops have very shallow roots, so it is best not to use a cultivating device close to the row, for you are apt to damage the surface feeder roots. In other words, it is best to pull the weeds close to the plants. Be especially careful not to disturb the bean plants after they begin to bloom—this can cause the blossoms to fall off before the beans are formed. Young seedling plants are susceptible to damage from both slugs and birds, so steps should be taken to protect them.

Pay special attention to watering vegetable crops. If you water thoroughly, it is not necessary to water as often. You can water by the irrigation method or by sprinkler. Morning is the best time to water, and if you are in doubt as to whether the crops need watering, simply scrape a small patch of soil between the rows to a depth of an inch or two to check soil moisture.

TOMATOES

As the weather warms a little later in the month of May, conditions become favorable for planting tomatoes. The key to success is the selection of

Select early-maturing varieties of tomatoes that will ripen during our short season.

early-producing varieties. Some extensive research has been done over the past few years to determine which varieties bear early, are productive, and are least susceptible to disease and other tomato problems. These tests have included some of the old-time favorites and some of the more recent new hybrid varieties. The research also included methods of growing tomatoes.

The following are a few of the varieties that received the highest ratings in the tomato research work done in western Washington:

IPB. This variety has been one of the researchers' favorites and consistently bears early year after year. The small to medium fruit is quite flavorful, but I think a little on the acid side. The skin tends to be a little tough. IPB is self-pollinizing and indeterminate in its growth habit, meaning that it can grow several feet high; so it will need staking of some kind. The leaves of this variety tend to look more like those of a potato than of a tomato.

Early Girl. Commercial growers say that they grow and sell more of this variety than any other tomato. It is an early medium-size tomato. The bright red, meaty fruit continues all season long. It is an indeterminate variety, so it will require some type of support.

Pixie. This variety grows only about 4 feet high. It is low in acid, has medium-size fruit that is sweet, and firm and mild in flavor. This is an excellent variety to grow in the garden or in containers on the patio or lanai. The sturdy plants have very attractive dark green leaves.

Pik Red (formerly Red Pak). This extra-large beefsteak-type tomato bears early in the Northwest garden. The firm fruit is low in acid and excellent for slicing. Like Pixie, it has a determinate growth habit, eventually obtaining a height of only about 4 feet. My favorite variety.

Sweet 100. In the Hume household, this is the favorite type of all cherry tomatoes. It gets its name from its sweetness and its ability to produce up to 100 cherry-size tomatoes per cluster if ideal tomato conditions exist. It is an indeterminate variety, so it may grow several feet tall and require some kind of support.

Other varieties that bear quite well include Solly's Red Dwarf Hybrid, Presto, Springset, and New Yorker, to mention just a few. Of the novelty tomatoes, yellow pear, patio, red cherry, Golden Jubilee, and Tiny Tim proved quite productive here.

It is exceptionally important that tomatoes be planted in a sunny, bright location in the garden. A south or west exposure is ideal, and, in fact, if you can grow them up against a wall or the side of a house or fence that faces south or west where they get reflected sunlight, they will do even better. Tomatoes can also be grown in containers on a patio, lanai, or sunny deck. Some varieties can even be grown in hanging baskets.

I think one of the biggest mistakes made in growing tomatoes is that of overfertilizing them. In my own garden I find that they do better if they are starved a little for food. At planting time I give them only a small quantity of 5-10-10 or well-rotted or processed manure along with one cup of dolomite lime. I do not feed them again all summer unless the foliage turns yellow during the summer growing season. I find that if the plants are continually fed, they tend to develop too much rank foliage growth instead of flowers and fruit. You might experiment a little to find out which method works best for you.

Give special attention to the watering of tomatoes. Sometimes there is a tendency to keep them too wet, which stimulates rank foliage growth. It is a good practice to water the plants thoroughly and then allow the surface soil to dry before thoroughly rewatering. Tomatoes will benefit from watering during the morning hours rather than at night. Proper watering during the morning hours allows the soil to warm up and dry out before cooler evening temperatures set in.

STAKING

The standard, conventional way of growing tomatoes is to place one to three stakes in the ground near the plant; as the tomato vines begin to grow, they are held in place by tying them with twist ties to the support stakes. Keep in mind that some varieties will do best without support of any kind, so avoid staking these. A common mistake made in staking tomatoes is to use stakes that are too small or too weak to adequately support your tomato vines. Be sure to select stakes sturdy enough and long enough to do the job properly.

CAGES

In recent years tomato cages have become a very popular way to grow tomatoes. Large-mesh fencing, concrete-reinforced wire, or hog wire is usually used for the cages. It is important that the wire have large openings so you can reach through and pick the ripe fruit at harvest time.

Select a wire that has about 4- to 6-inch openings. Three-foot-high fencing is generally used for the lower-growing varieties of tomatoes, while 5-foot-high fencing is used for taller-growing varieties. You will need approximately 5 feet of wire to make an 18-inch cage (which is generally suitable for most tomato varieties). However, if you prefer to make a 24-inch-diameter cage, it will require about 6½ feet of fencing. Simply form a circle with the wire and overlap and bend the ends. Set the cage over the plant so the tomato plant is situated in the center. Next, press the bottom edge into the ground about 2 to 4 inches. During the growing season, as the tomato plant grows up through the center of the cage, the wire provides all the support it will need, so it will not be necessary to stake or tie your tomato plants.

TIRES

Another excellent way of growing tomatoes. Actually, if you have an old automobile or truck tire, all you need to do is place the tire around your tomato vine, and simply allow the plant to grow right up through the center of the tire. The black of the tire radiates heat and creates an excellent environment for the plant, keeping the soil temperature warmer at night. Again, it is not necessary to support the plant in any other way. Tires provide sufficient support for small to medium tomatoes. For tall-growing tomato varieties, it is often a good practice to use two tires, one on

top of the other, for added support. It is not uncommon for plants grown this way to yield ripe fruit several days sooner than those grown by conventional methods.

TOMATO RING

This is really a method of growing tomatoes around a compost pile. To use this method, simply bend wire fencing into a 5- to 6-foot-diameter ring, then plant the tomatoes around the outside of the fencing. It doesn't make any difference whether you use small or large mesh in this case, because it is a completely different method from that of caging tomatoes. Throw all your garden refuse, including grass clippings, fallen leaves, and unused plant parts, into the center interior of the ring and actually build a conventional compost pile inside the ring. As this material decomposes, it will continue to feed the plants. As your tomato vines grow, tie them to the fencing with twist ties, nylon stockings, or similar tying material. You can space tomato plants about 2½ to 3 feet apart around the exterior of the tomato ring. Cucumbers and squash can also be grown in the same way by tying the vines to the fencing.

POTS

Over the years, I have had excellent success in growing tomato plants in containers on the patio, deck, or lanai, especially where they get reflected sunlight. Container growing of tomatoes is especially beneficial because you have complete control of watering and fertilizing of each individual plant. It also offers you the opportunity to grow tomatoes in the hottest, sunniest spot in the garden.

VEGETABLE GARDEN MAINTENANCE

As the weather begins to warm up in late spring, weed growth usually becomes more active. Keep weeds pulled or cultivated out of the garden area because they can be hosts to insects and diseases. Left unchecked, they will go to seed, compounding the weed problem later in the season. You can simply pull the weeds by hand or use a hoe or fork to remove them.

As your new seedling vegetable plants begin to germinate, they are very susceptible to damage by slugs. Special attention should be given to the task of controlling them. If baits are used, they should be applied at the perimeter of the vegetable garden to attract the slugs out of the garden or help control them before they enter the garden area. (See discussion of slug control on pp. 137–139.)

Black bean aphids and maggots may also be a problem at this time. Maggots attach themselves to and spoil root crops. To help avoid this problem, apply the correct amount of 4 percent Diazinon dust at planting time, following application directions carefully. Or organic gardeners can cover the crop with screen-door cloth, which keeps the moth from laying its eggs, hence no maggots. Use an all-purpose vegetable garden dust or spray to control black bean aphids. If you are in doubt as to which product to use, consult your local certified nurseryman, master gardener, or reliable garden clerk.

SEEDLING STARTER PLANTS

One way to get a head start on the spring gardening season is by planting out seedling starter plants of many vegetables. When you purchase these plants, take time to pick out sturdy, bushy, healthy ones. Avoid plants that appear stunted, off-color, or spindly in their growth habit. Keep in mind, however, that the largest plants are not always the best buy. In fact, they often go through a certain amount of shock in the process of transplanting, while the smaller, younger plants tend to transplant with little or no setback.

Some bedding plants are available in individual pots, while others are in seedling starter trays of two to nine seedlings per tray. The individually potted ones are generally those that are either more expensive to grow or difficult to transplant. The actual number of plants per tray will depend on the cost of the seed, growth habit, and amount of growing room needed. A label on the end of each flat should give you all the information about growing the particular plant: whether it grows best in sun or shade, its eventual height, and approximately how far apart the plants should be spaced to grow at their best. When it comes to the various varieties of vegetable plants, be certain that you select those varieties that will grow and produce in a relatively short growing season.

The soil around your seedling starter plants should be moistened before the plants are removed from their pots and trays so that the soil will cling to the roots, lessening transplant shock. In some cases, it will be possible for you to pull the plants apart with your fingers; in other cases, the roots will be so compact and vigorous that it will be necessary to cut them apart with a knife.

Be aware of planting times and locations before you plant outside. Get your vegetable garden off to a good start this spring by selecting top-quality seedling starter plants.

COMPANION PLANTING

As you are planting your vegetable garden, you may want to try placing the various vegetable crops so you can take advantage of their natural friends. This is called "companion gardening." If you already planted your vegetable garden, you may want to make some changes in subsequent plantings. Following is a list of the top twelve vegetables and their ideal companion plants:

Beans. Like celery and cucumbers, but dislike onions and fennel.

Beets. Bush beans, lettuce, onions, kohlrabi, and most members of the cabbage family are companion plants. Keep the pole beans and mustard away from them.

Cabbage. Celery, dill, onions, and potatoes are good companion plants. Cabbages dislike strawberries, tomatoes, and pole beans.

Carrots. Leaf lettuce, radishes, onions, and tomatoes are their friends. Plant dill at the opposite end of the garden.

Corn. Pumpkin, peas, beans, cucumbers, and potatoes are nice companion plants. Keep the tomatoes away from them.

Cucumbers. Like corn, peas, radishes, beans, and sunflowers; dislike aromatic herbs and potatoes, so keep them away.

Lettuce. Grows especially well with onions. Strawberries, carrots, radishes, and cucumbers are also friends and good companion plants.

Onions. Plant them near lettuce, beets, strawberries, and tomatoes; but keep them away from peas and beans.

Peas. Carrots, cucumbers, corn, turnips, and radishes, plus beans, potatoes, and aromatic herbs are their friends. Keep peas away from onions, garlic, leeks, and shallots.

Radishes. This is one vegetable that has a lot of friends. Radishes are excellent companions for beets, carrots, spinach, and parsnips. They grow well with cucumbers and beans. It is said that summer planting near leaf lettuce makes radishes more tender. Avoid planting radishes near cabbage, cauliflower, Brussels sprouts, broccoli, kohlrabi, or turnips.

Squash. Icicle radishes, cucumbers, and corn are among their friends.

Tomatoes. Carrots, onions, and parsley are companion plants. Keep the cabbage and cauliflower away from them.

BEST VARIETIES

The following are a few of the most popular types and varieties of vegetables for this region:

Artichokes. Green Globe (edible flowers), Jerusalem (edible roots).

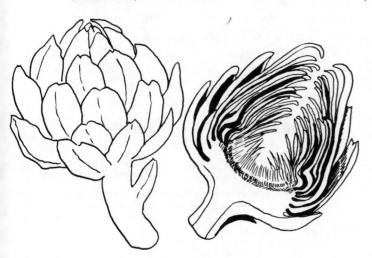

Asparagus. Mary Washington, California 500, Paradise, Washington Giant.

Bush Beans. Tendercrop, Tendergreen, Yellow Wax, Blue Lake.

Pole Beans. Blue Lake, Oregon Giant, Kentucky Wonder, Horticultural.

Beets. Detroit Dark Red, Cylindra, Early Wonder, Ruby Queen, Burpee Golden.

Broccoli. Waltham 29 (Northwest 29), Italian Green Sprouting, Green Duke.

Brussels Sprouts. Long Island Improved, Jade Cross, Green Gem.

Cabbage. Early Jersey Wakefield, Golden Acre, Danish Ball Head, Red Acre.

Carrots. Imperator, Danvers Half-long, Nantes, Spartan Sweet, Chantenay Red Cored.

Cauliflower. Early Snowball, Snow Crown, Snow King.

Celery. Utah (plant in June).

Chard. Large White Rib, Lucullus, Rhubarb.

Chinese Cabbage. Wong Bok, Early Hybrid G.

Collards. Vates, Georgia.

Corn. Early Sunglow, Golden Bantam, Spring Gold, Jubilee, Earliking, Morning Sun, Kandy Korn.

Cucumbers. SMR 58, Early Marketer, Burpee Hybrid, Burpless, Patio-Pik (Bush).

Endive. Green Curled and Deep Heart.

Garlic. Elephant, and standard varieties.

Kale. Dwarf Blue or Green Curled Scotch.

Kohlrabi. White Vienna, Purple Vienna.

Leek. American Flag, Giant Mussleburg.

Lettuce. Leaf: Grand Rapids, Salad Bowl.
  Bibb: Buttercrunch, Summer Bibb, Green Ice.
  Head: Great Lakes, Ithaca.
  Romaine: Paris Island, Dark Green.

Mustard Greens. Fordhook Fancy, Tendergreen.

Onions. Early Yellow Globe, Red Globe, Walla Walla, Sweet Spanish Strains, Evergreen White Bunching.

Parsley. Paramount, Triple Moss Curled.

Parsnips. Hollow Crown, Model.

Peas. Tall Telephone (Alderman), Little Marvel, Aspen, Green Arrow, Aurora; Edible Pod: Sugar snap, SugarRae (bush sugarsnap), Oregon Sugar Pod.

Peppers. California Wonder, Yolo Wonder, Hungarian Wax (hot).

Potatoes. Seed: Explorer.
  Early: Norgold, White Rose.
  Late: Netted Gem, Kennebec.
  Red: Red Pontiac, Norland, Red La Soda.

Pumpkin. Jack O'Lantern, Small Sugar, Big Max, Connecticut Field.

Radishes. Cherry Belle, Early Scarlet Globe, Comet, Champion, Icicle (long), All Seasons (white).

Rhubarb. Crimson Wine, Victoria, Strawberry, Valentine, Canada Red.

Rutabagas. American Purple Top.

Spinach. Bloomsdale, New Zealand, Northland, Winter Bloomsdale.

Squash. Summer: Zucchini Dark Green, Patty Pan, Scaloppini, Early Summer Crookneck.
  Winter: Acorn, Blue Hubbard, Butternut, Table Queen, Spaghetti.

Tomatoes. Pik Red, Early Girl, IPB, Pixie, New Yorker, Springset, Red Dwarf Hybrid, Willamette.
  Cherry: Red Cherry, Sweet 100, Tiny Tim.
  Novelties: Yellow Pear, Golden Jubilee.

Turnips. Purple Top, Tokyo Cross, Tokyo Market.
  Greens: Seven Tops, Shogoin.

Needless to say, countless other varieties of vegetables do well in the Pacific Northwest, and if you have a favorite variety that has been especially productive in your garden, by all means continue to grow it. At the same time you might want to try a few of these varieties so that you can compare results.

Spring-Flowering Perennials

It wasn't very many years ago that perennials were considered to be an essential part of landscaping. Current trends in modern landscaping often overlook them as a source of seasonal color in the garden, yet they still have a lot to offer. Perennials have many advantages. They are permanent plants. Most flower for a considerable length of time, and at a time when the garden is lacking in color. Many start to bloom in earliest spring, and others fill the gap between the spring-flowering shrubs and the summer annuals.

Since spring-flowering perennials come in such a wide range of sizes, shapes, and flower colors, they are really very versatile garden plants. The low-growing varieties are often used in rockeries, outcroppings, as ground cover plants, and as low border plants in flower and shrub beds. The medium-height spring-flowering perennials are often combined with the lower-growing varieties of evergreens and flowering plants, while the tall perennials are used as background color in landscape plantings. They can be used individually or in groups of three, five, or seven plants each for a pleasing mass effect.

The following are just a few of the varieties available:

Violets. Many of the common varieties have a sweet fragrance. The small delicate flowers and low leaves combine well with other shade plants. Since they are low-growing, use them as foreground plants.

Primroses. There is a wide selection of varieties and types of primroses. Many start flowering in the fall, continue throughout the winter, and reach their peak of bloom in springtime. Colors span the color spectrum. The three most popular types are English, Auricula, and Candelabra. They vary in height from just a few inches tall to the Candelabra types, which are often 3 or more feet. Although most varieties have single flowers, some are double. Most varieties do best in filtered sunlight.

Columbine (Aguilegia). This spring perennial adds interest to any garden. It comes in a wide range of brilliant and pastel colors. The combination of attractive colors and dainty foliage makes it especially nice in the garden.

Doronicum daisy. This variety has bright yellow single flowers that stand out above the dark green foliage. There are two popular varieties grown in the Northwest. One reaches a height of about 15 inches and the other may become 2 feet tall. These are colorful plants in the garden, and they make excellent cut flowers for use in the home.

Bergenia. The variety crassifolia is probably best known in this area. The large leaves give it the common name of Elephant Ears. Early flower clusters are often rose, pink, or lilac shades. It is often grown as a rockery plant but is suitable anywhere in the garden.

Lupine. Varieties of lupines range in shades of blue, white, pink, or red. The flowering season is generally May through July. Growing heights range between 2 and 3 feet. It is excellent in partial shade or full sun.

Wallflowers. Most do best in full sun or partial sun and shade. Heights vary by variety; some are low-growing while others grow to a height of 2½ feet. Orange is the predominant color, but they come in other colors as well. The normal flowering season is May to July. This is a biennial rather than a perennial. It is excellent to use in beds or borders, and is often started from seed in summer for the following year.

English daisies. They are available in red, white, and pink. Normal height is usually less than 6 inches. They are excellent for borders and rockeries. Some begin flowering as early as March. They do best in full sun or part sun and shade.

Bleeding heart (Dicentra). This is a very fine perennial for the shady garden. The delicate texture of the foliage is an excellent background for the hanging heart-shaped blooms. Pink and white varieties are the most common. They are native to many parts of the Northwest. Their ultimate height may reach 18 inches.

Here are a few of the low-growing perennials that you may want to consider for your garden These are especially good for borders and rockeries:

Phlox subulata. Better known as creeping phlox. Ohme Gardens in Wenatchee, Washington, is famous for its plantings of it. Phlox also does well on the west side of the Cascades. It normally comes into bloom around Mother's Day. It grows in a wide range of colors, including white, pink, rose, magenta, and lilac. An excellent rockery or ground cover plant.

Iberis. Better known as candytuft, it has pure white flowers that make it an excellent companion plant with other rockery perennials because it makes the other colors really stand out. It usually starts to bloom in midspring and continues into June.

Aubrietia. One of the most popular spring-flowering perennials, it comes in a wide range of colors. Violet, rose, and lilac are most often chosen. Some varieties have single flowers; others are double. They usually grow to about 6 inches in height and spread very rapidly. They can be used in any part of the garden, but are especially favored in the rockery because of their habit of cascading down over rocks.

Alyssum saxatile. It is often called Basket of Gold and is chosen for its bright yellow color. It grows about 1 foot tall. A light yellow variety, Lutea, is also available.

Arabis. Rock cress is the common name of this perennial. It has long been a popular spring-flowering plant. It is available in shades of pink, rose, and white, and it blooms profusely. Some varieties have single flowers; others are double. It is great with the other rockery perennials. It usually grows less than 12 inches in height and spreads rapidly. The foliage of many varieties is gray-green, making this an attractive plant throughout the year.

Forget-me-not. Several varieties are very colorful in the spring garden. They are easily started from seed. The taller varieties have long been favorites, but the new dwarf varieties in pink, white, and blue are popular for borders or mass plantings. They bloom about the same time as the spring-flowering bulbs. The regular varieties will reach about a foot in height, but some are even taller. The flowers on these varieties are generally bright vivid blue with white eyes.

Euphorbia. Several varieties are available, and many have brilliant yellow-green flowers. It is an interesting plant family.

Saxifraga. There are several varieties with a wide range of growing habits and a height of 3 inches to 3 feet. Foliage texture and flowers vary depending upon the one selected. White, pink, rose, yellow, or lilac flowers are available.

Lithospermum. Their bright blue flowers combine well with the other spring-flowering rockery plants. They make an excellent ground cover plant. Dark green foliage remains on the plant most of the year, and the flowers are a bright vivid blue.

Take care when selecting perennials. It is possible to choose them for sun, shade, or semisun and shade. Because many bloom in the spring, they are ideal companion plants for such spring-flowering shrubs as rhododendrons, azaleas, camellias, magnolias, and the spring-flowering trees and bulbs. They require very little upkeep in the garden.

Most of these perennials do best in well-drained soil. Dig an extra-large planting hole, because planting time is the only time to get nutrients directly into the root zone. The addition of a nonburning transplanting fertilizer, processed manure, or well-rotted manure to your existing soil is beneficial. Peat moss, compost, or leaf mold mixed with the soil is also useful to the plants. Be sure to plant your spring-flowering perennials so that the top of the rootball is level with the soil surface.

The best time to fertilize spring-flowering perennials is in late February or early June. A fish fertilizer or all-purpose liquid or dry garden fertilizer is generally used to feed them.

Any spindly growth that develops on these plants should be pinched back to encourage bushiness. When they have finished flowering, simply remove the dead flowers to keep the plants looking their best. The removal of spent flowers will often encourage additional blossoming.

Be on the lookout for slugs—they love the young tender growth of many perennials and also find the low-growing foliage of many perennials to be an ideal nesting place. It is often a good practice to initiate slug control procedures (see pp. 137–139) in areas where perennials are grown. Continue to be on the lookout for slugs throughout the spring, summer, and fall.

If you have some established plants that need to be divided, do so during early summer or early fall. July and August are most often set aside for this task. If you have some that are not doing well, it is probably because they need to be divided or need additional nutrients.

Water your garden thoroughly whenever the soil begins to dry. Do this early in the day if possible. An inch-thick mulch of organic material around perennials will reduce the need to water and will keep the weeds down as well.

Add a bright spot of color and some permanence to your spring garden by growing some of the spring-flowering perennials.

Selecting and Planting Annuals

Spring is the time when gardeners get anxious to begin planting summer-flowering annuals. Remember, an annual is a plant that completes its life cycle in a single year—it grows, flowers, goes to seed, and dies in a single season. A little extra-special care can keep them growing and flowering for the longest possible time. On the other hand, neglect of annual plants will generally result in their quick demise. They are tender, so be sure to wait until weather conditions are favorable before planting them outdoors. There are quite a few hardy types that can be planted quite early in the warmer areas of the Northwest.

If you live in the warmer metropolitan areas, you can often plant much earlier than someone who lives in cooler suburban areas. If you have lived in your area for any length of time you undoubtedly know how early you can plant. But, if you are new to the area, you may want to check with a neighbor or local nursery for advice about the best time to begin planting summer-flowering annuals.

If you find some particularly nice flowering annuals that you want to include in your garden but the weather is still too cold, keep them indoors in a nice bright spot until conditions are favorable for planting them outdoors. A utility room, a covered porch, a garage, or an unheated basement is an ideal place to keep them until the weather warms up. Some can be planted in March or April, but many need to wait until at least May.

Most annuals grow easily and bloom prolifically throughout the summer season. They are very versatile—there are types suitable for borders, massing, edging, background planting, and the rockery, and just about every hue in the color spectrum is available. With a little planning, it is possible to put together some outstanding combinations.

Among the most hardy annuals to plant out in late March or early April are the carnations, pansies, and violas. Snapdragons, stock, alyssum, and lobelia are all sturdy, hardy annuals and will do well in areas where the temperatures seldom go below 40 degrees. Remember, if the temperature drops suddenly and there is any chance of frost, these plants should all be covered with newspaper or some type of light cloth for added protection.

One of the earliest annuals to come into bloom is the marigold. Young seedling plants are often available in flower as early as April. Keep in mind that they are very susceptible to frost damage. If the weather suddenly turns cold, they will definitely need to be covered.

Petunias are undoubtedly one of the most popular of the summer-flowering annuals. They are moderately hardy, but will need protection should the weather turn cold. In most areas it is best to wait until late April to plant them.

Some varieties of annuals are excellent for low borders in the summer garden. They are available in a wide range of colors, and many can be planted during May. In the normally colder locations, planting should be delayed until all danger of frost has passed.

"Border plants" are generally those annuals that remain under 12 inches in height. Choose the ones that have a bushy, uniform habit of growth. Some of the most popular ones include dwarf lobelia, ageratum, alyssum, dwarf salvia, French marigolds, wax begonias, impatiens, pansies, verbena, and nemesia. Dwarf snapdragons and petunias are used for borders too, but these plants are more effective in mass plantings. Pansies, impatiens, and violas grow and flower best in the shade garden. Lobelia, wax begonias, and alyssum can be used in part sun and shade.

If you intend to plant annuals in the shade, be aware of the varieties meant for shaded gardens. Impatiens is one of the most popular summer-flowering annuals for the shaded garden. These colorful plants (commonly called Bizzy Lizzy) are available in a wide range of colors. Both single and double-flowering varieties come in pink, red, orange, white, and some that are two-toned. Their bushy habit of growth makes them excellent plants for borders, mass plantings, or container plantings.

The newer New Guinea impatiens are also popular shade plants. In addition to attractive flowers, many of these impatiens also have multicolored leaves. These plants can tolerate more sun and are often planted in semishade.

The multicolored foliage of the coleus makes it an attractive shade plant. This foliage color is generally obtained if the plant is situated where it gets indirect light. Coleus plants tend to develop seed heads, which should be picked off as they distract from the beautiful color of the leaves.

Cinerarias are another popular choice for the

shaded or semishaded garden. The clusters of daisylike blossoms come in a wide range of colors and color combinations. Their only drawback is that they are sometimes susceptible to aphid infestations.

Many varieties of annuals do best in full sun. Among the most popular sun annuals are marigolds, petunias, asters, zinnias, snapdragons, lobelia, and alyssum. Their wide range of growing heights and flower colors makes them very versatile. You will find the taller-growing varieties of godetia, clarkia, cosmos, zinnias, snapdragons, and marigolds among the best annuals for mass planting, background plants, and borders. If you want to grow annuals primarily for cut flowers, you will find marigolds, stock, zinnias, cosmos, and godetia excellent choices.

Some of the annuals that are all too often overlooked include salpiglossis, cockscomb, Iceland poppy, the new varieties of California poppy, nemesia, schizanthus, Marguerite daisy, moss rose, and Livingston daisy.

Both fuchsias and geraniums are popular summer-flowering annuals. The upright and spreading fuchsias are special favorites in the Pacific Northwest. They come in a wide range of colors and color combinations and enjoy a prolific flowering season. They do best in part shade, protected from the hot midday sun. The upright varieties are generally used for bedding or container plantings; trailing varieties are best for hanging baskets. Geraniums are considered moderately har-

dy, but if the weather turns cold all of a sudden, they will need some protection.

WINTERED-OVER ANNUALS

If you wintered-over fuchsias and geraniums from last summer, here are some suggestions to help get them off to a good start this spring. The old soil in which they are growing probably has been depleted of nutrients by now, so it is a good idea to repot wintered-over plants with fresh soil. A commercial potting or planting soil can be used or you can mix your own. If you mix your own, it should contain about one-third each of peat moss, sandy loam, and compost or leaf mold. The advantage of a commercial potting soil is that it has been sterilized, so there is no chance of introducing soil-borne insects or diseases around the roots of the plants. Place the plants in the soil at the same depth as they were previously growing. Be sure to leave enough space above the soil line and below the rim of the pot to allow for watering. Following are some more specific tips on the care of wintered-over fuchsias and geraniums:

Fuchsias. Prune severely around April. The old stocks do not produce green foliage and will remain bare and ugly if not removed. Severe pruning will result in abundant green foliage. Hanging basket plants should be cut back to the edge of the basket and approximately 6 to 8 inches above soil level. Place the plants in a light area where the temperature is between 55 and 65 degrees. Begin a monthly feeding program and a regular watering schedule. Pinch off any leggy or spindly growth that develops.

Geraniums. After repotting, the plants should be placed in a bright, sunny room. Temperatures should be between 55 and 70 degrees. Pinch off leggy growth to encourage bushiness. A regular schedule of watering and monthly feeding should begin. Plants kept over the winter are slow to begin flowering the second year, so it is important to bring them out of their dormancy as soon as possible in early spring.

STARTING ANNUALS FROM SEED

Many annuals can be planted from seed sown directly into the garden. Planting instructions on the backs of the seed packets will tell you where to sow, how to space, and approximate germination times.

After you have prepared the soil, you are ready to seed. Simply broadcast the seed over the prepared area, covering it with the correct amount of soil. Some seeds should not be covered with soil at all (see packet instructions), whereas others will require a light covering. Be careful to broadcast the seed as evenly as possible, firming the soil gently after broadcasting. This can be done with the back of a rake, with a hoe, gently with the palm of your hand, or with a flat board. Keep the seeds moist but not overwet until they have germinated.

Nasturtiums are probably one of the easiest of all annuals to start from seed. They will grow and flower at their best in rather poor soil where they get limited attention. Simply broadcast the large seeds and cover them with about half an inch of soil. Since nasturtium seedlings are difficult to transplant, it is best to start them in their permanent location, spacing them about 6 to 12 inches apart. The dwarf varieties are generally used for bedding. Tall varieties are used for containers or where a trailing or vining plant is desired.

Many other summer-flowering annuals are easily started from seed. One of my favorites is the godetia. Like the nasturtium, it thrives on a certain amount of neglect. The colorful flowers are quite prolific and offer a bright spot of color to the summer garden.

One of the quickest low-growing types of summer-flowering annuals is the alyssum. The white-flowering varieties are best known and most frequently grown, but there are also pink and lavender varieties. Sunflowers are another easy plant to grow. The tall varieties are especially spectacular, and the colorful flowers also provide food for the birds.

If you are looking for an unusual early-summer-flowering annual that is easy to start from seed, then salpiglossis (or "painted tongue," as it is commonly called) may be just the plant for you.

It is a real conversation piece in the garden, and the unusual flowers can be cut for arrangement. The plants range in height from 18 inches to 3 feet at maturity. The flowers are trumpet-shaped and often multicolored.

Clarkia and cosmos are two other annuals that are easy to start from seed. These old-time favorites are once again becoming popular summer-flowering annuals. Both can be cut and used in flower arrangements.

COLOR SPOTS

If you are looking for almost instant color, you should begin with seedling starter plants or "color spots." Seedling starter plants are often chosen because they give you about a 60-day jump on the normal growing season. They are available in trays of four, six, nine, or twelve plants each. You may also have some of your own that you started indoors earlier in the spring. Some of

the more difficult types of annuals to seed are almost always started in this way in March or early April. All seedlings can be set outside by late May.

Here are a few pointers to help those of you who want to choose seedling plants from your local nursery or garden centers:

1. Select bushy, sturdy, healthy-appearing plants.

2. Avoid purchasing oversize plants, or plants that have been overcrowded and are out of shape; they have been in containers too long and seldom do well in the garden.

3. Avoid plants that are too small to have had time to establish a good rooting structure in the trays.

Before removing plants from pots, moisten the soil thoroughly so that it will cling to the roots and minimize transplant shock.

4. Do not think that the plants you buy must already be flowering. Plants that are not yet in bloom will transplant better.

Before planting seedlings or seeds, take time to properly prepare the soil. First, rake the area to remove all debris, weeds, and large stones. Plants will do best if you cultivate to a depth of about 8 to 12 inches. This may be impossible if you are seeding between existing trees and shrubs; simply scratching the soil may have to suffice in such locations. Next add a little processed manure, peat moss, or compost if it is available. You should also add the correct amount of 5-10-10 or a rose fertilizer as you prepare the soil. A little dolomite lime or charcoal is also beneficial.

Planting and spacing requirements vary for the various annuals, so read the backs of the seed packets for directions. If you are planting seedling starter plants, you will find a label on the end of each flat that specifies location and spacing requirements for that particular plant.

Because annuals complete their growing cycle in less than a year, they need special care as to watering, feeding, and insect and disease control.

It is almost impossible to stand in one place and water annuals properly by hand. Instead, set the sprinkler and let it run until the moisture has penetrated to a depth of about 6 inches. Taller-growing plants that might be weighted down by overhead watering should be watered instead by the irrigation method.

Annuals are rapid-growing plants that benefit greatly from monthly applications of an all-purpose plant fertilizer. A rose, garden, fish, or all-purpose liquid fertilizer can be used for this job. Read and follow application directions on the label of the product you use.

Don't hesitate to pinch plants back if they get a bit leggy. This encourages bushiness, which generally results in more flowers as well. The older varieties often need to be pinched back at planting time. Many of the newer hybrid varieties grown today are self-branching, and pinching is not necessary in many cases. Once the plants go to seed, they will die. Therefore, spent flowers should be picked as they appear. This will also keep the plants looking nice and encourage bushiness.

If annuals are placed where the air is stagnant or if you choose a variety susceptible to mildew, steps should be taken to control the problem if it appears. A fungicide like Benomyl, Phaltan, Funginex, or Captan can be used for this purpose.

Young plants need protection from slugs, who love tender growth, so follow a slug control program wherever annuals are grown (see pp. 137–139). Weeds also compete with the plants for survival, so it is important to keep them pulled.

Insects vary from one plant to another. Should aphids, whitefly, root weevil, or caterpillars infest a planting, it is wise to spray or dust with an all-purpose insecticide. Be sure to apply the material at a time when the bees are not active in the garden, and follow application directions carefully.

Annuals are almost synonymous with summer, and spring is the time to seed or plant the ones you want to grow.

Roses

Spring is rose pruning time. Actually, timing will vary a little depending upon where you live. For example, in the warmer metropolitan areas, it is generally done between March 1 and March 15. In rural areas and foothills, the best time may be between March 15 and April 1.

It is very important that you take time to properly prune your rosebushes in the spring. One of the greatest advantages is that proper pruning results in a more compact, sturdy, denser-foliaged plant that develops long stems and large flowers. There is nothing uglier than bare rose canes, and you can eliminate most of them by pruning properly in springtime.

There are many different recommended methods of pruning roses. If you are using a method and having success with it, by all means continue to prune by that method. However, if you are confused or are not getting the results you desire, here are a few tips on how to successfully prune roses.

Before you start any pruning, it is important to have the right tools for the job. First you will want a pair of sharp, clean, sterilized pruning shears. Next you'll need a pair of gloves to protect your hands from the sharp thorns. You will also need a healing compound to spray on the areas where you cut the rose canes.

The first thing to do is check closely to see if the canes are still alive. Examine the canes carefully. The inner portion of a live cane will be white to green in color. The center of a dead cane will show browning. If you find this browning condition, cut further back on the cane until you reach live wood.

As with any type of pruning, always remove any dead, decayed, weak, or broken canes from your rosebushes. Also remove any tangled growth that would tend to cut off air circulation and sunlight exposure to the center of the plant. Another principle to remember is that pruning cuts are always made above an outside bud to force the growth outward and to open up the plant for better air circulation and sunlight exposure. When new canes develop, some of the old ones should be removed to keep the plant young, vibrant, and healthy. Suckers that develop below the bud union should be removed right away. The bud union is the swelling at the base of the bush where the hybrid graft was made. Shoots originating below the graft are suckers from the rootstock rather than the hybrid and will not produce the same flowers; instead, blooms will be generally small, single or semidouble, and insignificant in comparison to the hybrid blooms.

These canes often appear as long, straggly growth that develops quickly and produces foliage different from the hybrid variety. If allowed to remain, this growth will sap the strength of the plant.

There are several different types of roses, and each one is pruned a little differently. The most popular garden roses are hybrid teas, the large flowering types. These include such favorites as Peace, Tropicana, Helen Traubel, King Ransom, Mr. Lincoln, Sutter's Gold—and thousands of others. It is important to prune them severely if you want long flower stems and large flowers. Here is the rule of thumb I suggest: Canes the size of a pencil should be pruned back to 4 to 6 inches from the ground; any cane that is the size of your little finger should be pruned back to 4 to 8 inches from the ground; canes the size of your forefinger should be pruned back 8 to 12 inches from the ground; thumb-size and larger canes should be kept pruned back to 2 feet or less if possible. Sometimes they have to be pruned a little higher if you cannot find any growth buds on the lower portion of the canes.

You will find the small, prolific-flowering floribundas and polyanthus roses much easier to prune. It is not necessary to cut them back as severely, because all you are trying to do is produce an abundance of small flowers on the rosebush. Simply head the canes back about 12 to 18 inches from ground level. These roses will often produce multiple canes from the ground. Most of them can remain, but it is a good practice to remove a few of the weaker canes to allow for better air circulation and sunlight exposure. Just use good common sense in determining which ones should be cut out.

Climbing roses are probably the most difficult for the average home gardener to prune. Yet if you follow a few simple procedures, they really are quite easy to grow, train, and prune. Climbing roses have a tendency to grow rather upright, so spread the canes out when possible. This spreading encourages secondary growth to develop on the main cane, and it is the secondary growth that produces the abundance of flowers on climbing roses. At this spring pruning, simply cut back the secondary growth to just above the second bud. The main climbing rose cane is cut back to fit the trellis, wall, or location in which it is growing. Occasionally remove some of the old climbing canes to encourage new ones to develop.

Tree roses are pruned the same way as bush roses, except that cutting distances are figured from the top of the bud union rather than from ground level. In the case of a hybrid tea tree rose, prune by the size of the cane, figuring it from the bud union at the top of the tree stem.

Miniature roses are best pruned by removing approximately half of last year's growth. If your miniature roses are heavily branched, you should remove a few of the inner canes to allow for better air circulation.

Treat pruning cuts with a tree-healing compound to discourage the entrance of insects and diseases through the open cut. This also lessens the chance of evaporation.

Additional pruning can be done during the growing season as you cut the flowers. Prune back to the first five-leaflet stem.

Take time this spring to properly prune your roses. Maintain your plants at the proper height and you will be rewarded later on with bushes clothed in lush green foliage and lovely flowers.

Lawn Care

The cold weather of winter causes many lawns to look sad and ragged. By starting spring lawn maintenance in March and continuing it through April and May, you can help bring your lawn out of its winter doldrums. A planned spring lawn maintenance program is needed to reverse the situation and return the lawn to good green color.

The first and most important job is mowing the lawn. Because a lawn is the framework of the entire landscape, simple mowing can immensely improve the general appearance of the landscape. Be sure the mower is clean and sharp to start the season off on the right foot. One of the biggest mistakes is to use dull equipment; it pulls

at the grass instead of cutting it off cleanly, and results in ragged yellow grass tips.

Another common mistake in springtime is to let the grass get too long between mowings. The result is the same as when dull equipment is used: The mower cuts into the yellow grass stems, giving the turf a yellow appearance. Most Northwest lawns are composed of bent and fescue grasses, so the proper cutting height is ¾ inch. If you have a bluegrass lawn, the mower should be set at the 1½-inch height.

After mowing the grass, one of the best ways to determine what kind of care the lawn needs is to visually examine it. One way to do this is to cut a plug of your lawn about 4 inches square. (If there are several problem areas, it may be necessary to cut several plugs.) Examine the plug carefully to check the following: (1) how the grass is growing; (2) how deeply the roots have penetrated into the soil; (3) whether a layer of thatch has developed; (4) whether there are any disease or insect problems. This important step in lawn maintenance shows you what problems exist so you know where to start without wasting time and money on unnecessary projects. When you have finished with the plug, simply place it back in the lawn, and then step on it to secure it in position.

This turf examination is especially helpful in diagnosing the problem in areas where brown spots occur. Two possible causes of large brown patches are soil compaction and the buildup of thatch.

Thatch is the accumulation of dead grass at soil level between the roots and grass blades. It acts much like a thatched roof—shedding water, soil conditioners, and fertilizers so they cannot get to the root area where they will be of value. If your inspection of the turf reveals a layer of dead grass ½ inch or more in depth, it would be wise to thatch the lawn. If thatching is necessary, the job should be done when the turf is fairly dry. It is usually done in early spring when the weather is not too hot.

There are several ways to remove thatch. Most garden centers and rental agencies have power thatching machines available on an hourly rental basis, or an attachment that fits on rotary mowers can be purchased. A hand-thatching rake can be used, but thatching by hand is a tedious undertaking and should be attempted only by persons strong of body and long on patience.

The time required to thatch will depend on the severity of the problem. If accumulation is heavy, it may be necessary to go over the lawn more than once. However, the average 5,000-square-foot lawn can be power-thatched in two hours or less. Mow again after thatching. The thatched lawn may look rather unsightly for a period of several weeks, but fertilization, reseeding, watering, and regular mowing should help it recover and be much healthier.

Where soil compaction is the problem, the hardpan or clay soil must be penetrated by perforating the lawn area. Aerating the soil in this way allows for better penetration of fertilizers and water throughout the growing season. Lawn perforation can be done with a power perforating machine or by hand with a pitchfork, manure fork, or a root-feeding device that fits on your garden hose and perforates by water pressure. The perforations should be at least 3 to 6 inches in depth.

Spring lawn fertilizers may be applied if needed. A good indication that a lawn fertilizer is needed is a yellowish appearance of the grass after winter, indicating that the fertilizer has been used up or has leached out of the soil. The product label will indicate the amount to use and whether the material needs to be watered in after application. Be sure to follow directions carefully.

Another problem in many lawns is weeds. They should be pulled and destroyed immediately, before they have a chance to flower and go to seed. If there are too many to pull, use a lawn weed killer. Apply it when the temperature is between 45 and 65 degrees, and when there is no chance of rain for 24 hours. Watch the wind, too—if the mist blows onto your garden plants, it will kill them.

If your lawn has bare spots or yellow patches, it may be infested by the European crane fly. The larvae feed on the turf and, as the season progresses, may attain a size of up to 1½ to 2 inches. They have a very tough skin; hence the common name "leatherjacket." In the fall, the adult fly is very large with long legs; hence the name "crane fly."

These pests can devastate a lawn in just a few days. They remain underground during the day and sometimes appear aboveground on a damp, warm night. You may spot them by observing the lawn at night by flashlight, or infer their presence by noting discoloration of the lawn. They seem more prevalent in moist areas, and it is at this rainy time of the year that you get the best control of the crane fly. Substances recommended for control of this insect include liquid Diazinon 25 percent, granular Diazinon, or Dursban. Read and follow label instructions on the product you use.

If your examination of the turf reveals moss in your lawn, spring is a good time to eradicate it. Moss is generally caused by compacted soil, sour soil, overwet soil, too much shade, or improper fertilization. Through a process of elimination, you can determine which of these is responsible and then begin to correct the problem.

The first job is to kill the moss. Several chemical moss killers are available at local garden outlets. Ferrous ammonium-sulfate is the basic ingredient of most of these products, and it will turn moss black in a matter of minutes or hours. Once it has turned black, rake it out of the grass.

Once the moss has been eliminated, it is time to correct the soil condition that caused it to flourish. Moss will return until the cause is removed. If the problem is compacted or poorly drained soil, lawn perforation will help. If improper fertilization is the problem, start a regular feeding program at once. The grass needs to be fed in spring, summer, and fall with a quality lawn fertilizer. Avoid brands with a high nitrogen content—they tend to stimulate top growth only. If high-nitrogen fertilizers are used, they should have a calcium base and should only supplement the use of lawn fertilizers.

If the problem is sour soil, calcium should be applied to the lawn area as an additional corrective measure. It is a soil sweetener and can be applied after the grass has been fed. Dolomite or agricultural lime is often recommended for this job. It should be applied at the rate of 40 pounds per 1,000 square feet. One application will probably not be sufficient; a second application in the fall and a third the following spring may be required. The grass should be much easier to maintain once you have remedied the condition that caused the moss to flourish.

Once you have eliminated the moss and the insects, you'll want to eliminate those ugly bare spots that remain. Now is the time to overseed the lawn, making sure to use a grass seed mix that will blend with your existing lawn. If you are not sure what kind of grass you have, take a plug to your local certified nurseryman or master gardener, so they can recommend the correct type of seed. After you have your seed, broadcast it over the established lawn area as well as the bare spots, using about one pound of seed per 1,000 square feet. Keep the area moist until the new seed has germinated. One of the areas that benefits most from overseeding is the area under tall trees, especially evergreen trees where the lawn competes with the tree's root system.

Give the lawn the care it needs now, and you will be rewarded with a nice-looking lawn this spring and summer.

Shrubs and Trees

SHRUBS

Spring is an excellent time of year to brighten up your garden with some of the early spring-flowering shrubs. By choosing the right varieties, it is possible to have shrubs in bloom from January through the spring season.

Rhododendrons, the Washington state flower, are one of the most popular of all the early-spring-flowering shrubs. Probably the greatest advantage in using spring-flowering rhododendrons in the landscape is that they come in such a wide range of sizes: Some varieties grow only a few inches high, and some may reach a height of 20 feet or more at maturity. Another advantage is that some varieties begin to flower very early, some as early as January and February, and others following in March, April, May and early June. Flower colors of rhododendrons also vary—there are shades of white, pink, rose to red, purple, lavender, and some that are bicolored—as do foliage textures and leaf colors.

Rhododendrons are exceptionally popular for combining with other spring-flowering plants. They are ideal companions for azaleas, camellias, lily-of-the-valley shrubs, and magnolias. Primroses, violas, pansies, violets, and hosta are just a few of the popular perennials used as companion plants in rhododendron plantings.

Since there are so many varieties of rhododendrons, it is practically impossible to begin naming them. However, you will find that local nurseries and garden outlets have their finest selection of plants at flowering time. In addition to the common popular varieties, there are many new introductions that you may want to consider including in your garden.

Rhododendrons grow and flower best where they get partial sun and shade and are protected from the hot midday sun. If the location you have in mind gets quite a bit of sun, you'd do best to choose the darker-flowered varieties and those with dark leaves, which grow best in sunny spots. Avoid planting any rhododendron where it will get hot reflected sunlight, such as the south or west side of the home. Most varieties cannot survive that much sun.

Take time to properly prepare the soil before planting a rhododendron. First of all, mix generous amounts of peat moss, compost, and processed manure with your existing soil. Second,

Suggested Rhododendron Varieties

VARIETY NAME	APPROX. SIZE IN 10 YEARS	FLOWERING TIME	VARIETY NAME	APPROX. SIZE IN 10 YEARS	FLOWERING TIME
Reds			Hotei	3 feet	Early May
Jean Marie Montague	5 feet	Early May	Moonstone	3 feet	Late April
America	5 feet	Late May	Souvenir of W. C. Slocock	4 feet	Early May
Trilby	5 feet	Late May			
Markeeta's Prize	5 feet	Early May	*Lavenders and Purples*		
Halfdan Lem	5 feet	Early May	Purple Splendor	5 feet	Late May
Vulcan	5 feet	Late May	Blue Peter	5 feet	Early May
			Blue Diamond	3 feet	Late April
Pinks			Anah Kruschke	6 feet	Early June
Bow Bells	3 feet	Late April	Blue Jay	5 feet	Early June
Mrs. Furnival	4 feet	Early May	R. Impeditum	1 foot	Late April
Furnival's Daughter	5 feet	Early May			
Cynthia	7 feet	Early May	*Hardy Varieties*		
Mrs. G. W. Leak	6 feet	Late April	*(below −20 degrees)*		
Anna Rose Whitney	6 feet	Late May	American (red)	5 feet	Late May
			Boule de Neige (white)	5 feet	Early May
Whites			Catawbiense Album (white)	6 feet	Late May
Gomer Waterer	6 feet	Late May	English Roseum (lavender)	6 feet	Late May
Loder's White	5 feet	Early May	Nova Zembla (red)	5 feet	Early May
Loderi King George	8 feet	Early May	P. J. M. (lavender)	4 feet	Late March
Chinoides	4 feet	Late May			
Beauty of Littleworth	6 feet	Late April	*Dwarf or Low-Growing Varieties*		
Snow Lady	2½ feet	Late March	Scarlet Wonder (red)	2 feet	Early May
			Baden Baden (red)	2 feet	Early May
Yellows			Chikor (yellow)	1½ feet	Late April
Unique	4 feet	Late April	Ramapo (violet)	2 feet	Late April
Crest	6 feet	Early May	Riplet (rose-pink)	2 feet	Late April
Chikor	1½ feet	Late April	Shamrock (chartreuse)	1 foot	Late April

be certain to plant your new rhododendron so the rootball is right at ground level or a little above. Rhodies planted too deep develop only leaf growth and never flower. If your rhododendrons are not flowering, check their planting depth; then remove any excess soil or mulching material so the top of the roots are on the soil surface. About the only other thing that would keep them from flowering is too much deep shade. Be certain to moisten the soil thoroughly once the rhododendron is planted. The use of a transplanting hormone will help lessen any transplanting shock.

Established rhododendron plants in your garden should be fertilized during the spring growing season. The first application of a rhododendron-type fertilizer is made in late February or early March; if a second application is needed, do it after blooming in late May or early June. Be certain to read and follow manufacturer's instructions on the label—and be certain to water the fertilizer thoroughly after each application; do not rely on rain.

Most varieties of rhododendrons seldom need pruning; however, should a plant outgrow its planting location or become straggly in its growth habit, it can be safely pruned during or immediately after its spring-flowering season. There is no need to shy away from pruning rhododendrons if they do need shaping, but unnecessary and severe pruning can result in the loss of flowers for a year or two.

If notches appear on the edges of your rhododendron leaves, it often indicates the presence of the root weevil. Damage is done by the adult weevil at night, so you may never see the insect. It is best controlled by spraying the leaves and ground with the insecticide Orthene. As a result of research done in the Pacific Northwest, it is recommended that the spray be applied once a month from May through October. But be careful: Never apply this or any other type of spray when the bees are active in the garden.

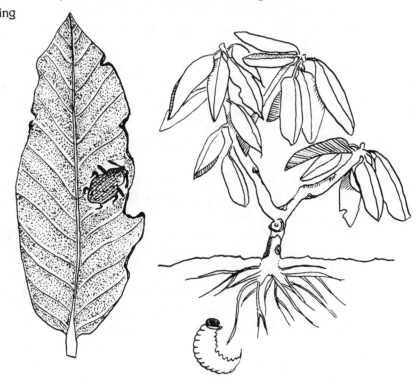

Notched leaves on rhododendrons and other evergreens indicate the presence of root weevil. Control both the larvae and adults with Orthene.

Camellias are another popular early-spring-flowering plant. The winter-flowering Sasanqua camellias start blooming around Thanksgiving, while the spring-flowering varieties begin early in the year. Their varying growing heights and habits, and their dark bold green foliage, make them a nice addition to the landscape. Flowers range in color from white to various shades of pink and red, with some that are combinations of two or more colors. These plants are especially nice for semishaded areas.

Another popular plant to use in the spring garden is the azalea. Two types are commonly grown here—the evergreen azalea and the azalea mollis. Evergreen varieties are often used in rockeries, foundation plantings, and landscaping beds, and their colors generally range through shades of white, pink, rose, and red, with some lavender varieties. Evergreen azaleas can be used in practically any part of the landscape to add a bright spot of color in springtime. You have undoubtedly seen them in full bloom in rockeries, flower and shrub beds, neatly grouped in landscape borders, or in containers. They grow and flower in practically any part of the garden, providing that the soil is well drained.

One of the greatest attributes of evergreen azaleas is that they are outstanding companion plants with other spring-flowering trees and shrubs. They are especially nice when planted at the base of rhododendrons, camellias, lily-of-the-valley shrubs, magnolias, and other spring-flowering plants. In the rockery, evergreen azaleas flower at the same time as most of the spring-flowering rockery plants, and make an outstanding flower display when combined with the blues, whites, yellows, and other colors of rockery perennials.

Evergreen azaleas provide the best floral display when used in groups of three, five, seven, or more plants. This is such an attractive spring-flowering plant that it can even be used individually in the garden for spot color.

By color, here are a few of the most popular spring-flowering azaleas. In red shades, a few of the popular varieties are Hino-Crimson, Hino-degiri, Sherwood Red, and Wards Ruby. In pink and rose shades, the varieties considered among the best are Glamour, Gaiety, Rose Bud, Twenty Grand, and Pink Gumpo. Varieties of Everest, Gumpo White, and Helen Close are a few of the best white-flowering evergreen azaleas. Buccaneer, Flame Creeper, and Sherwood Red are three colorful orange-red-flowering varieties of evergreen azaleas. The bright purple flowers of the variety Purple Splendor are a colorful addition to the spring garden.

The azalea mollis, also called the "flame azalea," loses its leaves during the winter months. Quite a few of the mollis-type azaleas have a very pleasant fragrance, while others have a rather strange odor. The large flowers of the azalea mollis appear on the tips of the branches and are very conspicuous in the garden. The flowers are in clusters much like a rhododendron truss and provide a mass of color during the spring-flowering season. The blooms of the plant develop at the same time or slightly before the new growth, so they are very noticeable on the plants. Flower colors range through shades of red, rose, pink, copper, orange, yellow, peach, apricot, and white. Both plant and blossoms are very sturdy and nicely withstand the wind and spring weather of the Northwest region.

Evergreen and mollis azaleas benefit from the same type of fertilizer you would apply to rhododendrons and evergreens. Fertilizer should be applied in late February or early March and again after they have finished flowering. If you use a dry-type rhododendron fertilizer, be sure to water it in thoroughly immediately after application. Again, do not rely upon rain to do this job.

Root weevils will sometimes affect azaleas just as they do their relatives the rhododendrons. Spray with Orthene if this happens. Should moss, algae, or lichen form on the branches of your azaleas, it is best to spray them with a copper spray when the temperature is between 45 and 65 degrees in early spring or late fall.

Still another popular spring-flowering plant is the magnolia. Of special interest in the early spring is the star magnolia and *Magnolia stellata* with its white or pink flowers. This variety has a mild fragrance. The larger-flowered varieties in shades of white, rose, and red are also popular spring-flowering garden plants.

Some outstanding daphnes flower during the spring season. Probably one of the most popular is the low-growing rock daphne, sometimes referred to as the "rose daphne." The prolific flowers and intense fragrance of this low-growing form of daphne make it ideal for a rockery or as a low ground cover plant. The taller-growing *Daphne odora* is also popular. It grows and flowers best in partial sun and shade.

There are other spring-flowering evergreen and deciduous shrubs that make nice additions to the early spring garden. Several different varieties are available.

Forsythia (deciduous). Its bright yellow flowers look like sunshine itself in the early spring garden.

Lily-of-the-valley shrub (Pieris japonica) (evergreen). This very attractive evergreen flowers in springtime. Its medium green foliage and attractive white cascading flowers make it an ideal companion plant with rhododendrons, camellias, and azaleas.

Quince (deciduous). There are some outstanding varieties that can be used in the spring garden. The newer large-flowering varieties provide an abundance of color in the garden, predominantly ranging from white to pink to red.

Winter-flowering heathers (evergreen). There are about fifteen or more varieties that provide an abundance of color at this time of the year. The low-growing varieties make excellent ground cover plants or companion plants for spring-flowering shrubs.

TREES

Besides spring-flowering shrubs, you might consider having some spring-flowering trees and fruit trees in your garden. We are fortunate in the Pacific Northwest to have a wide variety of spring-flowering trees from which to choose. Dogwood, flowering cherry, plum, magnolia, crab apple, and hawthorn head the list of popular types grown here, and many others also merit your consideration.

When you are planting a new landscape, always consider the trees first; it takes them the longest to become established, and remember that trees, in addition to their beauty, provide shade and privacy. Choose locations for them where they can best satisfy such needs.

I am often asked to recommend a fast-growing tree. I always try to point out that a fast-growing tree will usually become a very big tree, perhaps reaching 150 feet at maturity. Most home gardens cannot accommodate a tree this large. Instead, I suggest that a tree be chosen for its interesting foliage, color, texture, and/or flowers. Always keep in mind the ultimate size it will reach. Trees can be pruned, of course, but the fast-growing ones are still too large for the average yard.

Few places in the world have as broad a selection of flowering trees as here in the Pacific Northwest. The choice is almost unlimited.

Among the most popular types are the flowering cherries. There are many varieties—too many to name—but in the small-growing category, you will probably find the weeping varieties to be best. Their average height is around 10 feet, but I have one in my own garden that is already over 15 feet. Simple pruning will confine the growth somewhat. Both single- and double-flowering varieties are available.

One advantage of flowering cherries is the wide range of growing habits. Varieties like Mt. Fuji reach only about 20 feet in height but may spread wider. Amanogawa has an upright, columnar habit of growth. Its width is generally 6 feet or less, but its height may reach as much as 20 feet. There are a dozen or more varieties that will attain a height of 20 or 30 feet. Flowering cherries are available in a wide range of colors. There are whites, pinks, rose shades, plus one variety with chartreuse blooms. This tree also flowers at about the same time as rhododendrons, camellias, and azaleas, making it particularly nice in combination plantings.

A tree that deserves special consideration is the flowering plum. It is especially popular in the Pacific Northwest, probably because of its very attractive reddish foliage. Not all varieties have red leaves, but those that do seem to be the ones most often chosen. *Prunus blireiana* is a favorite because of its very attractive double pink flowers followed by reddish leaves. Thundercloud is another good one and has deep purple crimson foliage. Others that merit consideration are Newport, Hollywood, and Woodii. Most flowering plums reach a height of approximately 25 feet. Hollywood is an exception, often attaining a height of 40 feet. Pruning can restrict the growth of all of these trees.

Another tree that includes many varieties suitable for the Northwest landscape is the crab apple. In some varieties, the flowers are followed by small fruit that can be used for jams and jellies. Many of the newer hybrids will reach about 20 feet at maturity. *Malus floribunda* is a favorite of most landscapers. Its flowers are multicolored from white to pink to red, and the habit of growth is very interesting.

Our native dogwood trees are also very popular. *Cornus nuttallii* may attain a height of 50 feet. Rather upright in its growth habit, the advantage of this variety is that it flowers not only in the spring but often again in the fall. In addition, it has beautiful autumn leaf color and scarlet fall fruit, making it colorful almost all twelve months of the year.

The Florida varieties of Cornus are especially attractive, often with white flowers, generally a bit smaller than our native western dogwood. The best-known variety is the pink dogwood, *Cornus florida rubra*. It has a very interesting spreading habit of growth and beautiful pink flowers in the spring. *Cornus florida welchii* has interesting variegated foliage as well as beautiful flowers. It is sometimes chosen for its foliage color alone. There are several other varieties, all of which merit consideration in gardens here.

Do not overlook the value of fruit trees in the general landscape. Some of them are very attractive flowering trees. I remember when I was a youngster and our family had a montmorency pie-cherry tree in our garden. The spring flowers were as beautiful as any of the ornamental cherries, and we enjoyed the added bonus of the shimmering red fruit later on in the year. Many other varieties of cherry and apple trees are worth considering as flowering trees. The dwarf or semidwarf varieties are the best ones to grow in the home garden because of their more limited growth habit. Both can be controlled somewhat by pruning.

When fertilizing spring-flowering trees and shrubs, I find it a good practice to make perforation holes around large established trees and shrubs to help get the fertilizer down to the root zone. Usually a crowbar or pipe can be used to make holes between 12 and 18 inches deep. Apply the plant food directly into the holes, and water thoroughly. This encourages deep root growth, which keeps roots out of the lawn area and anchors plants firmly in the soil so the wind cannot easily uproot them.

When deciding what kind of fertilizer to use, follow these basic guidelines. Evergreen trees and shrubs are fed with a rhododendron-type plant food. This group includes rhododendrons, camellias, azaleas, cypress, junipers, conifers, and the broad-leaf types. Trees and shrubs that lose their leaves during the winter, commonly called "deciduous" plants, should be fed with a rose- or garden-type fertilizer. Included in this group are lilacs, forsythia, flowering trees, fruit trees, and shade trees. Processed well-rotted manure or organic manures can also be used for these basic categories of plants.

Spring is a good time to select and plant flowering trees and shrubs if you want to include them in your landscape.

Suggested Fruit Tree Varieties

VARIETY NAME	COLOR	USES
*Apples**		
Gravenstein (sometimes slow to bear)	Striped/Red	Eating, cooking, dessert
Jonagold	Yellow/Red	All purpose
King	Striped/Yellow (Fall)	All purpose, baking
Melrose	Red	All purpose, excellent for storage
Spartan	Red	All purpose, excellent for storage
Yellow Transparent	Yellow (Summer)	Pies, sauces
*Pears***		
Bartlett	Yellow/Bush	Eating, canning
Comice	Greenish Yellow	All purpose, storage
Flemish Beauty	Yellow/Hint of Red	Canning, eating
Cherries		
Van†	Black	Eating
Bing	Black	Eating, canning
Lambert	Black	Eating, canning
Rainier	Yellow/Red	Eating, canning
Royal Anne	Yellow/Red	Eating, canning
Montmorency (sour)	Red	Pie cherry

Need more than one variety for pollination.   †Needs pollinizer to produce cherries.
**All varieties need pollination.*

Planting and Caring for Bulbs

April is the month to plant dahlias and gladiolus. Plant both of these colorful summer-flowering bulbs in a bright, sunny part of the garden in well-drained soil. You will find that local nurseries and garden outlets have their finest selection of both dahlias and glads at this time of year. This is also the time for planting lilies, anemones, ranunculus, and other summer-flowering bulbs. Be certain to add bulb fertilizer and soil insecticide at planting time. Taller varieties of dahlias should be staked to protect them from whipping winds.

Suggested Fruit Tree Varieties (continued)

VARIETY NAME	COLOR	USES
Prunes and Plums		
Italian	Purple/Late	Eating, canning, freezing
Brooks	Purple/Early	Eating, canning, freezing
Blue Damson	Blue/Midseason	Jam, canning
Green Gage	Green/Midseason	Canning, eating
Shiro‡	Yellow/Midseason	Eating
Satsuma‡	Crimson	Jam, jellies, dessert
Peaches§		
Red Haven	Yellow flesh	All purpose
Veteran	Yellow flesh	Freezing, canning
Pacific Gold	Yellow flesh	Eating, canning
Apricots§		
Jannes	Golden Yellow	Eating, canning
Tilton	Golden Yellow/Red Blush	Canning
Wenatchee	Yellow	Freezing, canning

‡*Need pollination.*

§*All varieties are self-pollinizing.*

Lay dahlia tubers on their side in freshly prepared planting soil.

Plant the bulbs 6 to 8 inches deep, laying dahlia tubers flat on the soil. Gladiolus bulbs planted at two-week intervals will flower over a longer period of time late this summer and in early fall. Mix a shovelful each of peat moss and processed manure with your existing soil. A low-nitrogen, nonburning transplanting fertilizer or bone meal can be added at this same time.

Besides planting summer-flowering bulbs at this time, it is important to care for the bulbs that flowered during this season. When spring-flowering bulbs have finished their display in the garden, certain procedures need to be followed to ensure that the bulbs ripen properly. The correct treatment of the foliage is of prime importance.

When crocus, tulips, hyacinths, and daffodils are finished blooming, the leaves usually become rather unsightly. There is a great temptation to cut them back along with the dead blooms, but under no circumstances should this be done. The leaves play an important role in the future development of the bulbs—they function as a source of food for the bulbs, combining materials from the air with elements picked up from the roots. The us-

able nutrients return to the bulbs and help replenish the nutrients used up in the production of foliage and flowers during the past season. This food supply revitalizes the bulbs, allowing them to become larger and stronger so they will produce healthy flowers in future years. Thus, the leaves should be left alone until they have completely died back. Some gardeners tie them back or in knots to make them less conspicuous. Other gardeners plant annuals in among the bulbs to help conceal the deteriorating bulb foliage.

Sometimes a gardener wants to dig up the bulbs with deteriorating foliage and move them to a less conspicuous location. I do not recommend this unless there is a compelling reason to do so. I have on occasion found it necessary to move bulbs because I wanted to move other plants into the area or because I was changing the beds completely. I have never noticed any damage to bulbs I have moved, but the proper techniques must be used. Dig bulbs carefully— the roots must not be damaged in any way, and as much soil as possible should remain with the bulbs. There are two reasons why I do not recommend moving bulbs. First, it is a lot of extra work, and I firmly believe that gardening should be fun rather than a chore. Second, there is always the possibility of damaging the bulbs, and the risk seems unwarranted when there is no reason for moving them. Under no circumstances should bulbs be moved while they are in bloom.

The dead flowers of spring bulbs should be cut off before they have a chance to go to seed. Seed formation deprives the bulbs of growth needed to develop next year's blooms. Removing the dead flowers also improves the appearance of the planting area.

When the leaves have ripened and dried, the bulbs can be dug and stored until planting time in the fall. However, it is not necessary to do this each year; I have seen many plantings around the Northwest that have been left undisturbed for twelve years or more and they are still doing just fine. Digging and dividing become necessary only when the bulbs no longer perform at their best.

After blossoming, but before the foliage has completely died back, is the perfect time to fertilize with a liquid plant food. Fish fertilizer is suitable for this feeding.

Ensure the continued beauty of your spring-flowering bulbs in future years by treating them properly when flowering is over. Above all, let the foliage die back naturally at this time of year. Also, don't forget to plant those summer-flowering dahlias and gladiolus for continued beauty in your garden.

Houseplants

Because we are outside so much during the spring, it is easy to forget houseplants. Remember, they are completely dependent upon you for water, light, and nutrients. Most houseplants are beginning to come out of their winter dormancy, and any that need repotting should be attended to now. A good indication that a plant needs to be repotted is matted roots beginning to appear above the soil, or roots starting to protrude from the drainage hole. Lack of growth and poor leaf color are other signs to look for.

When repotting, transplant into a pot that is only one or two sizes larger than the original. Use an all-purpose houseplant medium for this job. If you use soil from the garden, it should first be sterilized so there is no chance of introducing soil-borne insects and disease into your home. To accomplish this, bake the soil in the oven at 170 or 180 degrees for about two hours. Then add peat moss and other soil conditioners as needed. Water the plant before repotting, so soil will cling to the roots. Then lightly tap the plant out of the pot. If the roots are matted, gently loosen them with your fingertips before repotting.

Now that houseplants are beginning their new growth, they can be fertilized more frequently. In fact, at this time of year, most houseplants will benefit from feeding about once every four to six weeks. Use an all-purpose houseplant fertilizer for this job.

Now is also the time to pinch back leggy, spindly, or misshapen growth on houseplants to encourage bushiness and improve the plant's shape and appearance. Pinch or prune just above a node (the point where a new leaf will develop). If a plant continually loses its lower leaves, the result will be leaves at the top and an ugly bare stem. To correct the problem, simply prune the plant back to 6 or 8 inches from the soil. New growth usually will appear from a node in a few weeks. Within a few months you will once again have an attractive houseplant. The tip growth you remove can be used to start new plants.

If you take good care of your houseplants this spring, they should remain healthy and good-looking for some time to come.

Herbs for Seasoning, Etc.

In addition to being useful plants, herbs are also attractive in the landscape. Many are quite easy to grow and have almost unlimited uses in everyday cooking.

One advantage of growing herbs is that they do not have to be confined to the vegetable garden area, although this is a good place to grow them if you have the room. Another good place for them is near the kitchen door in a flower or shrub bed. If your space is limited, they will fit into any small area that is available. In an apartment, they can be grown in a pot on a windowsill.

If you want to start herbs from seed, March is the time to get the project under way. Most seed racks at local nurseries or garden centers carry at least half a dozen varieties. Specialty seed companies carry a broader selection. I have found that if your local dealer does not have the specific seed you want, he can often order it for you.

Since some herbs are rather slow to grow from seed, you may find it better to buy seedling starter plants later in the spring. They are usually available at local garden outlets in April or May, and some growers feature as many as fifty varieties. Most are sold in individual containers or in trays of four to six plants each. Sometimes you can find mature plants in gallon cans.

What goes together better than cats and catnip? If you like herbs in the garden, don't forget the catnip for your cats.

If you prefer to start the seeds yourself, choose a room where the temperature is between 60 and 70 degrees. As the seedlings begin to develop, be sure to turn the containers every three or four days so that the plants will not grow lopsided toward the light. Once the seedlings reach an inch or two in height and have developed two sets of true leaves, it is a good idea to transplant them to individual containers or trays of four to six plants each. Do not set them out in the garden until all danger of frost is past.

Most herbs are not very fussy about soil. In fact, many do best in poor soil where they do not get very much attention. Too much care tends to stimulate rank leaf growth, which in turn may cause a shortage of oils in the plants. It can be said that herbs thrive on a certain amount of neglect. Spacing varies somewhat by variety; but as a general rule, plants should be spaced about 12 to 15 inches apart. Little soil preparation is needed, but it is a good idea to mix in generous amounts of peat moss and a nonburning transplanting fertilizer. Make certain the soil is well drained. Fertilizer seldom is required for established plants. However, if any plants show stunted growth or develop off-colored leaves, an all-purpose vegetable garden food can be used, preferably in late winter or early summer. To keep the plants bushy and compact, pinch or prune back any leggy growth that may develop. Most herbs are not susceptible to insect or dis-

ease problems, but if either appear, it is best to use a vegetable garden spray or dust. Follow application directions on the label, and never apply when the bees are active in the herb garden.

Parsley. One of the most popular herbs. Its attractive dark green leaves are often used to garnish salads and fruits. To add good flavor to soup and vegetable dishes, cut the leaves fine before you use them. Incidentally, parsley is nutritious and should be eaten whenever it is served as a garnish. Two types are commonly grown in the Northwest: moss-curled and the flat-leaf type. Dark green foliage and fine leaf texture make this an attractive plant in the landscape. It is hard to start from seed, but once it does germinate, it is easily grown.

Spearmint. One of the most popular varieties of mint. Its uses are unlimited. They include flavoring for tea, garnishes, jellies, and mint sauce. Mints are quite easily started from seed, but the most popular way to start them is from root divisions. They grow best in shade, and unlike most herbs they require quite a bit of moisture during the summer season.

Thyme. Can be used to flavor sauces, soups, and stews. Start from seed, or starter plants can be purchased. Foliage and pale pink flowers are rather attractive in the garden.

Lavender. Used quite extensively in gardens here. The flowers are fragrant and can be dried for use in sachet bags or as a moth repellent. It will grow very well in poor soil.

Chives. Another all-purpose plant. They grow well in pots as well as in the garden, and are easy to start from seed or by division. Established plants can be divided every year in the spring or in the fall. They have a nice compact growth habit. Their leaves have an onion flavor and are excellent for use in salads, cottage cheese, stews, fish dishes, or soups.

Basil. Probably the top-rated herb for culinary purposes. The leaves have a clove flavor and are often used for poultry, fish, meat, game, egg dishes, sauces, salads, and soups. The best time to cut the leaves is when the plants begin to bloom. Cut them back almost to ground level.

Sage. Makes an attractive garden plant. It grows best in full sun or part sun and shade. Sage is often used in soup, but is probably best known for its use in the stuffing that accompanies the turkey on Thanksgiving Day.

Dill. Very useful in the kitchen, but the flower arranger also likes this plant. It is used to flavor pickles, gravy, and sauces. For winter use, pick and dry the leaves in August.

Rosemary. A colorful landscape plant as well as popular herb. It grows best in full sun. The combination of attractive gray flowers and fragrant leaves makes it a good choice for the home garden. The leaves are often used in roasts and stews. It can be dried for use in sachet bags also.

Summer Savory. Easy to grow in full sun. The aromatic leaves are often used in salads, meats, stews, gravy, and dressings.

Borage. Plant this herb in sun or semisun and shade. The young leaves can be used in salads; the older leaves often are used to flavor lemonade. The flowers are excellent forage for the bees.

Marjoram. Plant this herb in full sun or part sun and shade. Fresh or dried foliage is often used to season soups, stews, meat pie, sauces, salads, poultry dressings, peas, and beans.

Needless to say, these are only a few of the herbs you might select. Planting some of them will add color, fragrance, and interest to your garden and, best of all, fresh flavorings to your kitchen.

Growing Your Own Berries

If you want to pick fresh berries from your own berry patch this summer, spring is the time to plant your favorite kinds. Almost all types do especially well here in the Pacific Northwest. Raspberries, strawberries, and blueberries are among the most popular, but grapes, currants, gooseberries, and many others produce quite satisfactorily here also. Berries are fun to grow and can be used for jellies, jams, desserts, garnishes, and to eat fresh. A few plants of your favorite will often provide enough fruit for the average family.

One of the major factors in growing berries in this region is the proper selection of varieties. When choosing strawberries or raspberries, this is really quite easy: The varieties that were hybridized and developed specifically for this area have been given Northwest names that you will quickly recognize. With the other berries, it is a matter of knowing which ones have proved best in trials conducted in this region.

There are many great varieties of berries, and the following are only a few of the best. For strawberries choose Northwest, Shuskan, or Hood. For raspberries choose Heritage, Willamette, Sumner, or others with Northwest names. Earliblue is one of the earliest blueberries. Another good blueberry choice is Bluecrop, or for great flavor choose Dixie. If you like white grapes, pick Interlaken Seedless or Seneca. For a dark grape, Van Buren or Schuyler is best. Aurora is a good blackberry, and Red Lake a good currant. A good red gooseberry is Poorman, while Oregon Champion is a good green gooseberry. With a little care and proper selection of variety, it is possible for you to have a bountiful berry harvest.

If you are planting berries for the first time, you will find that local garden outlets have their finest selection starting in March. Look for sturdy, top-quality, well-rooted plants.

It is especially important to take time to properly prepare the soil before planting berries. The addition of compost, processed or well-rotted manure, and peat moss to your soil is beneficial for the plants. Mix all these additives thoroughly with your existing soil to a depth of at least 10 to 12 inches.

At planting time, be certain to spread the roots out in the planting hole so that they have plenty of room in which to become established. (There is a tendency to crowd the roots into a small planting hole.) Be careful to set the plant right at ground level, at the same depth it was previously planted.

Many people do not realize that berries do not need a special area in the garden to grow successfully; many grow well alongside your other garden plants. For example, strawberries make a very attractive ground cover. Blueberry bushes are very showy landscape shrubs that flower, have nice leaf texture, and produce bright autumn leaf color. Grapes are nice when grown over an arbor as a patio cover or on a pillar or post. Even raspberries or vine berries can be grown in the landscape if space is limited.

Most berries do best in a bright sunny spot

with good air circulation. The soil should be well drained. A sandy loam type is ideal, but not essential. Most Northwest soils are satisfactory as long as good drainage is provided. If the soil in your garden tends to be a little on the wet side, it is important to mound the soil and raise the beds to provide the drainage berry plants need.

Early March is the best time for feeding most berries. You can use 5-10-10 or an all-purpose garden fertilizer for this purpose. A second application could be made in late May or early June if needed. Organic gardeners would mulch with manure in the fall.

Winter and early spring are the best times to dig and divide all types of berries with the exception of strawberries. Be sure you wait until early spring to late summer to divide and plant strawberries.

Birds and slugs are two of the biggest enemies of berries, so steps should be taken to try to eliminate them. Netting can be used over many of the crops to help protect the berries from being devoured by the birds. Flashing aluminum strips, scarecrows, and noise will often discourage them. If slugs are a problem, be sure to take steps to control them in areas where low-growing berries are being grown.

Weeds and grasses rob valuable nutrients from berry plants; they are also host to insects and diseases—an added incentive to keep them cultivated out of the berry patch.

Individual varieties require individual tech-

niques for pruning. Several methods are used, and if you are having success now, don't change your technique. On the other hand, if you have had limited success, perhaps these pointers will be helpful.

Raspberries. The canes that produced berries should be cut back to the ground level immediately after the fruiting season. The canes that developed during the summer will bear next year's fruit and should not be pruned. If the new canes get too tall and become weighted down by heavy foliage, snip off tip growth in the fall. In January or February, all canes can be cut back 4½ to 5 feet, cleaning out any weak or diseased canes.

Blackberries, boysenberries, and other vine berries. Grow one year and then produce berries the next. Immediately after the crop has been harvested, remove all of the vines that produced berries. The new vines that grew but did not produce berries should be left alone. Vine berries are robust growers and should be tip-pinched in spring when new growth starts. This encourages lateral growth and shortens the length of the vine. If a berry vine has gotten out of hand, I have found it best to cut it back to 2 or 3 feet from the ground and begin a regular pruning schedule.

Currants. The best time to prune is during the winter dormant season. Prune out old, dead, decayed, or weak canes. Leave a good balance of one-, two-, and three-year-old canes. They are the ones that will bear the fruit.

Blueberries. Berries develop on established growth, so it is advisable to encourage and save vigorous new growth. Weak or twiggy growth should be removed. Thin the growth to allow for good air circulation and light exposure. Remove approximately one-third of the old wood to encourage sturdy new growth to develop. The best time to prune is in February or early March. Try to avoid late pruning or the plants might become stunted. This could reduce fruit production.

Strawberries. The major pruning requirement is the removal of yellow, dead, or decayed leaves so that they will not affect the berry crop in any way. If too many runners develop, remove some of them. Runners tend to take strength from the parent plant, which can reduce berry size or quantity of fruit produced.

Grapes. Pruning should be done in winter or earliest spring. The actual amount of pruning will depend largely on where the plant is growing. Generally, the main cane is shortened to fit the trellis or arbor on which it is being grown. Be sure to thin out leggy or weak canes. As a guide, secondary growth is generally pruned back to the second bud. If too many canes are present, thin for best air circulation and sunlight exposure. Commercially grown grapes require more severe pruning than is suggested here.

When pruning any berries, always remove any dead, decayed, weak, or broken canes. Should any fruit remain on the plants as winter approaches, it should be picked and destroyed, as this is an excellent place for insects or diseases to winter over. If you want to enjoy the fresh flavor and nutritious value of berries from your own garden, spring is an excellent time to plant them.

Hanging Baskets for Summer Color

Colorful summer-flowering hanging baskets can add a bright new dimension to the summer landscape. For years hanging baskets were reserved for the porch or patio, but today imaginative home gardeners are using them for dramatic color effects in many other places around the garden.

In today's garden you will find baskets hanging from the eaves of the house, limbs of trees, from an old clothesline standard, or sitting on a pedestal or post. You are apt to see up to a dozen baskets hanging from specially constructed pipe frames. In fact, you will find half baskets tacked on fences, walls, or the side of the house for spot seasonal color. Spring is an excellent time to plant or purchase your hanging baskets to get them ready for summer's flowering season.

One of the key factors in successfully growing hanging baskets is to begin with a good soil mixture. Hanging baskets tend to dry out quickly because they are exposed to air on all sides, including the top and bottom, so it is important to use a soil mixture that will retain moisture. Commercial potting soils are often used for this purpose. If you plan to mix your own, use about one-half peat moss, one-fourth compost or processed manure, and one-fourth sandy loam. For fuchsias or begonias, it is best to use one-fourth each of compost, peat moss, processed manure, and sandy loam. Mix all of these ingredients thoroughly. Now you are ready to plant your hanging baskets.

There is often a tendency to be too skimpy with your planting, and, as a result, the baskets look too sparse most of the summer. If you are planting a combination basket, you can include up to a dozen to two dozen plants in a single basket. Use the trailing plants over the edge of the basket, medium-size plants next, and the taller plants in the center. If you are planting fuchsias, trailing-type begonias, or ivy geraniums, use four plants, one over each side of the basket. Although this may seem crowded as you plant the basket, it will provide an abundance of summer color as the plants begin their flowering period.

Hanging baskets can dry out easily. Make sure to give them special watering attention every day during the hot summer months.

Fuchsias, ivy geraniums, impatiens, trailing-type begonias, and combinations are probably the most popular types of hanging baskets for use in gardens here. Whether you make up your own or purchase one already made up, you will find that many local garden outlets have their finest selection of baskets and plants during the month of May.

Plants suited to hanging baskets are quick-growing and prolific-flowering, and will thus require more fertilization than most garden plants. It is generally recommended that plants in hanging baskets be fertilized on an average of once every three to four weeks. Usually, all-purpose liquid plant foods, fish fertilizer, or specialty plant foods are used for this feeding. It is important that you read and follow application directions on the label of the product you use.

Plants grown in hanging baskets sometimes tend to get a little leggy or spindly, so it is important to take time to occasionally pinch this irregular growth back to encourage bushiness and additional flowers. Also take time to remove any spent flowers on your hanging-basket plants—this keeps them from going to seed. If a plant dies, it is important to replace it with a new one so your basket remains bushy, healthy, and prolific-flowering.

Watering is probably the number one factor in successfully growing hanging baskets. During hot weather, it may be necessary to water at least once a day; during cool weather, watering is not required quite that frequently. Either extreme of watering can be fatal to your plants, so use good judgment. One of the best ways to test whether your hanging baskets need watering is simply to lift each one. If it is heavy, it has plenty of water. If it is light, the plants probably need water.

Be on the lookout throughout the summer months for any types of insects or diseases. Most hanging baskets will go through the entire summer without much trouble, but problems occasionally crop up. If you find either insects or disease, apply an all-purpose rose-garden or vegetable dust or spray. Since most insects appear on the undersides of the leaves, it is important that you concentrate your spray or dust in those areas.

Special consideration should be given to selecting the right plants for the location and exposure the basket will get. If you have a sunny location, be sure to choose plants that will grow and flower well in the sun. On the other hand, a shady location will require plants that tolerate shade. A combination of both groups will probably do well in a partial sun and shade spot.

Among the most popular hanging baskets for a sunny spot are ivy geraniums, lotus vines, ice plants, black-eyed Susans, and petunias. In combination baskets you can use all these plants plus upright geraniums, lobelia, marigolds, creeping Charlie, Livingston daisies, Marguerite daisies, verbena, ageratum, schizanthus, annual phlox, alyssum, and dwarf snapdragons, to name just a few.

Undoubtedly the most popular baskets for a shady location are fuchsias. In recent years impatiens baskets have also become very popular because of their prolific flowering habit and long flowering season. Trailing begonias also provide an abundance of color in the shade. Over the years the coleus with its bright multicolored foliage has been a popular hanging-basket plant in the shade. Combination baskets including impatiens, fuchsias, begonias, coleus, lobelia, alyssum, pansies, violas, and creeping Charlie also make an attractive display in the shaded garden. In a semisun location, hanging baskets receive part sun and shade, and protection from the hot midday sun. Most of the plants mentioned for shade or sun could be used in combination baskets. However, the best plants to use in the semisun location are ivy geraniums, lotus vines, ice plants, black-eyed Susans, petunias, lobelia, marigolds, creeping Charlie, upright geraniums, Livingston daisies, Marguerite daisies, verbena, ageratum, schizanthus, annual phlox, alyssum, dwarf snapdragons, impatiens, and the dark red variety of fuchsias.

You can certainly add a bright spot to your garden by including hanging baskets for summer color.

Diggin' in the Dirt—A Child's Garden

After being cooped up in the house most of the winter, the kids are as anxious as you are to get out and get their hands dirty. Most children really enjoy puttering in the soil, planting a seed or two, or putting a few plants into the vegetable garden—plants they can call their own. So let them do their thing. Give them a spot to try their

hand at gardening, but make it small. Young children will find a couple of square feet of garden space enough to handle.

Let them use your tools to mix the soil, add the fertilizer, and get things ready for planting. Be ready to lend a helping hand, but keep your coaching to a minimum. They will learn more by watching you first. Remember, it is up to them to water and care for the plants. But if they get busy playing games and doing other things and neglect their small garden, it's probably best not to say anything. Let them learn from your successes.

After they have prepared the soil, let them choose what they want to plant. Try to encourage them to grow those things that have a good chance of survival under any conditions—the types of flowers or vegetables that need only minimal watering and weeding. Sunflowers, for example, are a great choice. They grow huge and are easy to grow. Pumpkins are another great choice because of their robust growth and the large fruit they produce. Most flower bulbs are also easy to grow and provide a nice display. Dahlias and glads are especially nice to plant in springtime. Very young children need to see results in a hurry, so encourage them to grow radishes and lettuce.

Fast-growing, quick-flowering plants like nasturtiums, godetia, clarkia, alyssum, and marigolds are ideal for children to start from seed; it's a great learning experience for them to see the mir-

acles of Mother Nature when seed, soil, water, and sun interact.

Miscellaneous Spring Projects

After you have completed the major gardening projects, there are still other ones that can be done in the months of March, April, and May. Garden maintenance done in the spring and kept up will not only improve the appearance of your garden but also cut down on time that must be devoted to the garden when the warm summer weather arrives.

Probably one of the major projects that can be accomplished in the spring is the removal of moss from roofs, flower beds, and other parts of the garden. Whether the moss is growing on a cement walkway, the patio, the roof, or on trees and shrubs, it usually is quite conspicuous: It is a different color from the rest of the lawn, and it has a rather irregular habit of growth which many gardeners consider unattractive. In addition, it can deteriorate surfaces; and on cedar rounds and decks, it often becomes a slippery, slimy obstacle that could result in injury. Here are some ways of eliminating it wherever it is found. Chemical moss killers used on lawn areas cannot be used around flowers and shrubs, so moss growth in ornamental beds should be removed by cultivation. Then make an application of dolomite or agricultural lime to sweeten the soil and reduce the likelihood that moss will return. Mulching beds with bark or sawdust will also help. If the area is shaded by overhead trees and shrubs, removal of some lower branches will let in more light and discourage regrowth of moss.

Moss growing on the roof, on walkways, and on patios can be destroyed by using one of the specialized moss killers. It is very important to read and follow directions on the label, because moss killers contained in lawn fertilizers cannot be used on concrete or wooden surfaces—they would stain them. Therefore, be sure to get the right product for the particular job.

Moss, algae, or lichens growing on deciduous trees and shrubs can be sprayed during the dormant season with liquid lime-sulfur spray. Copper sprays can also be used. Remember that such sprays should be applied on most trees and shrubs only during the dormant season.

Because there are so many products that kill moss and most of them have limitations, I cannot stress enough the importance of reading the label and following directions carefully.

Over the years many gardeners have remarked to me that they enjoy the beauty of moss in the garden. If you are one of these, by all means let it grow unless it would create a hazard or adversely affect the appearance of your garden.

As you complete your major projects, don't forget the finishing touches. Destroy weeds before they have a chance to go to seed. Once the weeds are removed, herbicides can be used to help prevent their regrowth in many garden areas. For example, Casoron used in ornamental tree and shrub beds will help control hard-to-kill weeds, like horsetail and quack grass, for up to one full season. Another herbicide, such as Dachtal, can be used in some parts of the flower and shrub beds, and even in parts of the vegetable garden. However, all of these herbicides have limitations, so it is especially important that you read and follow application directions on the label.

Even though spring is the season for rain here in the Pacific Northwest, we do have occasional dry spells. Be sure your garden is getting adequate moisture. In many cases, plants under the eaves of the house or under tall evergreens or in containers are bone-dry and in desperate need of watering. Spring is a good time to check plants in such locations to see that they have sufficient moisture.

An excellent project for spring, especially during the rainy days, is greenhouse gardening. With a greenhouse you can take cuttings of many plants and flowers—azaleas, laurel, geraniums, fuchsias, heathers, coleus, chrysanthemums, gardenias, citrus plants, Marguerite daisies, poinsettias, and other houseplants. You can also seed annuals, perennials, and vegetables to get a head start on the season. It is a good time to pot many different types of plants—orchids, geraniums, fuchsias, begonias, African violets, and cactus.

Nice days of spring (and even the rainy ones) provide many opportunities to complete projects that will improve the appearance of your garden and make summer maintenance easier.

SUMMER

Summer is the time for beautiful weather, vacations, and water sports. It's easy to forget your garden with all the conflicting activities. However, the sun that you are enjoying can dry out your garden in a very short time. Watering and basic maintenance are two prime concerns.

The summer sun can be brutal, so be sure to give your vegetables, perennials, annuals, and lawn plenty of water. Roses, trees, shrubs, ground covers, and vines also need more water at this time of year. Houseplants and plants in outdoor containers dry out especially fast.

Summer maintenance includes weeding, fertilizing, and controlling garden pests. One way to cut down on watering is by pulling those water-consuming weeds. Adding fertilizer at appropriate times will promote sturdier growth during months of rapid growth. When controlling garden pests, try not to kill garden friends like bees, birds, spiders, and ladybugs. With this little bit of maintenance, your yard can look beautiful.

This is the time of year to enjoy the fruits of your labor. Don't make gardening a chore. Use the extra hours of daylight to keep your yard looking beautiful, while still enjoying all of the recreational activities summer has to offer.

Summer Vegetable Gardening

It is important to give vegetable plants the right care during the summer months. But by focusing on the essentials, you can maintain a beautiful vegetable garden and be assured of a bountiful harvest with a minimal amount of work.

Much of what was important in the spring is equally important during the summer. Watering and weeding should be continued. Insufficient water is one of the main causes of bitter vegetables. It is essential to run water on them long enough to get deep penetration. Two hours in the morning is usually sufficient. Don't forget to pull weeds this time of year—they consume water and can really hurt vegetable growth.

Since many vegetables grow quickly and mature rapidly, they need an occasional boost of fertilizer to keep them healthy and full of nutritional value. Organic gardeners often use a tea made of manure or processed manure for summer feedings. A 5-10-10 or general vegetable garden fertilizer is the type most often used by the chemical home gardener. Spread fertilizer along the sides of the crops, keeping it about 4 to 5 inches away from the plants. Read and follow label directions.

Mulching discourages the growth of weeds and grasses, and also helps retain moisture in the soil. Straw, sawdust, bark, shredded newspaper, and grass clippings are most often used for mulching the vegetable garden. (Never use grass clippings from a lawn that has been treated with a weed killer.) It is a good practice to check the mulching material every now and then to be certain that the soil is moist below.

Now is the time to make sure that tall-growing crops like beans have adequate staking. Tomatoes may also need support—often provided by circling the tomato plants with wire mesh or placing a tire around the plant's base.

Should any insects or diseases appear on your vegetable crops, they can be controlled by using a vegetable-garden-type spray or dust. Your local pesticide dealer or a certified nurseryman at your local garden outlet can recommend products that are safe for use on vegetables. When you get home, be sure to apply the product only as recommended on the label.

Slugs are active in the vegetable garden during the spring and early summer, and steps should be taken to control them (see pp. 137–139). Whatever method of slug control is used, it is important that you either get them before they enter your vegetable garden, or, if they are already in the garden, use methods to attract them out of it. Fortunately, slugs often go into a bit of a rest cycle during the warmer midsummer months, but you will find them nesting in the moist, cooler areas of the garden. Concentrate your slug control program in those areas.

It is important to prepare the soil and reseed as soon as one vegetable crop has finished. The second planting should be of quick-maturing crops. To prepare the soil, simply add additional fertilizer and spade or till to a depth of 6 to 8 inches, then reseed.

Second-seeding vegetable crops planted in June and July should be situated where they will get full sun and good air circulation. The following are a few of the most popular vegetables that could still be planted in June and July.

Beans. Bush green beans and wax beans can be seeded any time throughout June and July. However, it is too late by July to seed most pole beans.

Beets. Both the standard globe-type beets and cylindra beets can be seeded directly into the garden in June and July. Remember, you can enjoy beet greens as well the beets. If you cover the beets with evergreen boughs, straw, or some type of cloth during cold weather, you can continue to harvest them throughout the winter months.

Broccoli. This is one crop that can be seeded directly into the garden in June, or you can set out starter plants as late as July. The plants will withstand a light frost and gain flavor late in the season.

Chinese cabbage. It can be seeded directly into the garden in June, or seedling starter plants can be set out throughout the month of July—one of the best times of the entire year for seeding or planting Chinese cabbage. The plants have less tendency to bolt.

Carrots. This outstanding root vegetable can be seeded throughout the months of June and July. If they are given a winter covering, they may remain in well-drained soil over the winter and be harvested throughout the winter and early spring months. As with all root crops, be sure to thin them so that they develop properly.

Cauliflower. Seedling starter plants of this tasty vegetable can be planted throughout the month of June for a fall harvest.

Celery. Mid-June to early July is the best time for planting starter plants of celery. Late planting produces a crop that can be harvested in late October or early November.

Swiss chard. The red or white ribbed Swiss chard can be seeded directly into the garden throughout the months of June and July.

Collards. This is another excellent leaf crop that can be seeded directly into the garden during the months of June and July.

Kale. This nutritious crop can be seeded anytime throughout the month of June, or seedling starter plants can be set into the garden during the month of July. The flavor of this vegetable is intensified by a light frost, so July is an excellent time for planting.

Kohlrabi. Seed directly into the garden during June or July. Excellent flavor is obtained by late planting of this crop.

Lettuce. It is best to seed the leaf lettuce varieties. Bibb lettuce can be seeded throughout July and August. The typical leaf varieties can be seeded in July, August, and September. Seedling plants of both head and romaine lettuce can be set into the garden. Keep in mind that lettuce can be grown year-round if seeded in a cold frame or greenhouse, or if the plants are protected by covering.

Mustard greens. This is another crop that can be seeded directly into the garden from July through mid-September. Bok choy can be seeded until mid-August.

Green onions. These can be considered year-round plants, so you can count on them for winter harvest. Seed them in July and August.

Peas. Seed in June and again in early July for a second crop in the fall.

Radishes. All types and varieties can be seeded in July. The standard globe-type radishes can be seeded in August and September as well.

Spinach. Winter varieties can be seeded in September for winter or early spring harvest.

Turnips. Can be seeded in June and July for both greens and root crops.

Needless to say, if you have the space and the time, there are many other vegetables that can be planted or seeded during the months of June, July, and August; and they will provide fresh and nutritious vegetables in the fall and winter.

Perennials That
Flower in the Summertime

Are you looking for some permanent plants to provide color year after year? If you are, the answer may be the colorful summer-flowering perennials and biennials. These plants are relatively easy to start from seed, and June is one of the best months of the entire year for starting them.

Perennials are permanent garden plants. They will grow and flower year after year. The top growth of some types and varieties will die back during the winter, while others may maintain their leaves throughout the year. Biennials, on the other hand, complete their life cycle in two years. They will often reseed, however, providing flowers for many years.

For summer color, you can depend on such perennials as campanulas (Canterbury bells); chrysanthemums; coreopsis; many varieties of shasta daisies, carnations, and pinks; the magnificent delphiniums; gloriosa daisies, geum; baby's breath, lavender; lupines; phlox; Oriental poppies; painted daisies; and hardy asters. Whether used in perennial borders, massed in groups, or planted among trees and shrubs throughout the landscape, the various summer-flowering perennials add a bright touch and give permanence to the garden at the same time.

Some of the most popular biennials include wallflowers, sweet William, forget-me-nots, fox-glove, and hollyhock. Be sure you choose. the right exposure for each variety, whether it be full sun, part sun and shade, or full shade.

Many perennials and biennials are started from seed indoors in February or March. They can also be started outdoors in June. Soil temperature in June and July is generally warm enough to encourage rather fast seed germination and quicker development of seedling perennial plants.

Select a sunny spot in the garden to seed the perennials and biennials. It is a good practice to cultivate the soil to a depth of about 6 or 8 inches. The addition of peat moss or compost (if available) to your existing soil will be beneficial. Once you have cultivated the soil, rake it level and, if possible, hill it slightly so that it will warm up and dry quicker. Dusting the soil with an all-purpose fungicide, like Captan, will help control damp-off disease.

Once the soil is prepared, you are ready for seeding. It is easiest to scatter the small seeds over the prepared area, letting them run off your fingertips or between your fingers. Be sure to scatter them according to instructions on the seed packet.

After you have sown the seed, firm the soil with the palm of your hand or a board. Next, lightly cover the seed with a fine layer of soil or peat moss (or tamp down, according to the package instructions). It is at this stage that many gardeners make a big mistake. Never cover the seed with more than about 1/8 inch of soil. Again, the directions on the seed packet will be of assistance in determining how much soil should be used to cover the seed. If in doubt, however, cover with less soil than is recommended.

Some seeds of both perennials and biennials are hard-shelled and can be quite difficult to germinate. In the past it has been a common practice to assist their germination by either nicking or filing them to break through the hard outer shell. In recent years it has become more commonplace to freeze the seed, which helps hard-shelled seeds to germinate more rapidly. The ice tray from the freezer is usually used for this process. Fill the tray half full of water and freeze, then remove the tray from the freezer and scatter the hard-shelled seeds on top of the ice, leaving the tray out just long enough for the ice to begin to thaw. Fill the tray full of water and put it back into the freezer to freeze again—encasing the seeds in ice. Leave the seeds in the freezer for approximately two days, after which time they can be thawed and planted.

Plants started from seed this year will usually flower for the first time next year.

DIVIDING PERENNIALS

The summer months are an excellent time to divide spring-flowering perennials—primroses, aubrietia, candytuft, arabis, iris, and many others. The summer-flowering types are divided in the springtime, usually late in March or in April.

It is not necessary to dig and divide perennials each year. In fact, they will often go three, four, or more years before they become overcrowded or encroached on by weeds and need to be separated.

If perennial plants are not doing well, it is often because the nutrients in the soil have been used up. This can be another reason for digging the plants. Repreparing the soil with nutrients before replanting the divisions will result in healthier plants.

The third reason for dividing perennials is to increase the supply of plants. This is probably the most common reason for undertaking this task.

The actual digging and dividing is very simple. As you dig the clumps, be sure to start out far enough away so that you get all of the roots without breaking or damaging them. Gently shake or wash off the soil that clings to the roots. They are hairlike, very fragile, and can be damaged easily.

To divide the clumps, pull apart or cut away each division from the crown of the plant with roots intact. A few roots will break off and can be discarded. Discard the old center part of the clump—the young outer divisions are the healthy ones. The new divisions should be reset in the ground as soon as possible so that the air does not dry out the roots.

Each type of perennial has its own planting requirements: Primroses, for example, must be planted with the crown right at ground level; setting the crown too low will suffocate the roots and the plant will die. This is also true of other types. On the other hand, bearded iris should be planted with about half the rhizome in the soil. Be sure to note the planting depth as you dig each plant, so you can replant at the same depth.

After transplanting, soak the new divisions thoroughly with water. In the days that follow, watch the watering closely so the plants have a chance to become established. Mulching with peat moss will help retain moisture, and will discourage the growth of weeds. Avoid mounding the mulch up around the crowns of the plants, however.

Proper watering during the summer is the most important concern. Nearly all perennials, including summer-flowering types, need a good deal of moisture throughout the summer season. If you can let a garden hose run at the base of the plants for about five minutes, the soil will be thoroughly soaked. If the plants are in among trees and shrubs, you may find it more convenient to use a sprinkler. If so, try to sprinkle during the morning hours so the foliage will have time to dry before the cool evening hours set in.

As soon as perennials have finished flowering, it is a good idea to remove the spent blooms. Cut them back along with any leaves that turn yellow-brown or have an off-color appearance. If you remove the spent blooms before they have a chance to go to seed, the plant will often flower for a longer period of time.

Regardless of the plant types being grown, June or early summer is the time to feed perennials with fertilizer.

Insect and disease problems vary from one perennial to another, but generally an all-purpose rose dust or spray containing an insecticide and fungicide will give satisfactory control. Read and follow the directions on the label of the chosen brand. Be sure to spray or dust at a time when the bees are not active in the garden.

Take the time to properly care for your perennials this summer and they will continue to look nice in the garden all year long.

Annuals for Summer Color Spots

SUMMER CARE

It is hard to beat the prolific summer color that annuals provide in the Northwest garden. To keep them flowering for the longest possible time, special consideration should be given to feeding, watering, pinching, and cultivating them during their summer-flowering season.

Since annuals are fast-growing plants, it is important to fertilize them every two to four weeks throughout the summer. Fish fertilizer or a liquid all-purpose garden fertilizer is generally used. Make sure the soil is moist prior to feeding; and if fertilizer is to be sprayed, be certain it is done during the coolest part of the day.

Some annuals have special watering requirements. Many of the succulent annuals—like Livingston daisies, moss rose, and ice plant—require less water than the leafy types. As a rule, it is a good practice to allow water to penetrate to a depth of at least 6 inches each time you water. Early morning is by far the best time to water annuals. Avoid watering in the late afternoon or in the evening. Otherwise, moist conditions are apt to attract slugs and could create mildew.

Other things to be taken care of during the summer include pinching back leggy growth, removing dead flowers, and checking for slugs, insects, and disease. If the last three mentioned are present, take care of them as you did in the spring.

COLOR SPOTS

In recent years, commercial growers have been producing larger annuals in full bloom for late planting. These plants are referred to as "color spots" in the garden trade, and the advantage of using them is that they provide instant color. If you have an area in your garden that looks dull and drab, set out a few color spots this summer.

Color spots come in a wide selection of annual types and varieties. The lower-growing types are ideal for borders or low massing, while medium-size plants are ideal for big border plantings, foundation plantings, or mass plantings in landscape beds. The tallest-growing annuals are excellent for background plantings or seasonal cut flowers. Many of the color spots are also ideal for containers or hanging baskets.

When you get the plants home, be sure to follow these easy steps in planting them. Take time to properly prepare the soil so the plants will continue to grow with a minimum amount of setback. Dig a planting hole about twice as wide and deep as the actual size of the rootball. For a 4-inch-pot plant, this would mean preparing a planting hole about 8 inches wide and 8 inches deep. Into the planting soil mix peat moss, processed manure, and a little liquid fertilizer. Be sure to water the plant thoroughly while it is still in the pot; the moist soil will cling to the roots, reducing transplanting shock. Set the plant at the same soil level as it was previously planted. Then, with the palm of your hand, firm the soil around the plant. Finally, soak thoroughly with water.

Among the most popular color spots are zinnias, marigolds, salvia, impatiens, begonias, geraniums, ageratum, and coleus. Some petunias, dianthus, and dahlias are also favorites. If you have a sunny location, zinnias, salvia, geraniums, ager-atum, petunias, dianthus, and dahlias are the best plants to use. For a shady spot, choose impatiens, begonias, or coleus. Give these color spots the same care you would your other summer annuals. Give the annuals the care they need and they will reward you with nice foliage, bushy plants, and a profusion of summer-flowering color.

Summer Rose Care

Throughout the world the rose is undoubtedly one of the most popular flowering garden plants, and there are few places in the world where they grow as well as right here in the Pacific Northwest. If you simply observe their cultural requirements and give them the care they need, they will respond with attractive foliage and beautiful flowers during the summer-flowering season.

Roses grow and flower prolifically over a period of a few months, so they need more fertilizing, watering, and spraying attention than most plants. Here are a few ideas on steps you can take to keep them in top-notch growing and flowering condition this summer.

Whenever possible, keep water off the foliage of rosebushes; water by the irrigation method. Avoid nighttime watering—it keeps the soil too cold and moist throughout the normally cooler evening hours. Water deeply.

Fertilize roses monthly throughout their spring and summer growing season—until August, when only a light application of fertilizer should be given your roses so they'll have a chance to begin hardening off before cooler weather sets in.

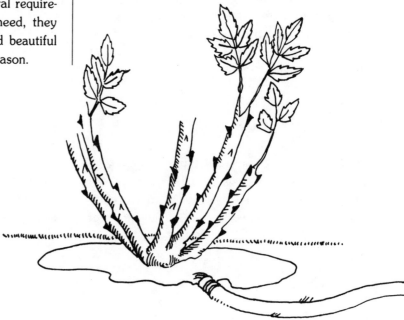

When a rose has finished flowering, cut the stem back to the first five-leaflet stem.

Severe pruning should be avoided during the summer, but roses will benefit from a little summer pruning, which can best be done at the time you pick the blossoms. As you are cutting flowers or removing faded blossoms, cut the flower stem back to just above the first five-leaflet stem so the plant will rebranch with new, long flower stems.

Special attention should be given to the control of insects and disease. Aphids, whiteflies, spider mites, and many other insects can be found on roses. A well-planned program of spraying or dusting is necessary to keep your roses looking their best. Systemic insecticides, often used to control sucking types of insects, are generally effective for three to six weeks. Since systemics do not control chewing-type insects, apply an all-purpose rose dust or spray to control them if they become a problem.

If you are in doubt as to which type of product to use to control a particular insect or disease, consult your local nurseryman, master gardener, pesticide dealer, or garden clerk. Be certain to spray or dust at a time when the bees are not active in the garden.

Cool, moist weather often aggravates mildew and black spot on rosebushes. Use a rose fungicide—Funginex or Benomyl—to control these problems. In order to effectively control the different types of mildew, the rose hobbyist will often alternate the use of these two fungicides, since some strains are apt to build up a resistance to one fungicide but seldom to both. Some brands of rose dust contain a combination of fungicide and insecticide and can be used to help control both insects and disease. Early morning is by far the best time to apply fungicides.

After removing the weeds, you can mulch your rosebushes with bark or sawdust. Mulching not only discourages weed growth but also helps to hold moisture in the soil. There are also several types of preemergent herbicides (see pp. 132–133) that will help control the regrowth of weeds. If you have a particular weed problem, check with your local nurseryman, master gardener, pesticide dealer, or garden clerk for recommendations on the best herbicide to use.

It is very important that roses be planted in a location where they get plenty of sunlight, good air circulation, and adequate drainage. If your rosebush is planted in the wrong location, wait until this winter to move it to a more satisfactory spot. It can be transplanted anytime between November and late February.

Roses grown in containers can be planted during the summer. Plant container and all at that time. In the fall after the first light frost, the plants can be dug and planted directly into the soil.

If you give your roses extra care during the summer season, they will flower well for you.

Lawn Care During the Summer

Since the lawn is the framework for the entire landscape, it is important to keep it looking nice all summer. Take time to plan a program of summer lawn care that includes scheduled times for mowing, watering, feeding, and general lawn maintenance. Summer lawn care need not be difficult, but haphazard maintenance does not give very satisfactory results.

The fertilizer that you applied to the lawn this spring has probably been all used up by June or July or has leached out of the soil; so summer is an excellent time for an application of a summer lawn fertilizer. If you are not sure which particular type or brand to use, ask your local garden clerk for suggestions. It is important to read and follow directions on the label as to how much to apply, when to apply, whether watering is necessary, and any other particulars that would affect the performance of the fertilizer you are using.

Avoid fast-acting types that stimulate rapid growth but have little lasting quality. Use one that contains slow-release nitrogen and it will not be necessary to fertilize as frequently.

One of the biggest mistakes in lawn watering is to water frequently for short periods of time. All this does is encourage shallow rooting of the

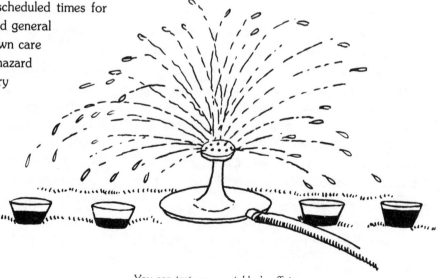

You can test your sprinkler's efficiency by the amount of water that lands in each container.

grass, and in very warm weather it dries up in a hurry. When you water the lawn, set a sprinkler for an hour or more or until the water has penetrated to a depth of 6 inches or more. You can check water penetration by using a straight-edge shovel to pull back the soil and examining it. After doing this once or twice, you will know how long the sprinkler should be set in one location for the deep water penetration you desire. Turf specialists say it takes only three days for the lawn to dry out, but about a month to restore it to good green color. So give the lawn the water it needs.

Sometimes you will find that water will run off the lawn if the sprinkler is set in one spot for a

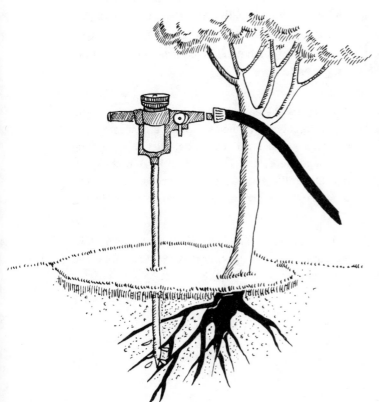

long time. Hard, compacted soil could cause the water to start to run off after a half-hour or less of sprinkling time. There are two ways to overcome this problem. One is a wetting agent that assists water penetration; one application is effective for about six weeks. The second is to punch holes in the turf with a perforating tool, pitchfork, or root feeder so water can get through the compacted soil.

Weed control is another major factor in keeping the lawn nice-looking during the summer. If you have just a few spotty weeds in the lawn area, they can be removed with a weed-pulling device, or you can cut them out with a kitchen knife. If, on the other hand, you have a lot of weeds in the lawn, you can use a liquid weed control product or a combination weed and feed product. Commercial weed control products must be applied under certain conditions of wind and weather, so it is exceptionally important that label instructions be followed to the letter. Be sure to do the job when the wind is not blowing—even a light breeze can carry the weed killer onto desirable plants and damage them—and when there is no chance of rain for at least twenty-four hours. Weak solutions are not effective, and solutions that are too strong will only burn your lawn weeds. Give the material time to work before it is diluted by water.

Toadstools are also a problem in many Northwest lawns. Unfortunately, there is no technical recommendation for their control. The best way to handle the situation, according to one specialist, is to "mow the lawn and forget about the toadstools."

Annual bluegrass (*Poa annuna*) can ruin the appearance of a lawn. During the summer months it is usually a lighter color than the rest of the grass and often grows a short seed head. The recommended control for this nuisance grass is the chemical Bensulide. It is contained in several lawn products.

Veronica, the blue-flowering weed, is another nuisance in some Northwest lawns. Dachtal is generally recommended for its control.

If miniature mounds of dirt (about the size of a quarter) appear in the lawn, this usually indicates the presence of nightcrawlers. Anything you might use to control them would also affect all beneficial worms. If possible, it is best to ignore the presence of nightcrawlers.

The number one complaint I hear during the summer months is: "How can I get rid of those brown spots in my lawn?" They can be caused by several different things, but most often soil compaction or thatch is the problem. One of the best ways to determine whether either of these is the cause of the brown spots is to remove a 4-inch sample plug of the lawn for examination. You can tell quite easily if there is a thatch build-up or the soil is compacted. If neither condition exists, there are other possibilities to consider.

Small to medium brown spots may be caused by the urine of female dogs. If you catch these spots early, you stand a pretty good chance of avoiding complete die-out in the affected area. Usually the grass will turn bright dark green and then take on a dull gray-green or blue-green color. Immediately saturating the area with water often dilutes the urine sufficiently to avoid killing the grass.

Lawn moths and sod webworms often appear in early summer. You can see them flying over the lawn; or in the morning, when dew is on the grass, their webs often can be seen. They resemble small spider webs. Diazinon and other lawn insecticides can be used to control the larvae.

Another brown-spot problem is lawn fairy ring, which is caused by an underground root growth. This condition appears in a circular pattern in the lawn in various sizes depending upon its rate of growth. The lawn within the ring is either darker or (usually) lighter than the rest of the lawn. Currently, the recommended control for lawn fairy ring is as follows:

1. Perforate the entire ring and about 1 foot beyond in all directions. The holes should be at least 6 to 8 inches deep and can be made with a perforating tool, a manure fork, or a pitchfork. A root feeder that fits on the end of a garden hose is ideal for this purpose. Place the holes approximately 4 inches apart.

2. Treat the entire area with a wetting agent. Following the application directions on the label, treat the area you have perforated.

3. Set a sprinkler, and keep the fairy ring area at least three times wetter than you would normally keep the rest of the lawn. This means that the fairy ring should be moist at all times.

4. Keep the entire area moist for a thirty-day period.

Set up a schedule of regular maintenance for your lawn this summer and you will find that it takes very little time to keep it in top condition. By providing a little extra care in the early summer, you can keep your lawn looking its best all summer long and give it a head start on the fall season.

Attractive Summer-Flowering Trees and Shrubs

Are you looking for some summer-flowering shrubs to add bright spots of color to your permanent landscape? Well, you don't have to look very far, because there are several summer-flowering shrubs that can be used in the Northwest garden to fill the gap between the spring-flowering rhododendrons, camellias, azaleas, and bulbs and the summer-flowering annuals and perennials.

One of the greatest advantages of summer-flowering plants is that they come in a wide range of sizes, so they can be used in many areas of the garden. Here are a few that are especially popular in the Pacific Northwest.

Heather. Some summer-flowering varieties are attractive not only for their flowers but for their interesting foliage. The golden tones plus the light, medium, and dark green shades are bright additions to the garden. The flowers are a bonus, and the season ranges from June until October, depending upon the variety grown. They are excellent for rockeries and borders or for spot color throughout the landscape.

Ceanothus. If you are looking for a shrub that flowers in late May and June, this is an ideal choice. Bright blue flowers and dark green foliage add a bright spot of color to the garden. There are several different varieties, including low-growing ground-cover types and taller upright varieties. Colors range from light blue to brilliant blue. This is one of those garden shrubs that thrive on a certain amount of neglect.

Hydrangea. Another popular plant here in the Pacific Northwest. They have large flowers and provide an abundance of color in the garden during the summer. The blue-flowering variety is the most popular, but they are also available in shades of lavender, pink, rose, and white. One of the great advantages of this plant is that besides providing color in the garden, the flowers can also be picked and used as cut flowers or dried for use in winter arrangements. Plant hydrangeas where they are protected from the hot midday sun.

Veronica. The various varieties are all attractive in the garden. Probably the most popular one here is Autumn Glory, a low-growing evergreen that will reach about 3 feet at maturity; however, it can be pruned and kept bushier. Beautiful blue flowers begin to appear in June and continue until frost if the dead flowers are kept picked. It does best in full sun or partial sun and shade.

Abelia. This is another plant that has a long flowering season. Two varieties are commonly used in gardens in the Northwest: Edward Goucher—a bushy, compact variety with dark pink flowers; and Grandiflora—a taller variety with lighter-colored flowers. Both flower almost continually from July until October. They grow equally well in full sun or part sun and shade.

Escallonia. This plant is especially popular because of the many varieties available. Some flower as early as June, while others do not flower until July or August. Although blooms vary by variety, the pink, rose, and red ones are by far the most popular. This is another plant that does best when placed in full sun. Most varieties will reach 5 to 7 feet at maturity, but they can be kept lower with pruning. This is an excellent evergreen for hedging, screening, or group planting throughout the landscape.

Callistemon. If you are looking for something different, this is an excellent plant. Commonly called "bottlebrush," its unusual bottlelike flowers are bright red and make an interesting contrast to most flowering evergreens. It must be placed in full sun, and it enjoys dry soil. It is a plant that thrives on neglect.

Smoke tree. This is a large shrub or small tree. Foliage colors are either green or red, depending on the variety. Pink to gray fruiting panicles cover the plant in midsummer and give the appearance of a cloud or puff of smoke. It likes plenty of sun, and it is deciduous. Yellow fall foliage color is nice.

Potentillas. The summer-flowering varieties make colorful garden plants. Flowers range in shades of cream, yellow, and orange. They flower from June until the first frosts of fall. The plants are deciduous but provide constant color during the summer months.

Convolvulus cneorum. One of my particular favorites for summer color, it is sometimes difficult to find. Commonly called "evergreen morning glory," it has a name association with a nuisance plant, but it is a beautiful shrub and not a pest at all. It is evergreen, has gray foliage, and is covered with pink flowers almost all summer long. It needs a bright, sunny location and thrives on neglect. If you can locate one, you should definitely consider including it in your landscape.

There are many other summer-flowering plants that could have been listed, but these give you some idea of the wide range of choices available. Visit local nurseries and growers during the summer so you can see the many varieties in bloom and decide which ones best suit your needs.

Before planting the new shrub or tree in your garden, take time to determine which is the front and which is the back side of the plant. Be sure to face the best side forward. You would be amazed at how many plants are incorrectly faced in the landscape. Such plants take several years to adjust their growth habits so they look as nice as they should. Also be sure to choose the proper location for your plants—and remember that deep watering and feeding are essential for trees and shrubs during the summer.

CARING FOR SPRING-FLOWERING TREES AND SHRUBS

Besides planting and caring for summer-flowering trees and shrubs, it is necessary to continue to care for your spring-flowering trees and shrubs. Rhododendrons in particular need extra care in the summer. They go through a rather ugly time right after they have finished flowering. Dead flowers on plants ruin the appearance of attractive leaves, and the removal of spent flowers will divert the energy and nutrients of the plant from seed production to the development of new growth and possible buds for the next year's blossoms. You will find that Mother Nature has provided a special place to snap off the dead flowers, indicated by a series of rings around the stem just at the base of the flower. Be especially careful when you snap off spent flowers—it is very easy to damage new growth if you are not. On close observation you will find that the new

growth develops right below the point where you snap off the dead rhododendron flower.

Mid-June or right after the rhododendron has finished flowering is an excellent time to feed them. Use a rhododendron-type fertilizer for this job. Organic gardeners may prefer to use fish fertilizer or cottonseed meal. Since rhododendrons, azaleas, and camellias are all surface-rooted plants, it is important that the fertilizer be applied out at the dripline of the plant to avoid spreading it up under the plant where it is likely to burn the surface feeder roots. If you use a dry fertilizer, it is very important to water the fertilizer in thoroughly after application. Never rely on the rain to do this job. Be sure to apply only the recommended amount of fertilizer.

SUMMER MAINTENANCE

One of the biggest problems a Northwest gardener experiences is plants that grow out of bounds, become misshapen, or remain sparse. Such conditions can often be corrected simply by pinching or pruning at the proper time of the year. Late spring and early summer are excellent times to prune many garden plants—junipers, conifers, some broad-leaf evergreens, rhododendrons, azaleas, camellias, and others. Common sense is the key to good pruning. Never prune unless it is necessary; trim to enhance the beauty of the plant when it is needed. Of course spent flowers, sucker growth, and any dead or decayed branches should be removed as they appear.

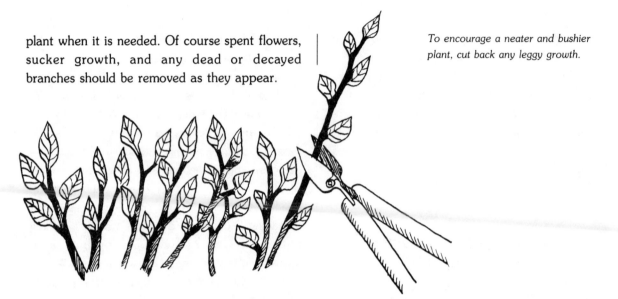

To encourage a neater and bushier plant, cut back any leggy growth.

Forsythia, spirea, mock orange, quince. Light pruning of any of these spring-flowering deciduous shrubs and others that bloom before June can be done immediately after flowering. Heavy pruning of such plants should wait until the winter dormant season. Leggy growth on any of these plants should be pruned back to encourage bushiness. Up to one-third of the old growth can be removed to encourage new flowering growth to develop.

Lilacs. Remove the spent flowers, being careful not to cut too far back or you might remove next year's flowers, which are forming during June. Limited pruning can be done on lilacs, but severe pruning should wait until the winter dormant season.

Junipers and conifers. Plants that need pruning can be attended to in June. Simply pinch tip growth of junipers to encourage secondary growth. This in turn

encourages bushiness and a more compact growth habit. Often, established plants tend to become quite straggly with only three to five leaders. Tip pinching often enhances the beauty of the plant. If necessary, trimming can be done again in July.

Fruit, flowering, and shade trees. There is a tendency among many to let sucker growth develop on these trees, and wait until the winter dormant season to remove it. I think it is better to remove suckers as they appear. Those that develop from the base of trees and roots should be snapped off cleanly. Water sprouts that develop from limbs should be cut back to the branch from which they originated. If you leave any stubs, they will return in increased numbers.

Rhododendrons. If they need severe pruning, the best time to do it is immediately after flowering. Cut back to the point where previous season's growth originated. They are very easy to prune. When they get out of hand or are not maintaining the shape you desire, pruning may be necessary. Keep in mind that 95 percent of the rhododendrons grown in the Northwest will never need pruning of any kind, so use good sense in deciding whether to undertake this project. Severe pruning will result in the loss of flowers of at least one year.

Warmer summer months are often problem months for insects and diseases on both trees and shrubs. In recent years, pine-shoot moth has been quite troublesome in parts of the Pacific Northwest, distorting or killing new growth on pines. Close observation will show that some of the new candles have been undermined at their base. A blob of pitch may be present. Actual entry holes made by the insect may be visible, and the larvae may even be found inside the stem.

This insect is rather difficult to control because it emerges from the stem, deposits its eggs, and disappears within a twenty-four-hour period. The recommended control is to spray at two-week intervals, from May 15 to June 15, using 25 percent Diazinon or the insecticide Sevin (I am hesitant about recommending Sevin because it is so deadly to bees). Thoroughly drench the affected trees with insecticide. Distorted or dead candle growth should be clipped off immediately and burned.

Lecanium scale is another possible insect prob-

lem. The brown to black egg cases, about the size of a pencil eraser, can often be found on numerous types of trees in the spring and early summer. As long as insects are in under the cover of the scale, there is no way to control them other than to peel the egg off the branches, and this would be a tedious job. Usually from about mid-June on, insects begin crawling out from under egg casings, and it is at this point that they can be controlled. The actual crawling stage of this insect varies somewhat from one area to another, so it is a good idea to check with a magnifying glass to see whether the insect is on the move. An all-purpose insecticide like Diazinon, Malathion, Orthene, or other multipurpose insecticides can be used to control this insect. On fruit trees, be certain to use only a safe product like fruit or berry insect spray.

The insect that ruins the appearance of lilac and holly foliage is the leaf miner. This insect generally lays its eggs on the midrib or veins of the leaves. As it matures it tunnels through the inner layers of the leaf. A systemic insecticide like Orthene is generally used to help control this pest on nonedible plants.

You can brighten up your summer garden by including a few of the permanent summer-flowering shrubs, and early summer is an excellent time to select and plant them. Be sure to give your trees and shrubs the care they need during the summer and they will reward you with healthier, sturdier, more attractive growth.

Houseplants

If you plan on putting any of your houseplants outdoors during the summer, it is very important that you wait until weather conditions are suitable. The weather up until mid-June is too cold for most houseplants. Nighttime temperatures should remain consistently near or above 60 degrees or your houseplants are apt to suffer.

It is especially important to select a spot for them in the garden that closely resembles the location in which they were situated in your home in terms of light. Most tropical houseplants cannot tolerate continual exposure to bright sunlight. Provide protection for them from the hot midday sun; in fact, a location where they get filtered sunlight from noon until 5:00 P.M. is ideal. It is also important to place them where they will be protected from strong winds.

If you are looking for suitable outdoor locations for your houseplants, consider placing them under flowering or shade trees, evergreens, or between trees and shrubs in flower beds. Other good locations are a covered patio, entry area, or under the eaves of the house. Be careful to avoid locations that get reflected sunlight.

Quite a few houseplants will definitely benefit from being outdoors during the summer. Among the most popular are these:

Poinsettias. Place them where they get full sun. As they grow during the summer season, prune back any leggy growth that develops. Cuttings can be taken from tip growth.

Ferns. If your ferns are suffering from their indoor environment, move them outdoors during the summer season, choosing a shady location.

Christmas cactus. Another plant that does especially well outdoors during the summer is the Christmas cactus. Be certain it is protected from hot midday sun. Easter and Thanksgiving cacti can also be placed outdoors in the summer. Often, this move encourages the development of flower buds and eventual flowering.

Citrus plants. The various types of citrus plants also seem to benefit from being outdoors during the summer. Be careful not to place them in an area where they would be subject to mite infestation. When it is time to take them back into the home in late summer, be sure that they are taken in gradually; otherwise they are apt to lose their leaves, keeping them in a cool room or covered porch for a few days to acclimate them, before placing them in the house where the air is hot and dry.

Jade plants. These do very well if they are placed outdoors during the summer season. Give them a spot in the garden where they are protected from hot midday sun but receive regular bright light. Watch watering, as there is a tendency to water them too much.

Don't forget your houseplants when you go on vacation. Remember, they are completely dependent upon you at all times for food, water, light, and proper air circulation. One way to provide for plants in your absence is to arrange for a neighbor or friend to care for them. But if you will be away for only ten days to two weeks, you can provide for them yourself. Place a piece of polyethylene in the bathtub, shower, sink, or washtub, and put a few damp newspapers on top of the polyethylene. Water the plants moderately and place them on top of the damp newspapers. This will provide them with moisture and humidity while you are away. If a covering is placed over the plants, or if the pots are enclosed in polyethylene, they will be safe even longer. With either of these methods, houseplants should be kept out of direct sun or bright light.

Away on a short vacation? Your houseplants can take care of themselves using a simple method of polyethylene, damp newspapers, and the bathtub.

HOUSEPLANT VINES

Vining houseplants can be used to accent the decor and add color and texture to the home along with other houseplants. Vines are usually grown in hanging baskets, but they also do well on a high shelf or windowsill. They can be trained upward or left to hang naturally. Actually, vines can be trained to do just about anything you want them to do.

One of the best uses for a vining plant is the one most often overlooked: to hide the bare stem of an upright houseplant that has lost all of its lower leaves. The vine not only covers the stem but can also provide an interesting texture variation and second leaf color.

When selecting a vine, there are several things you should consider. Location, light exposure, humidity, and eventual size are some of the concerns. Some thought should also be given to leaf texture and color, flowers, shape, and bushiness. By considering all of these things, you can choose just the right vine for any given situation. Should there be several houseplants in the room where you want to place a vine, be sure all of them are compatible and complement each other.

The specific care of any vining houseplant will depend upon where in the room it is placed. Plants on low tables near the floor require different care from those sitting on high shelves or hanging from the ceiling, because the air is hotter and dryer the higher you go in a room. Humidity and watering requirements increase with the height of the plant. Soil conditions, light exposure, and pot size are other contributing factors in the care of vines.

The hardest decision for the indoor gardener is determining the watering requirements of vines. There is no set rule to follow. Requirements differ from one plant to another, based on the conditions listed above. You will need to experiment a little to set up a suitable watering schedule for each plant in your home. Generally, I have found it best to water vining plants thoroughly, then determine when they need rewatering by lifting the pots to test their weight. A dry plant will be much lighter than one that is sufficiently moist. There is a tendency on the part of many to water as recommended by someone else. Don't rely on such advice; determine a watering schedule based on your own observation under your specific home conditions. Each situation is different.

Should a vine become spindly or grow out of shape, don't hesitate to pinch back the straggly growth to encourage bushiness. You can train a vine to grow upward with the aid of a wood or plastic trellis, or wooden stakes. If the vine does not have its own natural tendrils, the branches can be held in place with twist ties, string, or coated wire.

The following are a few of the most popular houseplant vines you may want to consider:

Bridal veil. Care is similar to that for wandering Jew. Ample humidity is needed, but be careful not to overwater this vine.

Clerodendron. It has nice deep green leaves and clusters of white flowers, each with a bright scarlet tube in the center. It requires bright light and high humidity. Keep it moist but not wet.

Ferns. Although not considered to be vines, they are often used as hanging plants. To grow at their best, they need a cool location. Protect them from direct sunlight and provide more humidity than for most of the other plants mentioned here.

Grape ivy. A bushy, compact habit of growth and glossy dark green leaves makes this plant excellent for hanging baskets or for training up a post. Place in bright light or semishade. Keep the soil moist but never overwet.

Again, houseplants are completely dependent on you for proper care. Provide it by setting up a proven schedule for watering, and by taking into account each plant's needs for heat, light, food, air, proper location, and humidity. Consider setting some of your houseplant vines outside for a summer break, but be sure to remember that those inside will need special care as well.

Drying Flowers
for Summer Arrangements

EVERLASTINGS

A popular flower for drying is the everlasting, because the flowers provide an abundance of color in the garden during the summer and can then be dried and used indoors as cut flowers year round. Easy to grow, everlastings thrive on a certain amount of neglect.

The following are a few of the most popular old-time favorite everlastings:

Strawflower. These come in a wide range of varieties that grow from 2 to 2½ feet in height. Colors range from white through yellow, gold, rose, and wine—an assortment that provides an abundance of color both fresh and dried.

Moneyplant or *Honesty.* This plant is an old-time favorite biennial that is grown and treated as an annual. It is best known for its silvery white flat seed pods, which are dried for use in arrangements.

Cockscomb or *Celosia.* This plant comes in two different varieties: the feathery plume type and the cockscomb or crested type. They are very durable as dried flowers and very attractive as garden annuals.

Statice. This plant grows to about 1 to 2 feet in height and produces clusters of parchmentlike small flowers in shades of rose, blue, pink, yellow, and white.

Bells of Ireland. These have very colorful green bell-shaped bracts, which turn straw-colored when they are dried.

Many of the everlastings can be grown from seed or from plants in the spring. Local garden outlets often feature seedling bedding plants of many types. Select a spot in the garden where the soil is well drained. The various types of everlastings will grow best in full sun. Take time to properly prepare the soil by mixing ample amounts of processed manure, compost if available, and peat moss into your existing soil. Spade or till to a depth of about 8 to 10 inches just before planting. At planting time, mix in the correct amount of an all-purpose garden fertilizer. Further fertilizing should be done strictly on a need basis. If the plants are healthy and growing abundantly, there is no need for further fertilizing.

Because there is a tendency to overwater everlastings during their growing cycle, it is best to plant them in an area where they are apt to be somewhat neglected. This will give them a chance to toughen up and harden off so they will last longer as dried flowers.

Everlastings are not really susceptible to many insects or diseases. However, if either should occur, you can use an all-purpose rose or vegetable-garden dust or spray.

DRYING FLOWERS

Late summer is an excellent time to dry some of the flowers from your garden so you can enjoy their beauty in your home during the fall and winter. They will last up to a year or sometimes even longer. Marigolds, zinnias, pansies, violas, and hydrangeas are just a few of the most popular flowers for drying. Indeed, almost all flowers can be dried successfully.

The key to drying flowers is to withdraw 50 to 90 percent of the water from them without destroying the appearance of the flowers or foliage. Keep in mind that as the flowers dry and lose water content, they become smaller in size; therefore, many more will be needed to create an arrangement than you would use with fresh material.

You will need a sharp pair of scissors or garden shears to cut the flowers. After drying them, you will need thin wire and green florist tape to prepare the flowers for arrangements. Following are a few of the easy methods for drying flowers in your home:

Air drying. To use this method, simply hang bunches of flowers upside down in a cool, dry room. Among the most popular for air drying are baby's breath, bells of Ireland, cattails, Chinese lantern, globe thistle, hydrangeas, strawflowers, and money plant. Herbs, such as mint, thyme, and sage, can also be dried in this manner. Generally, it will take about two or three weeks for these flowers and herbs to dry properly.

Silica sand drying. This is one of the most overlooked methods of drying flowers, though it is easy and relatively inexpensive. Many of the more delicate flowers, like zinnias, browallia, marigolds, lobelia, heathers, and just about any other flower can be dried by this method. Silica sand can be purchased at almost any masonry store or building-material center. The flowers are simply buried in the silica sand for one to four weeks. My wife uses this method quite frequently in drying her flowers and finds they do exceptionally well with a minimum amount of attention and last for a year or more.

Borax and *cornmeal drying.* This has been one of the most popular methods of drying flowers in recent years. Generally, a cookie or fruit cake tin is used to dry the flowers.

Silica gel. This is a granular material that quickly absorbs moisture from the flower petals. The drying time varies from two to seven days, depending on how many and what kind of flowers you are drying. The stem is removed from the flower, and just the flower is dried. After drying, they are attached to thin wire covered with green florist tape. Daisies, roses, larkspurs, marigolds, and zinnias are just a few of the most popular flowers dried by using this method. It is especially important to follow label instructions when using silica gel or you are apt to burn the flowers.

In addition to these methods, you can also dry flowers in dehydrators and microwave ovens. It is important that you refer to the manual for specific instructions on temperatures and timing. Many

One way of drying flowers is with silica sand. While supporting the flower with toothpicks, pour the sand slowly to avoid tearing any petals.

flowers can be dried by the pressing method. Flowers are simply placed between two sheets of typing paper and pressed within the pages of a book. My wife puts them directly into old telephone books, thus eliminating the need for typing paper to protect the pages.

When drying flowers for the first time, you will find that the pink, lavender, yellow, orange, or white flowers are the easiest to dry successfully. Some of the best to start with are single marigolds, zinnias, daisies, pansies, and violas.

By far the best time to pick flowers for drying is on a warm, dry day at a time when the flowers are not moist. The best flowers to choose for drying are new flowers when they first come into bloom. When possible, avoid using those that have been in bloom for several days, as they tend to lose some of their color during the drying process.

It is best to pick the flowers of everlastings for drying when they are open but not fully matured. Strip off some of the lower foliage from the stems, and hang the flower clusters upside down in a well-ventilated spot to dry.

Examine any flowers closely before picking them. It is important that they be blemish-free, since discolored areas or insect bites will show to a much greater degree after drying.

You can enjoy the beauty of flowers from your own garden during the fall and winter by drying and arranging them.

Summer Gardening in Containers

Container gardening can be an important part of your landscaping, whether you live in an apartment, mobile home, or urban or suburban house. Containers can be used for permanent trees and shrubs, summer annuals, spring-flowering bulbs, or vegetable gardening. They are an excellent means of creating a small garden in a very limited space.

If you have a lanai, deck, or patio, containers soften the area and add color where it might otherwise be drab and uninteresting. Properly planned, it is also possible to gain privacy or create a focal point around which to form an overall landscape design. The entry area is one of the most important with regard to landscaping. It is said that 90 percent of the people who enter the front door already have an impression of you and your home. Containers can dress up the entry and help create that good first impression. Container planting is especially useful and popular with apartment dwellers and mobile-home owners because it is possible to grow plants, flowers, and even vegetables in containers where gardening space just isn't available. Sometimes it is a decorative container on the ground, patio, deck or lanai. Sometimes, it is a permanent, built-in container, such as a window box or planter. At other times it may be a decorative hanging flower basket.

One of the major factors in container gardening is the selection of the container. There are some outstanding types of containers, including some attractive old ones. Today, containers are made of practically everything, from old tires to ceramic, wood, and plastic. Their sizes and shapes also vary considerably: Some are low and spreading; others are round, square, rectangular, or even upright. There is a style and shape to suit just about any need. Of course, there is always the option to make your own if you don't find one that you like. Some of the most attractive containers I have seen in recent years include drain tiles, old crocks, milk buckets, and wicker baskets. My ninety-year-old aunt makes the most beautiful concrete containers, forming the design with stones, driftwood, and shells. With a little imagination, the possibilities are just about limitless.

Be sure to select planters large enough to grow things successfully. If the pot is too small, the plants will become top-heavy and a strong wind could topple the container. It is difficult for plants to establish suitable roots when confined in this way, so choose pots that are large and heavy enough for your plants.

Your next step is to decide what you want to plant in your containers. There are many possibilities. Evergreens are often chosen for containers because they are permanent plants and interesting all twelve months of the year. If the planters are large enough, they will also accommodate a few seasonal plants to add color to the setting.

Consider any of the junipers or cypress plants for the focal point in a permanent container planting. I particularly like Hollywood juniper and Hinoki cypress because of their irregular growing habits. Pines, *Nandina domestica,* heavenly bamboo, viburnum, and stranvaesia are other possibilities. Alpine firs and pines are also popular because of their slow growth. Probably the most

popular deciduous plants are the various types of Japanese maple. In a shaded area, camellias, azaleas, dwarf rhododendrons, skimmia, acuba, fatsia, and the sasanqua winter-flowering camellias are good choices.

Seasonal color can also be added to containers. During the summer the emphasis is on annuals and other summer-flowering plants. Petunias, lobelias, marigolds, ageratums, geraniums, fuchsias, begonias, and impatiens provide color until the first frosts in fall. In winter you might use flowering cabbage, kale, or the winter-flowering types of pansies. For color in the spring, plant bulbs around the permanent plants each fall. Tulips, daffodils, hyacinths, and crocuses are very colorful in the early spring.

As you can see, it is possible to have color all twelve months of the year against a backdrop of interesting evergreens. Of course, seasonal plants can be used exclusively, and changed as the seasons change. This will be the better plan if you are using rather small planters.

If you are going to grow vegetables in containers, some of the best ones to grow are radishes, beets, carrots, onions, chives, bush tomatoes, and most herbs. Tomatoes do exceptionally well in containers, and it is best to select the lower-growing hybrid varieties like cherry tomatoes, patio-type tomatoes, or one of the hanging-basket varieties.

A container garden can include just about any combination of plants. For example, at our house we have one container that contains a tomato plant surrounded by lettuce, onions, radishes, and chives. From this container it is possible for my wife to go out and pick an entire salad for dinner several times throughout the summer. In another container we have a dozen different herbs, so we can take two steps out of the kitchen door and pick any herbs needed for seasoning or garnishes.

A number one concern in container gardening is the soil. It is important that a proper mixture be prepared. Plants in containers are exposed to drying air and temperature extremes on all four sides plus the top and the bottom, so they can dry out in a hurry. The soil must be able to hold moisture for the longest possible time. If good soil is not readily available, you can purchase an all-purpose commercial potting soil that will meet your needs. If you do have access to good soil, a mixture of about one-third compost or peat moss, one-third sandy loam, and one-third processed manure or leaf mold is best. Mix into the soil a slow-release nonburning transplanting fertilizer to encourage root growth.

During the summer months you must be concerned about watering. Water thoroughly each time, allowing the soil to soak to a depth of 6 to 8 inches. Shallow, frequent watering does more harm than good. It encourages shallow rooting, and during warmest weather they will dry out very rapidly. If you water deeply, it is usually not necessary to water as often. But do not overwater. Plants that sit in water for extended periods are in trouble, and drowning the roots will eventually be fatal to them. Always use good judgment in watering. Sometimes containers dry out rapidly during the winter months. It is important to check watering needs all twelve months of the year. This is especially true of broad-leaf evergreens, which tend to shed water.

Because of the limited root space, it is also a good practice to feed container plants more frequently than those growing in the ground. For this feeding you can use an all-purpose garden fertilizer or a liquid fertilizer. The important months for feeding are May, June, July, and August.

Check the plants occasionally for the possibility of insect and disease infestation. If either should occur, take steps to correct it. If you are in doubt as to which product to use, check with your local nurseryman, master gardener, or garden clerk.

If any of your container plants develop leggy growth, pinch or prune them back to encourage bushiness. Also remove the dead flowers before they go to seed.

It is possible to enjoy container gardening with a minimum of maintenance. When planning your containers, an abundance of seasonal color can be combined with attractive permanent foliage plants and vegetables to create interest in areas that otherwise would be rather uninteresting. You can enjoy a harvest of fresh produce from vegetable plants grown in containers and add a bright spot of color to your patio, deck, lanai, or entry area by including container-grown plants.

Ground Covers for Low Maintenance

Ground covers provide one of the easiest ways to cut down on garden maintenance. They supply attractive leaf color and texture, help retain moisture in the soil, discourage the growth of annoying weeds and grasses, and give a finished appearance to the area. If you want to spend more time fishing, hunting, camping, traveling, or whatever, you will find that many types of ground covers can be used to cut down on garden maintenance.

A wide range of ground covers can be used here in the Pacific Northwest, and the many different varieties make it easy to find suitable plants for just about any location, including steep banks, rock areas, and between steppingstones. Ground covers can even be used as grass substitutes. Some varieties of ground covers grow especially well in full sun, others can be planted in partial sun and shade, and some do exceptionally well in the shaded part of the garden. Leaf texture is a prime consideration when selecting any ground cover. Whether you choose one with fine, medium, or bold foliage depends upon the surrounding area. The foliage should contrast with nearby plants. For example, if large-leaf rhododendrons are in the planting area, use a fine- to medium-foliaged ground cover to make the planting more interesting and to add foliage variety.

Leaf color is another consideration. You can add interest and appeal to the landscape by selecting a ground cover with foliage that is a different color from that of the surrounding plants. It is possible to choose from green, gray, gold, silver, and variegated foliage.

Take into consideration whether the plant is evergreen or deciduous, whether it has flowers and/or berries, and whether the foliage color changes with the seasons.

In addition to evergreen and deciduous plants, there are also many perennials that serve as excellent ground covers—such as the spring-flowering aubrietia, snow-on-the-mountain, candytuft, basket-of-gold, coral bells, and many others.

Ground covers hug the ground, choking out weeds and shading the soil between plants, which helps to retain moisture. Possibly one of the greatest advantages to using ground covers in the landscape is that they give a finished appearance to flower, tree, and shrub beds.

In the past, the most popular use for ground covers was to cover a sloping area where soil retention was a problem. Deep-rooted ground covers were often used to help solve this problem. Of course, ground covers are also useful on sloping areas where it is difficult to maintain a lawn.

One large problem in landscaping is to fill the areas between steppingstones or between a rockery and walkway. In such spots, low-growing ground covers are often the ideal grass substitutes. Ground covers like thyme and sagina moss fill these areas rather quickly with a nice low, compact habit of growth. Both are suitable as grass substitutes in small areas. Thyme comes in varieties with flowers in shades of pink, white, lavender, and red. The variety of woolly thyme has very attractive gray foliage. Sagina moss comes in two varieties, one with dark green mosslike foliage and the other with chartreuse green foliage.

Ground covers are especially useful wherever it is difficult to mow a lawn or where the lawn does not grow well. A typical spot is under tall evergreens or deciduous trees.

Some ground covers grow very rapidly, others quite slowly. If you are covering a large area, you will want a fast-growing variety. If the area is small, slower-growing types may be suitable. Actually, the selection of a ground cover for a particular area depends upon the size of the area, location, rate of growth, height, and amount of time available to devote to maintenance.

If you want to put ground covers where you have moist soil areas, *Andromeda polifolia, Kalmia polifolia*, and ferns are recommended. Ground covers like kinnikinnick, cistus, genista, hypericum, and santolina are often recommended for dry areas. Pachysandra, gaultheria, sarcococca, and *Vinca minor* are often selected as ground covers for the shady garden. In full sun, you might want to use fast-growing plants like ivy, cotoneasters, kinnikinnick, ajuga, or any one of a dozen other varieties. Saint-John's-wort (*Hypericum calycinum*) is a popular ground cover for a sunny hillside. It can die back during a severe winter, which results in a rather unsightly appearance, but its dense habit of growth chokes out most weeds, and it is a good plant for hard-to-maintain areas.

English ivy is another popular fast-growing ground cover that can be used in large planting areas. Generally, it requires a minimum amount of maintenance. It has large leaves, but several other varieties of ivy are available that have smaller leaves. You will often see cotoneaster, kinnikinnick, and English ivy along freeways where steep banks are a problem.

For this region, one of the most suitable ground-cover choices is the heather family. Hundreds of varieties grow here; and by selecting several different ones, you can have them in bloom all twelve months of the year. Some are very low, while others are medium to upright. They all require well-drained soil.

To cut down on garden maintenance and improve the overall appearance of your landscape, summer is a good time to select and plant ground covers. Planting them in the summer gives them time to become established before cooler weather arrives in the fall.

Vines for Special Places

Are you looking for an annual vine that will provide a bright spot of color in your garden this summer? If so, you will find at least half a dozen different types that can be used for this purpose. Annual vines are generally quick-growing, prolific-flowering, and colorful. They are especially nice for providing privacy around a patio, screening out or covering unsightly objects like old tree stumps, or to cover patios, carport posts, pillars, or arbors. Some annual vines are also often used in hanging baskets to provide seasonal flower color.

Some type of support is usually necessary when growing these vines. When the first tendrils form, they must have something to cling to. Wood, string, netting, or wire mesh can be used. There are also clear plastic disks available with twist ties that are very effective, blend with the surroundings, and are relatively inexpensive. Called "wall ties," they glue onto cement, brick, or wood surfaces.

Prior to seeding or planting annual vines, it is very important that you take time to properly prepare the soil. Dig a planting hole at least 2 feet deep and approximately 2 feet wide. Mix generous amounts of peat moss, compost (if available), and processed or well-rotted manure into the planting soil. Also mix in the correct amount of a transplanting fertilizer or rose-type fertilizer as stated on the label. Since most annual vines grow quickly and flower prolifically, they need special feeding attention. Fertilize every four to six weeks throughout the summer, following application directions on the label.

Should any insects or diseases become a problem on your annual vines, use an all-purpose rose or vegetable-garden dust or spray to help control them.

The following are a few of the most popular annual vines to use in the Pacific Northwest garden:

Scarlet runner bean. The clusters of scarlet flowers are shaped like typical bean flowers. The vine will grow about 6 to 8 feet tall. The beans that form from the flowers are edible, but tend to be tough if allowed to fully mature. This vine is easily started from seed.

Cup-and-saucer vine, cobaea. Its pink to purple flowers are large and colorful. It must be planted in a sunny spot in the garden. Starting from seed is easy; just stand the seed on end and barely cover with soil.

Climbing nasturtium. These colorful, fast-growing vines provide an abundance of color with minimum care—in fact, they thrive on a certain amount of neglect. They are easily grown from seed. Nasturtiums are sometimes susceptible to black aphid.

Morning glory. Grow these vines in a container on the patio, deck, or lanai. They are easy to start from seed, but it is a good practice to nick the seed coat with a knife before planting. The blue and red varieties provide an abundance of color in the garden.

Sweet pea. This vine grows exceptionally well in this area. Plant in early March. It is a good practice to soak seeds overnight in water. The attractive flowers have a pleasant fragrance.

Black-eyed susan. The golden flowers are highlighted by a black center, providing a color display in the garden. Starter plants are available in most garden outlets from late April to early May. In full sun or partial sun and shade, they will provide a floral display for months.

Cardinal climber. Red, trumpet-shaped flowers and ferny foliage combine to make the cardinal climber an attractive annual vine. Nick the seed coats with a knife and soak them overnight in water before planting.

Gourds and hyacinth beans are two other popular annual vines that can be used to provide summer color.

Tip-pinching summer annual vines when they are about 12 inches high encourages them to branch and produce additional flowers. Besides annual vines, there are also evergreen, deciduous, or permanent vines that will add an abundance of color to your landscape. The four most popular permanent evergreen vines are ivy, fatshedera, *Clematis armandi,* and *Euonymus radicans.* Fatshedera is a shade plant and should be used only in a spot where it is protected from the sun most of the day. The other three will all take the sun. *Clematis armandi* needs shade around its root system and protection from severe cold weather. None of the four requires much pruning except to keep them shaped and suited to their location. Required pruning should be done after flowering.

Feed evergreen vines with a rhododendron-type plant food. February and June are the best times to apply it.

There are several types of deciduous or permanent vines:

Clematis. It is available in a wide range of colors, and a few have showy stripes of another color. They like plenty of sun. Prepare the soil deeply and plant the rootball deeper than ground level. Severe pruning encourages more flowers and a bushy vine. Pruning time depends upon variety. Shade the roots.

Climbing hydrangea. Has flat, lacy, cap-shaped white flowers. The Japanese varieties are the most popular here. They are available in several colors.

Wisteria. This is really a late-spring-flowering vine rather than a summer-flowering vine. White and blue-lavender varieties are most popular. They are also available in pink. Sometimes they flower again in midsummer. They like plenty of sun and a deep planting hole. Heavy pruning of secondary growth during early spring is advantageous.

Passion vine, trumpet vine, silver-lace vine, and the Japanese blackberry (*Akebia quinata*) are other excellent choices in this category.

Most deciduous vines should be fed with a general garden fertilizer. Feed the permanent types in June or early July. The annuals should have at least one feeding during the early summer, and do best if given monthly feedings. Avoid high-nitrogen fertilizers; they tend to stimulate foliage growth instead of flowers.

Because vines are rapid growers, they require generous quantities of water during the summer growing season. Water permanent types more sparingly late in the summer to give them time to harden before colder weather arrives. Soil, location, and weather conditions will determine how often you should water any vine.

Vines provide an abundance of color in the home landscape. Just about every garden has a suitable place to grow one of the many that are available.

Creating Privacy with Plants

Quite a few different types of trees and shrubs can be used to provide seasonal or year-round privacy or to screen out an unsightly area. Shrub fence rows, borders, and hedges, an integral part of landscaping for many years, are once again becoming popular in modern-day landscaping because of their value for separating areas, providing privacy, screening, dividing property lines, reducing noise, or providing a barrier to animal and human traffic.

Before you begin planting a screen, there are four questions you should ask yourself. First, do you want year-round or seasonal privacy? Second, should the planting be a hedge or a rather inconspicuous combination of shrub plantings that will provide privacy? Third, how tall should it grow? Fourth, how much time do you want to devote to its maintenance?

If you are looking for only seasonal privacy, there are many beautiful small- to medium-size flowering deciduous trees and shrubs that will do nicely. Lilac, forsythia, spirea, beauty bush, butterfly bush, and mock orange are just a few of the plants in this category. These plants lose their leaves during the winter, so they offer little or no screening at that time of year.

There are several evergreens that will provide year-round privacy. Some flowering varieties include the upright escallonias, stranvaesia, rhododendrons, camellias, and photinia. In addition, there are many nonflowering junipers, conifers, and cypresses that are ideal for hedging and provide interesting foliage textures and leaf color. If you are looking for taller trees to provide high privacy, the best choices are fir, hemlock, spruce, pine, and cedar.

If you are thinking about growing a hedge to provide privacy or a barrier between properties, you will find the laurel, privet, escallonia, hemlock, bamboo, *Thuja pyramidalis*, Portuguese laurel, and photinia among the best plants for this purpose. Using a combination of shrubs rather than a hedge will create an interesting mix of leaf colors, textures, and flower colors, providing an inconspicuous but attractive privacy screen.

If you decide on a hedge for privacy, remember that it will require pruning and shearing, whereas a combination planting should require a minimum amount of such maintenance.

Using trees and shrubs for privacy has several advantages. The most important advantage is the increased height that can be obtained. Most cities and counties have ordinances restricting the height of conventional fences, but there are usually no height restrictions on trees and shrubs unless there is a view to consider. When an unsightly view cannot be fully screened out by a 6-foot fence, plants may be the best solution to the problem. When you plan screening in the landscape, however, it is important not to interfere with the neighbors' view. It is also important that the screening not obstruct automobile vision in any way.

The height of the screen will depend on the situation. For example, to screen out the house next door that is higher than your house, planting tall trees on a mound of soil may be required. In such cases hemlock, fir, spruce, or pine trees can be used. If you are screening a fire hydrant or water faucet, low-growing plants like juniper, daphne, viburnum, low rhododendrons, and similar plants may be all you need. There are also narrow deciduous and evergreen trees and shrubs that can be used to screen small areas. Remember, while tall evergreens do provide high privacy, many are overpowering in the garden and provide too much shade, or may interfere with your view or that of a nearby neighbor. Take time to select plants that will fit the needs of the particular areas you are trying to screen for privacy.

One of the biggest mistakes is to select plants that are fast-growing. So often I hear people say they need the fastest-growing plant to provide summer privacy or shade in their garden, but they forget that fast-growing trees and shrubs become big trees and shrubs that can be completely overpowering in the garden. By all means, take time to select the right trees and shrubs for your particular screening or privacy needs.

Animals in the Garden

PESTS

If you are being plagued by animals in the garden, many humanitarian methods can be successful in overcoming them. Here are some suggestions given by readers of my newspaper articles.

One reader writes that the best way she has found to keep dogs from fertilizing her yard is to make friends with them. She says, "I give them meat scraps, pet them, talk to them, and now the only piles that are left behind are from an occasional wanderer which my neighbor's dogs quickly shoo on their way. An added benefit is that they also guard our house and property as though it were their own territory. We don't have a dog of our own."

Another reader states: "Dogs dislike the smell

of lemon. I found that spraying around the border of the yard with an inexpensive lemon wax works wonders, and rain doesn't wash it away. It needs to be replenished about once a month."

Here is still another suggestion: "Sprinkle cayenne pepper on the cleanup. It works! We had dogs that made a private potty of our parking lot, and they never came back after this treatment. My neighbor's kitty used my flower beds, which are out of the rain; but when other cats discovered it, I used my system and they never came back either."

Several readers commented on their success using naphthalene flakes around flower beds. The only drawback mentioned is that they must be replaced fairly often. This method was especially useful in controlling cats and squirrels.

On close observation you will discover that dogs tend to establish a regular path through the yard. Repellents should be used in those runs when attempting to discourage them. Here are two other suggestions: "Through past experience I have found the best repellent is raw blood meal. You can find it at any nursery outlet. Sprinkle it as if you were feeding chickens. It keeps cats, dogs, and squirrels out of areas where they are not wanted. After using this product, I found that animals, especially dogs, use the sidewalks instead of making a path through the yard. I also have found that the strong odor of pepper seeds discourages squirrels. You can purchase the seed at markets where spices are sold."

If you are having a problem with cats in a particular area, it may be because that area is very dry. Often the problem can be remedied by keeping that area moist for several weeks.

Every now and then I get a request for information about how to control rabbits. They can ruin shrubs and trees in a very short time. A recent recommendation from the East suggests the use of Rabbit-aid, a new combination of fungicide and repellent that remains active for at least two months. According to reports, this product has been very effective where there have been problems with rabbits girdling small trees and shrubs during the winter.

Some readers have reported a problem with squirrels that ruin garden crops. Aside from naphthalene flakes, wire mesh placed over plants helps deter squirrels. However, one of the most humane ways to get rid of squirrels is to trap them. The regional offices of state game departments usually have cages that you can borrow for this purpose. They also will suggest a suitable place to release the trapped squirrels.

Over the years one of the most popular means of controlling deer has been blood meal. It can be hung in cloth bags from the branches of nearby trees.

Science Products has a product called Rabbit and Deer Repellent that is available in 8-ounce, pint, and quart containers. Many home gardeners report excellent results using this.

Perhaps one of the most frustrating animals in

the garden is the mole. To wake up in the morning and find a molehill in the middle of a neatly kept lawn is very discouraging. Understanding mole habits makes it easier to deter them or to know how best to catch them.

In this area the two most common types of moles are the Pacific mole and the California mole. Both are meat-eating mammals, consuming soil insects for their food. One type raises the soil in a clumped-shaped mound; the other burrows just below the soil surface, raising the ground slightly as he goes along his merry way. The biggest concern with moles is that they often leave plants high and dry, and they provide runways for field mice. It is the field mice, not the moles, that are the culprits who sometimes eat bulbs and other vegetation.

Moles are in your garden for one purpose only: their source of food, live insects. Eliminate the insects and the moles will go away.

To date there are only two recognized alternatives for controlling moles. One is the use of a plant called the "mole plant" or "gopher plant" (*Euphorbia lathyrus*). The other method is trapping them. The mole plant is a very prolific plant and in fact may be considered a nuisance because it multiplies so rapidly. However, it does an effective job of controlling moles. Plant it in your flower beds around the edge of your property.

If you want to try trapping moles, first remove the top cone of soil and reach down with your fingers to determine how deep the passage is and whether it runs in a straight line or at an angle. A main runway will go in a straight line; a secondary runway will angle in another direction. Don't bother to set a trap in a secondary runway—set them in main runways only. Standard mole traps, the alligator-type mole traps, or out-of-sight traps are considered the most effective. Most

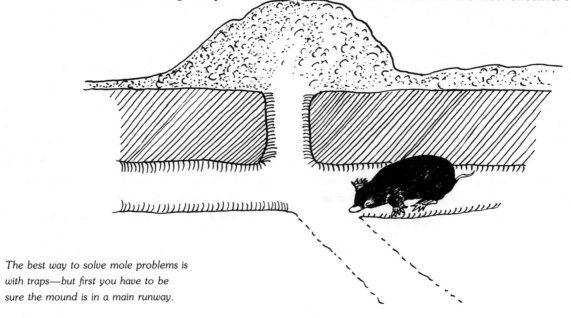

The best way to solve mole problems is with traps—but first you have to be sure the mound is in a main runway.

garden outlets, feed stores, and garden departments carry these traps.

Moles generally nest under the patio, at the bases of trees, under fence rows, under old clumps of grass, and other similar places. In the home garden, they are most often found underneath trees, walkways, or near the patio area. Concentrate your efforts in those areas where the mole is apt to be most active.

Once the mole trap is set at the correct depth in a main runway, it is important to cover the top of the trap with a bucket; otherwise a bird is apt to land on the trap handle, which could set it off. A second reason for placing a bucket over the trap is so that children are not as apt to pull it out of the ground.

Catching one mole does not guarantee that you have eliminated the mole population. In fact, it is more likely that a whole family of moles are present. Moles have a very pliable skin, so when you do catch one, be sure that it is dead before removing it from the trap. Too often, people remove moles from traps, bury them, and within a few hours they are working once again in the garden.

Many gardeners have used gases, exhaust fumes from the car, or liquids to drown moles. In fact, in recent years human hair has been recommended as a means of discouraging moles. However, trapping still remains the best method of control. If liquids or gases are used, remember that if they kill moles, they could kill other ani-

mals. Follow directions on the label of any material you use. Gases, mothballs, and other odorous substances used in mole runways often simply chase the mole to other areas.

FRIENDS

While there are many animals you want to discourage from entering your garden, there are some beneficial friends. Birds, bees, ladybugs, snakes, praying mantises, and fowl are among the most common ones. By adopting some commonsense approaches to gardening, you can help protect these desirable insects and animals that are a natural part of our environment.

When aphids, whiteflies, cornworms, and other nuisance insects become a problem, you can eliminate them with a minimum of damage to garden friends. Use insecticides that have a short residual period or choose the organics, like rotenone or pyrethrum. Which type you use depends upon the pest you are trying to control—check the labels.

When using an insecticide, apply it at a time when the birds are not as active in the garden. Avoid spraying when a plant is in bloom, because the bees are sure to be busy during that time. Early morning or evening is the best time for spraying. Use only the amount needed, as specified on the label. Use only a quality sprayer that mixes the proper proportions with water, or one in which you can premix the entire solution, such as a tank or trombone type.

Many new varieties of annuals, perennials, and vegetables are recommended simply because they are more resistant to particular problems that have plagued them in the past. Snapdragons are a perfect example: The new varieties are quite resistant to rust. Rose hybridizers have also produced some fine varieties that tend to resist mildew or black spot. If you choose to grow a plant that is susceptible to an insect or disease, treat only that plant with a spray, not the entire garden.

Keeping the garden clean is a major answer to both insect and disease problems. Pull weeds regularly and do not allow debris—rotten fruit, old leaves, and plant parts—to accumulate. Insects can incubate in such areas, and disease infestations are more likely to appear.

Natural predators like ladybugs and praying mantises can be purchased for use in the garden. A quart container has about 25,000 ladybugs, enough to protect ·the average garden against aphids, mites, scale, and several other insects. Each one of the adult ladybugs will consume up to fifty insects per day. Eight praying mantises will produce about three thousand voracious offspring.

Birds are great friends to encourage because they feed on insects. You can help attract them to your garden by planting various trees and shrubs that they can feed on. Pernettya, fire-thorn, blueberries, and many other such plants are usually attractive to them. Of course bird feeders, birdhouses, and birdbaths will also encourage their presence.

Onions, garlic, and leeks are often planted in the garden to discourage insects because of their strong odors. Chickens and ducks are also useful because they feed on small insects and even baby slugs.

Take steps during the summer to control animals in your garden, but also be sure to protect the beneficial critters.

Miscellaneous Summer Gardening Projects

The summer months of June, July, and August are a time to sit back and enjoy the garden and the fruits of your earlier labor. Of course, there are some things that everyone needs to do if the garden is to be kept in top shape. Watering, lawn care, care of the vegetable garden, and harvesting early crops, plus insect and disease control, are the main concerns. If these have been done and maintenance is well under control, you might consider some of these possible projects.

June, July, and August are excellent months to take cuttings of rhododendrons, camellias, aza-

You can start new plants by taking tip cuttings of evergreens, but be sure to cut just below a node.

leas, junipers, conifers, and many other garden plants. Take tip cuttings 3 to 4 inches in length. Dip them in a rooting hormone before starting them in sand, vermiculite, or sponge rock. You can place the containers of cuttings out in the open garden or in the greenhouse during the summer months.

Weeding is particularly important in all parts of the garden and in the lawn. Do not let weeds flower and go to seed or they will become a nuisance for many years to come. Cultivate, pull the weeds, then mulch the beds to help cut down on water evaporation and give a neat appearance to

the area. Be careful not to mound the mulch material up around the crowns of the plants or vital air may be cut off from the feeder roots. The most common materials used for mulching are peat moss, bark, sawdust, and straw.

It may be necessary to start watering plants in June, especially those under the eaves of the house and under tall evergreens. In many cases the plants in those areas are bone-dry. Check to be sure all your plants are getting enough moisture. When you water, let a hose run near the base of each plant for about five minutes.

Summer, especially June, is an excellent time to start fall plants from seed: winter-flowering pansies, flowering cabbage, or kale. Fall crocuses (colchicum) also become available in August. Their crocus-like flowers add a bright spot to the August and September garden.

Slugs sometimes go into a summer resting period, but not always. They like damp, cool weather, so if the summer meets those conditions, be on the lookout for them. Since they reproduce several times a year, it is important to keep them under control. Baiting, salting them, and collecting are the three most popular methods of controlling slugs. With some of the new slug control devices, like slug fence, it is quite easy to bait for slugs without contaminating the soil or attracting animals or birds. (See pp. 137–139 on slug control.)

One major project that can begin in August is the hardening of plants for the winter. August seems like a funny time to do it, but there is no better time to begin. Most garden plants should be given just enough water to keep them healthy. An Indian summer is not unusual, and prompts us to water too heavily late in the season. This should be avoided around the spring-flowering plants like rhododendrons, camellias, azaleas, laurestinus, and many other broad-leaf evergreens. It is especially important to cut back on watering of spring-flowering plants, because the additional water late in the season often tends to stimulate growth, which may cause the plants to bypass their flower buds. Thus, from mid-August on you should water with care.

Late pruning also stimulates new growth, which is apt to be too tender when the first frosts come. It is a good practice to avoid extensive pruning of broad-leaf evergreens until next spring. That is not to say that some limited pruning cannot be done in order to keep plants within bounds.

Most of your garden shrubs should have been fertilized much earlier in the season. Late fertilizing or fertilizing with the wrong type of fertilizers can lead to freeze damage, on your broad-leaf evergreens particularly. If it is absolutely necessary to fertilize your garden plants, be sure to use a low-nitrogen fertilizer. Actually, if you are concerned about whether a few of your plants are hardy enough to survive the winter, you could use a low-nitrogen or no-nitrogen fertilizer to help harden them. In the past I have used a 0-10-10 formula, which contains no nitrogen, to actually help harden plants. Just remember, a healthy plant can survive severe weather better than a plant that is not healthy, so use good judgment in fertilizing during the summer.

While you are outside enjoying both the nice weather and your garden, you might think about planning and starting a "spare parts garden." Such a garden will not fit the needs of every gardener, but it can help solve problems for some homeowners. One of its greatest advantages is that it is an excellent source of cut flowers for the home. Without a spare parts garden, the flower arranger of the house is often out raiding blossoms from plants that have been groomed to their peak of beauty. With a spare parts garden, display plants can be left intact. Another benefit is that it also provides plants that can be dug and used to replace any plants that have been damaged by pests, storms, or other causes. This same area can also be used to test a few annuals so you can determine whether they have merit for future use in your flower and shrub beds for summer color.

A spare parts garden should include not only some of your favorite summer-flowering annuals but also perennials and bulbs. By properly planning this part of your garden, you can include seasonal flowers that will bloom during the spring, summer, and fall.

When you first plant your spare parts garden, be sure it includes a few of each of the plants that you are setting out for summer color, and be sure to plant them at the same time you set out your bedding plants, so they are the same size in case you have to use them as replacements. Then, take time to plan which types and varieties of annuals, perennials, and bulbs you want to include as a source of cut flowers.

By setting aside a small part of your garden as a spare parts section, you will also have an area where you can try your hand at growing a few plants from cuttings or divisions. And if you have a shrub or plant that isn't doing well, the spare parts garden is a perfect place to put it until it recovers.

FALL

Fall is one of the best and busiest times for gardeners. With shorter days and weekend football games, it can be tough getting everything done. Autumn leaves add beautiful colors to the landscape but can increase your workload.

The vegetable garden is a good example of the highs and lows of fall. Fall is harvest time in the garden—all your previous hard work pays off with spectacular results. It is also the time to rip out dead and decaying matter and make a compost pile. You are finished weeding and watering, but now it's time to protect your winter vegetables. There are many other jobs to be done between September and December, such as finishing up lawn care for the year and pruning some trees and shrubs. This is also the best time for planting spring-flowering bulbs and drying flowers. Cuttings can be taken from many plants for propagation.

Fall brings major weather changes that affect your gardening. Houseplants continue to need care, and most must be brought back inside gradually, to protect them from shock. If rainy weather chases children indoors and ruins their plans, an indoor garden can give them something to do when fall weather turns nasty. Mulching will be necessary to protect many plants from the winter chill. Dead leaves that are cluttering up the yard often make good mulch.

When the weather gives you a break, or during halftime of your favorite football game, take some time to enjoy your garden and prepare it for winter. This really is one of the nicest times of the year.

Vegetables

HARVESTING

For fullest flavor and nutritional value, it is important to harvest your vegetables at the right time. Many can be harvested at just about any stage of their growth, but others do not have their best taste if they are picked when they are underripe or overripe; they must be harvested at exactly the right point in their development.

If you want the vegetables you have grown to arrive on your table at the peak of perfection, the following are a few suggestions and basic rules on how and when to harvest them:

Asparagus. Plants started from roots should not be harvested until the second year. Plants started from seed are not harvested until the third year. The asparagus spears are ready to harvest when they are about 8 inches long. Mound dirt up over the bases of the spears if you want them to be white and tender.

Beans. Pick the snap type when the pods are young and succulent. For dry beans, let the bean pods mature on the vines, but be sure to harvest before they get so dry that they shatter.

Beets. Best quality and food value are obtained if they are harvested when the beets are no more than 1 to 1½ inches in diameter. If you are canning them, add just a little dill for flavor.

Cabbage. Cut and harvest cabbage heads when they are firm.

Carrots. They can be harvested at any size; however, it is best to harvest them before they reach 1 inch in diameter if you plan to eat them fresh. Larger carrots are good for canning or storage.

Corn. For best flavor, most varieties should be picked when they are a creamy yellow instead of an orange yellow. Another sign that corn is ready for harvest is when the silks are drying. Fullness of the tip kernels and firmness of the unhusked ears are other signs to look for. Corn should be prepared immediately if you want to enjoy full flavor and nutritional value.

Cucumbers. They can be harvested at almost any stage of development before they begin to turn yellow.

Eggplant. Be sure to harvest eggplant while the fruits are still glossy.

Lettuce. The young, succulent leaves can be picked at almost any stage of development. If left too long, however, they will go to seed and lose their best flavor.

Onions. Pick the green bunching type about seven to nine weeks after planting. Most dry onions take two to four months before they are ready. Let the dry onions hang upside down for several days before storing them.

Peas. For best flavor and food value, peas should be picked while the pods are still green and before the peas begin to harden. Check the vines regularly for maturity. Use them immediately if you want to enjoy the best flavor and nutritional value.

Peppers. They should be harvested when the fruits are nice and firm.

Potatoes. Young potatoes can be harvested at about the same time as the peas ripen, but mature potatoes are not harvested until the vines die. Store them in a dark location that is well ventilated and where temperatures are between 40 and 50 degrees. Do not store them near apples. Discard or use all bruised and damaged potatoes; do not store them.

Pumpkins. Allow them to mature on the vine. Harvest them with part of the stem intact before the first severe freeze.

Radishes. Check them regularly because the large radishes become pithy and unusable.

Spinach. Spinach leaves can be harvested as soon as they are large enough to use.

Squash. Summer squashes should be used when they are young and tender with a rind that is easily penetrated by a thumbnail. Fall and winter varieties must have hard rinds. Pick them when they are mature, when the stems begin to turn brown and shrivel.

Tomatoes. Fruit can be picked either when fully ripe or when pink.

STORING VEGETABLES

Many vegetables can be stored for use during the winter. Practically *every* home has at least one spot where vegetables can be safely stored. Some ideal spots are an unheated basement, a garage, or the crawl space under the home. A cold, dark attic, a spot under a staircase, or cupboards in the utility room also are often suitable for storing vegetables.

Most vegetables should be stored in boxes or on shelves. Never place vegetables on a dirt or cement floor, as both tend to be too moist. Some root crops like carrots and beets can be stored in a pit, barrel, or box in vermiculite, sand, or light soil in a cool, well-ventilated room.

Ideal temperatures for storage are between 35 and 50 degrees. The room should be dark and well ventilated. Avoid storing vegetables in a humid room, but the air should have a *little* humidity. Vegetables that show any sign of decay or bruising should be used immediately and not placed in storage. Decay can very rapidly spread to your healthy vegetables, spoiling them also.

It should be pointed out that this is only one way to keep vegetables for an extended time, and not all vegetables should be kept in this way.

Many vegetables can be specially treated to help retain a higher percentage of their natural flavor and food value. Blanching, freezing, canning, and drying are some of the techniques you can use to accomplish this. Refer to a reliable cookbook or the homemaking section of your newspaper, or obtain information from the Cooperative Extension Service for exact processing procedures.

RIPENING TOMATOES

One of the most frequently asked questions during the fall is "What should I do with all those green tomatoes?" Green tomatoes can be used for quite a few cooking purposes, or there are a couple of methods you can use at the end of the season to ripen the tomatoes indoors so that they do not go to waste.

Before the first frost, provisions should be made to either use or ripen your green tomatoes. Once the tomato vines and fruit are touched by the first light frost, they are of no value in the ripening process.

Green tomatoes are extensively used for relishes, pickles, preserves, mincemeat, and sometimes green tomato pies. Their uses are practically limitless; in fact, many cookbooks now feature several green-tomato recipes.

The outdoor ripening season for tomatoes can be extended by covering the vines with either polyethylene or newspaper. Protected this way, they can usually withstand the first frost before ripening indoors. However, late in the season, when it's colder, the fruit generally takes longer to ripen, and there's a chance that a heavy frost may completely damage the plants. Instead, there are methods you can use to successfully ripen your tomatoes indoors.

Probably one of the easiest ways to ripen tomatoes is to simply pull out the vine and all, shake off the excess soil, remove the leaves, and hang the plant upside down in a cool, well-ventilated room, like the basement or garage. Removing the leaves is important because they are apt to draw moisture from your green tomatoes or transmit disease, thus making the tomatoes unusable. When green tomatoes are allowed to ripen on the vine this way, they must be picked as they ripen; otherwise they will drop to the floor, creating quite a mess.

You can also pick green tomatoes from the vines outdoors and bring them in to ripen. Contrary to popular belief, the best place to ripen them is not on a windowsill. They ripen better in a dark, cool, well-ventilated place, where the temperature will remain above freezing. Green tomatoes with blemishes of any kind should be discarded to avoid spreading disease to the others. Tomatoes that are turning white are the best for ripening indoors; immature, dark green tomatoes seldom ripen properly. Also keep in mind that a tomato ripened indoors will not have quite the flavor of a tomato that is vine-ripened outdoors.

It is a good practice to place a ripe apple with the green tomatoes you are ripening; the ethylene gas given off by the apple gives a boost to the ripening process. It is also a good practice to wash and dry green tomatoes before beginning the ripening process. If they are left on the vine upside down, you can wipe each tomato with a dry cloth instead.

Don't let your green tomatoes go to waste. Take the time to ripen them indoors. It is not uncommon for some of them to ripen so slowly they may not reach their maturity until close to Thanksgiving.

FALL AND WINTER VEGETABLES

There are quite a few things you can be doing in the vegetable garden during the fall and early winter so it will be in tip-top shape for spring planting. In fact, a little special attention to the vegetable garden now will greatly reduce the amount of work that will need to be done in the spring.

If you would like to get an early start on summer vegetables, or extend the harvest of fresh vegetables from your garden in the fall, winter, or early spring months, consider growing some of them in a cold frame in your garden. Construction is really quite basic, the vegetables will require minimal care, and you can use the cold frame for growing other plants in the off-season. Cold frames are unheated shelters for plants. Glass or plastic covers admit sunlight during the day and conserve heat and ward off frost damage at night.

You don't have to be a carpenter to construct a cold frame. There is a good possibility that you may have the materials on hand, and, if not, they can be easily obtained from a salvage yard. Begin with an old window sash—dimensions are not really important; if you have a window sash that is 3 feet wide and 6 feet long, make your cold frame that size. If the sash does not have glass in it, you can substitute fiber glass or polyethylene.

Use 2-by-6's, 2-by-8's, 2-by-10's, or 2-by-12's to construct the sides of the cold frame. If you don't have lumber on hand, you can use secondhand

Vegetables can be grown in the winter using a cold frame or hotbed.

lumber or pick up some old lumber at a salvage yard. Build the cold frame so that it is higher at the back—ideally, 18 inches at the back and 12 inches at the front. The slope allows rain to run off and affords a better angle for sun exposure. Set the cold frame 3 or 4 inches into the ground to provide better insulation for your vegetable crops. The boards that are buried should be treated with a wood preservative so they won't rot as rapidly.

One of the major factors in building a cold frame is its placement in the garden. Whenever possible, the cold frame should face the south; and for maximum sunlight exposure, its glass face should not be flat but sit at an 8- to 10-degree angle. If a southern exposure is not available, the second choice is a western exposure. Third choice is an eastern exposure, and the least desirable is a northern exposure because of insufficient light. Also select a location with a slight slope to provide adequate drainage.

You can add a good fertile commercial planting soil to the cold frame, or, if you have a good base soil to begin with, simply mix generous amounts of peat moss, compost, or processed manure into your existing soil. Cultivate to a depth of at least 8 to 12 inches. It is a good practice to renew the soil every year.

You can turn your cold frame into a hot bed by placing a heating cable in the soil to provide additional protection for your winter vegetables and encourage faster growth and quicker maturity of crops. If electricity is not handy, it is important that the cold frame be covered with burlap, blankets, or some other type of cloth during winter cold spells. The extra covering should be removed as soon as the weather has subsided.

It will also be necessary to provide ventilation for your cold frame during sunny or warm winter weather. Use a stick or a wedge to prop open the window sash on warm days; otherwise it will get too warm inside the cold frame.

You will have to experiment a little to determine how frequently to water, because the water requirements will vary from day to day and season to season. Generally during the winter season the cold frame will need to be watered only about once a week; or you can let Mother Nature do the job by opening the top of the frame on a rainy day.

The warmth of the cold frame can be inviting to slugs and insects, so it may be necessary to take steps to control them throughout the winter. (See pp. 137–139 on slug control.) If any type of bait or insecticide is used, be sure to follow label instructions. Only vegetable-type products can be used on edible crops.

Leaf lettuce is undoubtedly one of the most popular crops to grow in a cold frame or hot bed during the fall and winter season. This can be a real money saver for you, because of the cost of winter lettuce. When you harvest leaf lettuce, cut it an inch or two above ground level and the plants will develop new foliage for a second crop. Spinach, green onions, and radishes are other crops that do well in a cold frame. It is a good practice to devote only a portion of the cold frame to each crop and to plant at intervals so the vegetables do not reach maturity all at the same time.

In addition to growing vegetables, a cold frame is an excellent place to start new seeds in springtime or to root cuttings of your favorite evergreen plants in the fall and winter. In fact, the propagation of new plants—including rhododendrons, camellias, azaleas, and other broad-leaf and conifer evergreens—can take place in a cold frame as early as September. The cuttings can be taken at any time from September until early February. You will find the cuttings will root better with bottom heat from a submerged heating cable.

You can cut costs and enjoy the harvest of fresh vegetables from your garden by growing a few of them in a cold frame during the winter.

Fall Lawn Care

MAINTENANCE

There isn't a great deal that needs to be done in the lawn area during the fall. However, if you do spend a little extra time grooming it, the lawn will look better during the fall and winter and be in better growing condition by the time spring rolls around.

There are several lawn diseases you should be on the lookout for in the fall. Should dirty, white, tan, or brown patches appear, this is often a sign of snow mold, fusarium patch, or pink snow mold. A lawn fungicide should be applied to help control any of them. If pink spots or webbing appear on the lower blades of the grass, red thread is probably the cause; a good application of a fall fertilizer usually helps clear it up. This disease should not be mistaken for the redness caused by early frost damage.

Be sure to keep an eye out for insects. If you notice that an insect has damaged the lawn, an all-purpose lawn insecticide such as Diazinon should be used, following directions on the label.

Large-leaf weeds and any weeds that are in flower are an eyesore. They should be pulled or destroyed before they go to seed, or they will become an increasing nuisance. Occasional weeds here and there can be pulled by hand or with a weed puller. Heavy infestations probably are removed most easily with the help of an all-purpose lawn weed killer.

September and October are good months to feed the lawn with a fall or winter type of lawn fertilizer. The fall feeding is one of the most important of the entire year because it helps stimulate root growth throughout the winter season—

and it stands to reason that the better the root system, the better the top growth and the healthier the lawn will be the following year. This fall feeding also helps keep the lawn looking nice throughout the fall, winter, and early spring. Most nurseries, garden centers, and garden outlets feature special fall or winter types of lawn fertilizer.

One other thing that can be done in the fall is to make an application of dolomite or agricultural lime. This will help correct the pH of the soil and eventually should help reduce the incidence of moss and mushrooms. This application should be repeated in the spring if moss or mushrooms persist.

November should be about the last time you'll need to mow the grass this fall. If you can, mow it in a different direction than you mowed it during the summer. This helps to keep its growth habit more upright and uniform. Be sure to use a grass catcher each time you mow, or rake up the clippings after mowing; otherwise they are apt to become a yellow slimy mess.

If it is your weekend to mow and the lawn is wet, that is no excuse for not mowing the lawn. All you have to do is pull the garden hose, a rope, or a wire across the lawn; the water droplets on the blades of grass will drop to the soil below, and in a relatively short period of time—about fifteen minutes or so—the lawn will be dry enough to mow.

As the leaves begin to fall onto the lawn from

nearby trees, it is a good idea to rake them and add them to the compost pile, because they offer no winter protection to the lawn. In fact, they become a wet, slimy mess if left on the lawn, smothering it and ruining its appearance.

By giving the lawn a little extra care during the fall, you can keep it looking in tip-top shape all during the autumn and winter months.

PLANTING OR RESEEDING LAWNS

Fall is an excellent time to seed or sod a new lawn, and for reseeding bare spots in an established lawn. September is often one of the best times of the year for lawn planting, because the cooler fall weather encourages good, sturdy root development.

Reseeding small bare spots in the lawn is a simple process. All you need do is scratch the bare areas with a rake, add a little fertilizer, reseed, and cover with a light layer of peat moss. Keep the areas moist until the seed has germinated.

Seeding a new lawn area is quite a different matter. By the time you have read all the steps listed for new lawn construction, you will probably be ready to hang up the rake and say, "To heck with it, it's too much work." But remember, soils vary considerably from one garden to another, and many of the steps I mention may not be necessary in your situation. Simply eliminate the

steps that do not apply. But don't cut corners, because planting time is the only opportunity you will have to get the soil in top-notch condition. Proper soil preparation at planting time can save you much money and maintenance time in the years to come.

Soil preparation is of prime concern whether you seed or sod your new lawn. A deep, porous, nutritious soil bed will give the new grass a better opportunity to develop a strong, sturdy root system over the fall and winter months. It is a good idea to have your soil tested before you begin, so you'll know exactly what's needed to put the soil in best condition.

Here are the basic steps for seeding or sodding a new lawn:

1. Pick up any debris, sticks, stones, and large clumps of weeds.

2. Begin establishing drainage patterns and contours by scraping off any high areas and filling in any low spots.

3. Till the entire seedbed to a depth of at least 8 inches. It is best to do this in two directions.

4. Roughly rake the entire area to eliminate any stones or debris brought to the surface when you tilled.

5. Add topsoil or any other soil additives if needed. Sandy loam, sawdust, bark, or other similar soil additives are sometimes added at this point to help break up clay or hardpan.

6. Apply new-lawn fertilizer, following directions on the label for new lawns.

7. Mix the fertilizer and topsoil into the seedbed by tilling again.

8. Rake once again to remove any debris, stones, and other matter brought to the surface by tilling.

9. Begin contouring and establishing drainage patterns. To do this, take either a weighted ladder or make a frame of 4-by-4's and begin dragging the entire seedbed to establish a final grade. Take as much time as necessary to do this job correctly.

10. Lightly roll the entire area with a water-filled lawn roller. By doing this, you determine the high spots and low spots that still exist in the seedbed area. (A lawn roller is often available at the place where you buy your garden supplies or at a nearby rental agency.)

11. Rake the entire seedbed area again. Barely skim the surface of the soil this time, removing any medium-size debris and establishing your final grade.

12. Again, make a light application of lawn fertilizer. For this step, usually about 40 pounds of fertilizer is used to cover 5,000 square feet of lawn area.

13. Now you are ready to put down new sod or sow your grass seed.

14. If you are seeding, lightly cover the seed with peat moss. About 1/16 inch or less is sufficient to do the job.

15. Roll the lawn with a lawn roller half filled with water.

16. Be sure to fence the entire seedbed area to keep children and animals off the soft ground.

17. The entire seedbed should be kept moist until the seed has germinated.

Sod can be lightly fertilized immediately after it has been set in place, but a new lawn started from seed should not be fertilized until after the first or second mowing.

Never apply a weed killer to a new lawn until it has been mowed at least three to five times. It's not unusual for a few weeds to appear when the lawn first comes up, but don't worry, because they will usually disappear with the first or second mowing.

I have found it a good practice, when seed is spread with a fertilizer spreader, to thoroughly mix by hand any seed that remains in the hopper at the end of each pass. Otherwise, the heavier seed will tend to settle to the bottom of the spreader, and you are apt to get something of a patchwork lawn rather than an even blend. Another way to avoid the possibility of a patchwork pattern is to apply half the seed in the spreader in one direction, then apply the other half in a crisscross pattern.

It's a good idea to make one or two passes with the spreader at each end of the lawn, or around the circumference of the entire lawn. This gives you enough space to make your turn with the spreader off and start your next pass before you turn the spreader on, thus eliminating any overlap of fertilizer or seed.

Planting a new lawn takes time, but doing the job right can save you a great deal of time and money over a period of years.

Trees and Shrubs

Fall is an excellent time to plant or transplant trees and shrubs. Before you do, however, there are several points to consider in determining which tree is best for use in your landscape. Eventual size, rate of growth, shape, and planting location are the major factors in determining the type and variety of tree to use.

When selecting a tree, you must first decide what you want it for: whether you want to use the tree for shade, as a windbreak, for food, to provide flower color, to add interesting foliage texture or color, and whether you want the tree to have attractive autumn leaf color.

A second important factor in selecting a tree is whether you want it to be deciduous or an evergreen that will provide year-round foliage. There are certain advantages to both types.

Deciduous trees provide shade and privacy during the summer, but lose their leaves during the winter, thus allowing maximum winter sunlight into the area. Some have outstanding au-tumn leaf color; others produce fruit; and many have very attractive flowers. Deciduous trees come in a wide range of growing heights, habits, and shapes.

Evergreen trees also have many advantages: They provide year-round foliage, are excellent windbreaks, and are ideal for providing permanent privacy.

Since all trees have advantages and disadvantages, it is important to give careful consideration to the selection of one for your garden. Take time to select a tree with a suitable growing habit. Tree shapes vary from upright to spreading. If you are trying to provide shade, a round or spreading tree will do a better job than an upright one. On the other hand, if you are seeking privacy or a windbreak, a dense, upright-growing tree will probably be the better choice. You should also know a little about the ultimate size of a tree you're considering, and its planting requirements. Does it require special soil conditions? Is it subject to certain insects or diseases? Does it require any special maintenance?

In selecting a location for your tree, keep in mind overhead power lines, underground water lines, septic tanks, and sewer lines. Consider what effects the roots will have on walks, driveways, and paved surfaces. What effect will the tree have on your neighbors? Will it block their view? Will the falling leaves become a nuisance in their yard? Will the tree encroach on their property? Does the tree have a tendency to throw root suckers that will become a nuisance in their garden?

We are fortunate here in the Northwest to have such a wide range of types and varieties of trees and shrubs to choose from. Select some that add interest to the landscape all twelve months of the year. Include some that provide color in the spring, others that flower and have interest in the summer, those that provide color in the fall, and a few that add interest in the winter months as well. Fall is an excellent time to choose fall and winter trees and shrubs. Of special interest will be the flowering plants, those that have colorful berries, or the types with colorful fall and winter leaves.

Following are some of the best plants for seasonal color:

Sasanqua camellias. Of special interest during the fall will be the winter-flowering varieties. Many of them begin to bloom as early as late October; some start to flower in November; and others in December. They come in a wide range of colors, with single, semidouble, or fully double flowers. There is also a wide range of growing heights and habits, making them very versatile garden shrubs. Some are low and spreading, while others have a more upright habit of growth. They are more tolerant of wind and sun than the spring-flowering types. They are ideal plants to use in containers on the patio, deck, or lanai; or they can be planted in the open landscape. A few of the branches can be cut and used for indoor flower arrangements.

Viburnum tinus (commonly called *Laurestinus*). This is another of the really outstanding winter-flowering plants. You can generally count on the first flowers beginning to appear in late October or early November. The plant then continues to flower periodically throughout the winter months during warm spells, and comes into full bloom in late March or early April. Clusters of pinkish white flowers show off nicely against a background of dark green leaves. This shrub grows well in full sun or partial sun and shade. Its eventual height can be up to 12 feet, but can be kept lower by pruning, which is best done in March, April, or May.

Heather. The winter-flowering varieties provide an abundance of color in the garden in the late fall and early winter. There are a dozen or more varieties that flower during the winter in shades of white, purple, lavender, red, and pink, and several with in-between shades. At least two varieties flower for six months during the late fall, winter, and early spring.

Helleborus niger (Christmas rose). This is one of the holiday season's outstanding flowering perennials. The small single flowers appear from November to February and resemble the old-fashioned single wild rose. The attractive white flowers with tinges of greenish or purplish rose are offset by showy yellow flower stamens. This perennial herb, a member of the buttercup family, has attractive dark green foliage that is divided. Outside, these plants need a lot of room. Cut, they are excellent for flower arrangements, decorating, and corsages.

Nandina domestica ("heavenly bamboo"). This is another plant that adds interest to the garden in the fall. Although the leaves are evergreen, they do take on autumn colors in shades of orange and red combined with the green leaves. Occasionally the summer flowers are followed by fall red berries. For best leaf color, plant in full sun or partial sun and shade. Heavenly bamboo is a compact, neat-growing shrub and does not become a nuisance like some types of bamboos.

There are good reasons for planting during the fall. The most important is that whenever the temperature is above 45 degrees, root growth will take place over the winter. A good root system is needed for sturdy top growth, so plants that are set out in the fall have a head start on the next growing season. You can expect sturdier, healthier plants in the years to come.

Deciduous trees and shrubs—fruit trees, flowering trees, shade trees, roses, lilacs, and hydrangeas—are best planted after they have lost their leaves and have started their winter dormant season. Evergreens—like rhododendrons, azaleas, heathers, camellias, andromedias, junipers, and cypress—are best transplanted after a light frost has stopped their normal growth cycle. It is quite safe to assume that once the deciduous trees have lost their leaves, the evergreens can be safely planted or transplanted.

There are many reasons for transplanting trees or shrubs. If they have become overgrown and begun to crowd one another, you can either prune them or move them. Pruning may ruin their shape and appearance, whereas transplant-ing enables you to preserve their appearance and yet provide adequate spacing.

Transplanting may also be called for when a plant is not doing well. Poor drainage, competition with other plants, wrong exposure, sun reflection, and inadequate air circulation are only a few of the reasons why a plant might not be thriving in a certain spot and should be moved to a more suitable location. All too often a plant is placed in the garden without considering its light requirement. For example, skimmia is a beautiful shade plant, yet it is often placed where it will be exposed to full sun. Consequently, the plant loses its bright color and appears sickly. It should be

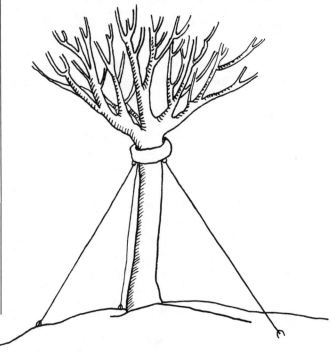

Newly planted or transplanted trees and bushes need support should a harsh storm arise.

moved to correct the problem. Note that container plants can be planted or transplanted almost any time throughout the entire year, except when the ground is deeply frozen.

When digging up a plant for transplanting, it is generally a good practice to begin digging approximately one-third to one-half the distance from the trunk of the plant to the drip line. If you encounter large roots, dig out a bit farther; otherwise you will be removing too many of the feeder roots and taking a much greater risk of the plant's not surviving. Once the plant is dug, pack the root system with burlap, an old blanket, black polyethylene, or a similar plastic or cloth material so that the soil does not fall away from the roots. You can use a wheelbarrow or handcart to move most plants. For an extra-large plant, it may be necessary to make a sling with burlap or 2-by-4's, and you will probably need two or more people to help with the moving. Be sure to get the plant into the new planting hole as soon as possible, so the roots do not dry out.

Planting
Spring-Flowering Bulbs

If you want to enjoy the beauty of tulips, daffodils, hyacinths, crocuses, and other spring-flowering bulbs, you'll have to plant them in the fall.

September, October, and November are the months for planting spring-flowering bulbs, but most Northwesterners prefer late September and early October to take advantage of better weather and the better selection of varieties available. If you wait too long, the supply will be picked over.

There is such a wide range of types and varieties of spring-flowering bulbs that their uses in the garden are almost unlimited. Give some thought to the overall garden plan and then select the types and varieties to meet your needs. It is just as important to know what to plant as it is to know where to plant it. In other words, you will want to know what effect you are trying to achieve before you make up your list of spring-flowering bulbs.

Plan your garden to include some of the early-flowering varieties like species crocus, glory-of-the-snow, snowdrop, and winter aconite. Then plan on some midspring bulbs like daffodils, early double tulips, muscari (grape hyacinth), Imperial Crown lily, Triumph, and Darwin tulips. Late spring color can be obtained by including such bulbs as double late tulips, ixia, lily-flowering tulips, cottage tulips, and Dutch iris.

Try to group bulbs by variety and color for spectacular effects. A mass of one color is especially pleasing to the eye. Small groupings are very effective to highlight various areas of the garden. In the naturalized garden, random drifts are most effective. In the established garden, one of the finest places to plant bulbs is in the perennial borders, because once the spring bulbs have finished their flowering season, the early spring perennials begin to bloom. Plant the bulbs in clumps of five, seven, nine, or a dozen or more. Ideal bulbs for such spots include daffodils, grape and other hyacinths, and tulips.

One of the best spots in the entire garden for planting spring-flowering bulbs is in the same area where you had your summer-flowering annuals. These open areas in landscape planting are spots you have usually selected as the focal points of your entire garden. In larger areas the bulbs can be planted in mass plantings, while in the smaller areas they will be most effective in group plantings, using one color to each group.

There is often at least one spot in the garden where low plants are needed for early spring color. Some of the interesting spring-flowering bulbs might be chosen to meet this need. Crocuses, grape hyacinths, dwarf tulips, daffodils, and snowdrops are the ones most commonly used. Others might include anemones, ranunculus, winter aconite, snowdrops, and glory-of-the-snow.

Some types and varieties are excellent for use in rockeries. I single out rockeries because they are ideal places to grow bulbs: The bulbs show off well, and drainage is usually quite good. In my own relatively flat yard, I have created two rockeries because they are such a good way to display my bulbs, which produce an almost un-

beatable burst of spring color combined with spring rockery perennials. Suitable bulbs for the rockery include the dwarf varieties of tulips, daffodils, hyacinths, crocuses, anemones, glory-of-the-snow, snowdrops, and many of the other specialty bulbs.

Bulbs are also very effective when placed among ground cover plantings. Many of them will grow just tall enough to reach above the ground cover, giving the impression that the cover itself is flowering. Crocuses, grape hyacinth, and the dwarf varieties of tulips are ideal for this purpose. They can be used in plantings of ajuga, sagina moss, thyme, ivy, sedums, and *Vinca minor* to name only a few. As an added bonus, these plants conceal the leaves of the bulbs as they die back after flowering.

Tulips, daffodils, hyacinths, and crocuses are undoubtedly the favorites of all the spring-flowering bulbs. By careful selection of types and varieties, it is possible to enjoy blooms from January through May.

Tulips. These colorful spring-flowering bulbs are undoubtedly the most popular. By selecting and planting a few of the different classes, it is possible to have them in flower for over two months during the spring-flowering season. Among the first tulips to bloom are the species types, followed by the single and double early tulips. Next to bloom are Triumphs, Darwins, hybrids, and lastly the late-flowering tulips: the double late, the lily-flowered, Darwin, cottage, parrot, and breeder. Double-flowering tulips are nice for rockeries, borders, or mass plantings; taller varieties are more suitable for mass planting or in groups for spot color.

Hyacinths. In addition to their stately beauty, one of the outstanding characteristics of hyacinths is their intense fragrance, which can best be enjoyed when they are planted near the entry area, driveway, or wherever foot traffic is heavy. Hyacinths have a formal, upright habit of growth. They tend to be a little too formal at times, but this can be overcome by including them with other spring-flowering bulbs in informal groupings. They are most effective in groups of a half-dozen or more. They also make excellent container plants for the patio, lanai, or entry areas, not only because of their flowers but also because of their fragrance. They can be planted individually or mixed with other spring-flowering bulbs. Save a few bulbs and pot them, forcing them for early indoor color in your home. It takes only about three large bulbs per 6-inch pot, and the beauty and fragrance of forced hyacinths is unbeatable.

Daffodils. Daffodils are one of the first large-flowering bulbs to show their color in the springtime. In addition to the large yellow trumpet daffodils, there are now many beautiful new varieties in shades of pink and lime, and some with delicate color combinations. Daffodils are ideal for group plantings, mass plantings, or for spot color throughout the garden. They are one of the finest spring-flowering bulbs for naturalizing. The lower-growing varieties are sometimes used for borders, while the taller ones are used for midbed plantings. Many varieties can be forced for indoor color.

Crocuses. One of the first signs of spring is when the crocuses burst into bloom. Although the Dutch crocus is by far the most popular in Northwest gardens, the new little species crocus is gaining in popularity. Species crocuses begin flowering in January or early February and are available in a wide range of colors and color combinations. They are much smaller than the later-flowering Dutch crocus—about 4 inches tall—so are excellent as border plants in rockeries or as edgings in containers. The larger-flowering Dutch crocuses are most often used for borders, rockeries, or for spot color in the low planting areas.

Often the beauty of tulips, daffodils, hyacinths, and crocuses makes us forget about some of the lesser-known bulbs that also supply abundant color for the spring season. Using some of them can also extend the bulb season. For an interesting focal point, conversation piece, and variety in the garden, a specialty bulb may be just what you need. Happily, the cost of these bulbs is considerably less than the more popular types. Growing heights and flower sizes vary considerably, so uses for specialty bulbs are almost boundless. Here are a few that merit consideration for use in your garden.

Fritillaria. The most popular variety is the crown imperial lily, which is quite large. However, there are smaller varieties that are also quite nice. Crown imperial lily has an interesting habit of growth: large leaves at the base, a flower stem, then very attractive bell-shaped flowers that are topped with a tuft of green leaves. Flower colors vary considerably but are found mostly in shades of yellow and orange. This is a real eye-catcher in the garden.

Ixia. The cut blossoms of this plant will last for weeks, so they are excellent for flower arranging. The flowers appear in spike clusters, reminding one of small gladiolus. Available in shades of pink, red, orange, cream, and yellow, they need well-drained soil and winter protection. This can be provided in the form of a bark or peat moss mulch.

Snowdrops (galanthus). This is a popular low-growing bulb that you probably remember from grandmother's day. Bell-shaped flowers are white with green tips and they grow on stems 6 to 9 inches tall. The bulb does best in a shady, moist, but well-drained area. It is often used for borders, rockeries, or naturalized settings.

Grape hyacinths. The small bright blue flowers of the miniature hyacinths provide an abundance of color in the early spring garden. They are nice for massing and bordering, or can be used in groups along with other spring bulbs. They prefer a well-drained soil but are not fussy about location.

Eranthus (winter aconite). Buttercuplike yellow flowers appear early in the spring season. The plant grows only about 3 to 6 inches tall. It prefers a partially shaded location where the soil is moist but not overwet. Flowers may attain a width of 1 to 1½ inches.

Glory-of-the-snow (chionodoxa). The flowers appear early in the spring in shades of pink, blue, and white. Often there are up to eight or ten blooms per 6-inch stem. The bulb grows and flowers best in partial shade. It is often used for bordering and is very attractive in rockeries and container plantings.

Sparaxis. Late spring flowers are gladioluslike with spike clusters. They are ideal for cut flowers and will last up to a month or longer in the garden. Flower colors include purple, blue, red, yellow, and white. They need well-drained soil and winter protection in the garden.

Ranunculus and anemones. Both should definitely be considered for use in the garden. They flower for a long period of time in the late spring, are an excellent source of cut flowers for the home, and are also very colorful. Both are available in a mixture of bright colors. Growing height varies from 15 to 24 inches. Plant them in well-drained soil in a sunny part of the garden. *Anemone blanda* and several other varieties are lower growing and are available in individual colors. The bulbs of both can be planted in the fall or very early spring.

Trillium. Some of the new varieties are outstanding. They are available in shades of white, lemon yellow, and reddish purple. Most of them flower in March or April. They are ideal for use in a naturalized setting in a moist, partly shaded area. Specialty growers list over a hundred varieties from which to choose. The fall dormant season is the time to plant them.

Calla lilies. Roots can be planted in fall or late winter in a warm, protected area of the garden. Although the white-flowering varieties are the most common, yellow and pink grow and flower here. Most varieties grow 2 to 2½ feet tall. Mulch plants with bark, sawdust, straw, or evergreen boughs for added winter protection, and make sure the planting soil is well drained.

Oxalis. Flower colors range from shades of pink, rose, and red to shades of yellow, white, and violet. This plant is best known for its glossy cloverlike leaves. Can be grown in the garden or in pots for early color in the home.

Erythoniums. Commonly called the "dogtooth violet," several varieties are native to the West. A few varieties adaptable to home gardens are available for planting during the dormant season. Specialty growers often list a dozen or more varieties. Some American species are known as avalanche lilies or trout lilies. Varieties range in height from 4 to 15 inches.

Hardy gloxinia (Incarvillea delavayi). These are grown from perennial roots. The magenta, trumpet-shaped flowers are much smaller than the tuberous gloxinia. They generally appear in clusters of two, eight, or more flowers per stem. They need well-drained soil and a sunny location in the garden.

Hybrid lilies. Hybridization over the past fifty years has resulted in some outstanding recent introductions. The world-famous lily grower Jan de Graaff, of Gresham, Oregon, has introduced some excellent ones. Flower size, color range, and height vary considerably from one variety to another. By careful selection, it is possible to have them in bloom from May to October. Most of the new varieties range in height from 1 to 6 feet or more. They are excellent plants to use for garden color or cut flowers.

Lily-flowering tulips. This is one of my favorite types of tulips. They seem to last a long time in the garden or as cut flowers in the home, and have long pointed buds with petals that curve upward, giving them a distinctive flared appearance in the garden. They come in a wide range of colors and combine well with other spring-flowering bulbs.

Cottage and Darwin tulips. These are probably the most popular and best known of the spring-flowering tulips. They are noted for their large flowers, consistent flowering habit, and sturdy stems. It is not unusual for some varieties to have huge flowers of up to 6 or 7 inches across.

Parrot tulips. These novelty tulips are quite popular because of their unusual ruffled, feathery appearance in the garden. Some varieties are finely fringed, making them very attractive garden conversation pieces. They come in a wide range of colors and color combinations. Their unusual shapes and textures add interest to any garden.

Double-flowering tulips. The early and late varieties of double-flowering tulips look like little peonies. They are very attractive flowering plants. Place them where they get some protection from strong winds, because the heavy double flower can sometimes be damaged by wind whipping. Since most of the varieties grow only about 6 to 12 inches high, this type of tulip should be used for foreground in your bulb planting. Early-flowering varieties of double tulips can also be used for forcing in the home.

Bouquet tulips. This new series and type of tulip sometimes produces three, four, or five flowers per stem. Of course, the flowers are considerably smaller than most tulips, but the profusion of flowers provides an abundant display of garden color. Plant in an area that is protected from strong winds, because the new flowers are sometimes too heavy for their stems. This tulip is sometimes very difficult to find.

If you are planning to add new bulbs to the garden, there are a few things you should know about selecting the best ones. The new crop of spring-flowering bulbs begins arriving at local garden outlets in early September. You should make your selection of bulbs early so you get the pick of the crop. Sometimes there is a tendency to wait to buy bulbs because the area in which you plan to use them is still colorfully planted with summer-flowering annuals, and it would be a shame to disturb them. Keep in mind, however, that if you wait too long you will end up with what is left over and the quality may not be everything you desire. It's better to buy your spring-flowering bulbs early and then wait to plant them until after the summer-flowering annuals have passed their peak.

Buying spring-flowering bulbs is much like buying potatoes or tomatoes at the supermarket. You should first check to see that the bulbs are of top quality and that they are not bruised or damaged in any way. In other words, visually check the bulbs over thoroughly. Look for diseases, too. If you find that some of the bulbs have a bluish-gray or tannish fungus growth on them, don't buy them.

You can also tell if spring-flowering bulbs are of top quality by simply feeling them. There is no need to squeeze or pinch; just touch them. Look for nice firm bulbs and avoid purchasing soft ones. If you are new at gardening, you may need a little help with this because some bulbs—lilies, for example—tend to be soft; but tulips, daffodils, hyacinths, and crocuses should be firm. Selecting bulbs in the Pacific Northwest should not really be a major problem, because many of the spring-flowering bulbs are grown right here. In addition, local garden outlets go out of their way to purchase high-quality bulbs; and most of them make it a policy to regularly eliminate any inferior bulbs.

When selecting bulbs, you may notice that some of them are cleaner than others. This is really nothing to be concerned about. The type of soil in which the bulb is grown and the cleaning process used by the grower are the factors that determine how clean the bulb will be. What you should be concerned about is selecting good, healthy bulbs. You may also notice that the skin of some bulbs is loose and falling away, while the skin on others is intact. The skin is no gauge of the bulb's health and makes no difference as long as the bulb is firm and not bruised.

Here are some pointers on selecting some of the individual types of bulbs.

Crocuses. Bulbs approximately ¾ inch in diameter or larger are considered the best-flowering size.

Tulips. Select bulbs an inch in diameter or larger for the best flowering. Smaller bulbs will need an additional year of development before they produce nice-size flowers.

Hyacinths. These usually come in a wide range of bulb sizes. The largest bulbs are ideal for potting to force for early indoor color. In the garden, large bulbs produce flowers that are too large and bend or fall over during a heavy rain or strong wind. So for outdoor purposes use small- or medium-size bulbs.

Daffodils. It's not unusual for daffodil bulbs to cling together. Each point is called a "nose." Garden outlets often feature single-, double-, or triple-nose daffodil bulbs. Generally, the more bulbs that are attached together, the more flowers. As a rule of thumb, it is generally considered that double-nose daffodil bulbs will produce an average of one and a half to two flowers, and that a triple-nose bulb will produce an average of two flowers. Since these different-size bulbs are often mixed together and offered at the same price, it is to your advantage to pick the double- or triple-nose bulbs.

It is best to get your spring-flowering bulbs into the ground as soon as possible. There are several reasons for early planting, one of the best being that weather conditions are more suitable; as the season progresses and the weather gets wetter and cooler, working outside becomes less appealing. Another good reason for early planting is that it gives the bulbs a chance to get established and develop a more prolific root system before cold winter weather sets in.

Spring-flowering bulbs are easy to plant and they grow very well in the soil of the Pacific Northwest, as evidenced by the commercial bulb fields of Washington and Oregon. Most do best in well-drained, light, sandy loam, but with a little extra care they will grow in almost any type of soil. In clay or hardpan, it is best to place a small amount of sand under each bulb to improve drainage.

When preparing the soil, it is a good practice to mix in ample amounts of peat moss, compost, or leaf mold. Add the correct amount of bulb fertilizer or bone meal. To cut down on insects and disease, use a complete soil insecticide/fungicide dust at planting time. Mix all the ingredients together thoroughly.

Bulbs can be planted individually in rows, or a large hole can be prepared for planting a dozen or more at one time. Whichever way you choose, be certain to plant at the correct depth. As a rule, plant three times deeper than the greatest diameter of the bulb. A 1-inch crocus bulb should be planted about 3 inches deep. A tulip or daffodil bulb with a 2-inch diameter should be planted 6 inches deep. When in doubt, plant deeper rather than too shallow.

*You can plant several bulbs in one hole
instead of digging individually for each
bulb.*

To add additional color in the off-season, plant winter-blooming pansies where you have planted bulbs. This is a nice combination planting, because the pansies will flower sporadically during warm spells throughout the winter, and then burst into full bloom about the time the bulbs come into bloom. Flowering cabbage and kale or winter-flowering varieties of heather are other nice companions for your bulb plantings.

FORCING BULBS

For bright color in your home during the winter, you can pot a few of the spring-flowering bulbs for forcing indoors. Bulbs started in October will flower indoors in January or February. Hyacinths, crocuses, dwarf tulips, daffodils, snowdrops, grape hyacinths, scilla, glory-of-the-snow, and paper-white narcissus are a few of the most popular bulbs for forcing. Probably the hyacinths, daffodils, and tulips are the most popular. Hya-

cinths are especially nice because of their attractive flowers and intense fragrance.

When selecting bulbs for forcing, it is important to choose the largest, plumpest, and most solid. Check them over carefully to see that there are no blemishes, bruises, or spots of decay. The number of bulbs you will need will depend upon the size of the pot you use.

A commercial potting soil is best for planting your bulbs. If you decide to use your own garden soil, be sure it is sterilized to avoid introducing soilborne insects or diseases. At our home we always use a good commercial potting soil because it provides adequate drainage and enables the bulbs to develop good fibrous root systems.

It will generally take about six tulips or daffodils, three hyacinths, or fifteen crocuses to fill a 6-inch pot—about the average size used for forcing bulbs. When planting tulips, place the flat side of the bulb toward the outside of the pot.

The first leaf that forms will thus face outward, and ultimately you'll have an attractive ring of leaves all the way around the pot.

As you place the bulbs in the pot, make certain they are not touching each other or the edge of the pot. Plant them as close together as possible, however, so you get a nice full display when they come into bloom. Give them plenty of root room; the tops of tulip and daffodil bulbs can even protrude above soil level. Do not press the bulbs into the soil; simply set them on the soil and then fill in around them. Be certain not to pack the soil—just gently firm it around the bulbs. Leave ½ inch or so at the top of the container for watering purposes.

The most important part of forcing bulbs is the conditioning cycle, where they are stored away for a period of 8 to 12 weeks. Water the bulbs thoroughly first, then bury them, pot and all, 4 to 6 inches deep, or mulch 4 or 5 inches deep with bark, sawdust, straw, hay, or leaves. If you live in an apartment, leave the bulbs in an unheated basement, garage, or other storage location. Be certain you place them in a spot that has little or no light.

Another method is to place newspapers or sheets of plastic on the floor of the basement, garage, or storage room. Cover the pots with a sheet of black plastic, surrounding the sides, tops, and bottoms for total darkness.

Wherever you store them, be sure to check them occasionally to see when they are ready to be brought in for forcing. A good sign to look for is the emergence of new roots from the drainage hole at the bottom of the container, or the emergence of shoots to about an inch above soil level. At this point they are ready for forcing.

After the eight- to twelve-week storage period, bulbs can be brought back into the home. Choose a spot where the temperature is around 60 degrees. It is the combination of cool temperatures and good light that helps the development of the flowers. If temperatures are too warm, the forced bulbs often develop long, spindly, weak flower stems and poor foliage. You can extend the flowering season by taking only a few pots from the storage area at a time. If you remove pots at two- or three-week intervals, you will be able to have bulbs flowering in the home for a much longer time. Be sure to leave them in the storage area until you are ready to use them; otherwise they will begin top growth right away.

Once the bulbs have gone through the forcing process, they are seldom worth keeping. However, if you want to plant them outdoors into the garden, they will eventually flower again.

Houseplants

Houseplants are a major source of enjoyment because their presence is much like having a part of the outdoors inside. Varying leaf textures and colors, plant sizes, and growing habits make plants attractive additions to the home decor.

Many houseplants enter their dormant period in the fall, so they need less care than during the rest of the year. They should not be completely neglected, however. Houseplant care is really quite simple if you use common sense. They need regular care, not sporadic attention. Enjoy your plants, but don't become a slave to them. This idea of misting three times a day, watering three times a week, and moving plants continually is for the birds. They are not worth having if they need that much attention.

If you have put a few of your houseplants out on the patio, deck, or lanai during the summer season, it is important that they now be returned to their regular spot in the home. Be sure to do this before the evening temperatures get too cold—and certainly before the first frost. The longer you wait, the more difficult it is for your houseplants to make the adjustment from a natural environment outdoors to the hot, dry air in your home. A word to the wise: Be sure to check your houseplants for insects before you bring them indoors, or you are apt to infest your entire collection of houseplants.

One of the major factors in fall houseplant care is watering—a real dilemma for many people. There is no set rule that can be applied to any given plant. Soil mixture, location, exposure, room temperature, type of heat, pot size, and hu-midity are all factors in determining how often any plant should be watered. Two plants of the same type in similar locations may even require different watering care.

I often hear someone complain that a neighbor has the same plant and gives it the same care but gets much better results. There are too many factors involved to expect the same care to give the same results. To test this for yourself, place three alike plants in the same room, one on the floor, one on a table, and hang one from the ceiling. You soon will discover that the needs of these plants differ considerably.

There is a tendency on the part of many to overwater houseplants; in fact, national surveys indicate that the number one cause of houseplant fatality is too much water. Therefore, learn how to tell when a houseplant needs water. Wilting leaves can be a sign, but it should be pointed out that an overwatered plant that is drowning also will develop wilted leaves, so this is not always the best guide. Touching the surface soil to see if it feels dry is not a very reliable guide either: The surface soil is exposed to the air and often dries out quite rapidly; and with some of the soil mixtures now used to grow tropical plants, the soil at the bottom of the pot can be soaking wet when the top soil is dry to the touch.

One of the most effective ways I have found to test the need for water is to lift the pot periodically to estimate its weight. If the soil is wet, the pot will be much heavier than when the soil is dry. The toothpick method of checking water is popular with many people. Simply insert a toothpick into the soil and pull it out; if there are any soil particles clinging to it, the soil is still moist; if the toothpick is dry and comes out clean, the plant needs water. This is the same method that cooks use to determine whether a cake is ready to come out of the oven.

In most cases it is a good practice to water until the excess begins to run out the drainage hole, then not water again until the plant has dried sufficiently. Experiment a little to determine how long this takes. The watering schedule will not be the same for all plants.

Several types of gauges are available to help determine the amount of moisture in soil. Some work by sound, while others give scaled meter readings. You may want to examine some of them and purchase one for your home.

We water large houseplants and ferns in our home by submerging them in water. To do this, simply fill the kitchen sink with room-temperature water before you go to bed at night, then submerge each plant so the water just runs over the top of the pot. When air bubbles stop coming out—usually after one to three minutes—set the plants on the drainboard and go to bed. Next morning the excess water will have drained away and the plants can be returned to their regular places. Using this method, we water our plants only about once every ten days to two weeks, depending on the temperature indoors. You'll have to experiment a little to establish an exact schedule for your home conditions.

Here are a couple of telltale signs that may help you recognize either extreme of watering. If your houseplants tend to get yellow toward the base or center of the leaf, this often indicates overwatering. On the other hand, if the soil separates from the container, or if the tips of your plant become dry and crisp, this often indicates lack of water.

It is a good practice to set aside a container of water each time you have finished watering your houseplants. By letting it sit for several days, the water reaches room temperature and any undesirable sediments tend to settle out.

Humidity is another prime factor in the care of houseplants during the fall. As the temperatures get colder outside, there is a tendency to turn the thermostat up indoors; consequently, the air becomes very hot and dry. Since most houseplants—especially the tropical ones—are not accustomed to hot, dry air, humidity must be provided for them.

You can add humidity in several different ways. For hanging plants, a vial or glass of water hidden in the foliage will be helpful. For plants on the floor or on a table, a container of water can be placed nearby.

Probably one of the best ways to provide adequate humidity for plants is to fill a saucer with gravel and pour water halfway up the gravel, then place the pot on the gravel bed, making

Simply placing a glass of water near your houseplants will give them the humidity they need.

sure the water does not come in direct contact with the base of the container. This provides humidity all around the plant.

I generally do not recommend misting plants as a means of providing humidity. My reasoning is that too much moisture on the leaves can encourage diseases like mildew; and when the leaves are dry, the combination of moisture and indoor heat almost seems to cook them. Unless you have a greenhouse or you keep your home cooler than average, I would suggest you avoid misting. Other methods of providing humidity are far better.

Fertilizer requirements of houseplants will not be as great in the fall as they are during the spring and summer growing seasons. Most green foliage houseplants should be fertilized a maxi-

mum of about once every three months during the fall and winter. A gray or white deposit on a pot or on the soil usually indicates a buildup of fertilizer salts. This means the plant has been overfed, so cut back on fertilizing if this occurs.

Fall is the time of year to be on the lookout for insects on your houseplants. As the weather gets cooler outside, insects often move inside. In fact, they are more prevalent in the home during the fall than at any other time of the year. They might come inside with houseplants that have been outdoors for the summer, or fly in when doors are open, or arrive on new plants that are infested. Insects can also be introduced to houseplants from containers that have not been cleaned properly or soil that has not been sterilized. When potting or repotting plants, always clean containers thoroughly, and be sure to use sterilized soil.

When searching for insects, check first on the undersides of the leaves, because about 90 percent of all insects are found there. Also check the leaf stem, main branches, and trunk of the plant. Some insects are so small that it is impossible to see them with the naked eye. A magnifying glass will greatly help in your search for them.

Some of the signs to look for are discoloration or malformation of leaves, drooping or rolled leaves, webs on foliage, and leaves that have been nibbled. A sticky substance on the leaves, pot, or surface around the plant is another indicator. Spider mites, mealybugs, scale, or aphids can be responsible for this. Sometimes a black sooty mold begins to grow in this substance, and this is still another clue to what is wrong.

Infected houseplants should be isolated immediately. Leaves that are malformed or discolored due to insect damage should be pinched off and destroyed because they seldom, if ever, will recover. Leaving them on the plant spoils the appearance of the plant in addition to harboring trouble.

The major chemical insecticide companies have regular brands of houseplant insect sprays specially formulated to control insects common to most houseplants; however, I cannot stress strongly enough the importance of reading the entire label carefully to be sure the product will control the insects you have identified as causing the problem.

Many insects reproduce at an amazing rate in a relatively short time. They often appear in three cycles, so corrective steps must take this into account. Repeated applications will probably be needed, and these should be given as stated on the label as well.

If any of your houseplants are leggy, spindly, or out of shape, they may need tip-pinching or pruning. This will encourage bushiness and improve the appearance of straggly plants.

Pinching should begin at the first sign of irregular growth. Too often plants are left to grow out of shape without any attention whatsoever. When needed, simply pinch the tip growth of the branch back to the first node—the point at which a leaf or stem arises. Pinching at this point encourages side branching, and a bushier, neater plant is the result. Very few plants do not respond to occasional pinching.

Sometimes, more severe pruning is needed. For example, dead, decayed, or broken branches should be removed as they appear. Pruning may also be called for when a large dieffenbachia, philodendron, or rubber plant has lost most of its lower leaves, leaving an unattractive stalk with only a few leaves at the top. Simply cut the plant back to within about 6 inches of soil level. Within a few weeks new buds will appear and new growth will develop.

As with outdoor pruning, use common sense in pinching and pruning a houseplant, lest you ruin the natural growing habit of the plant. Prune and pinch as Mother Nature intended the plant to grow.

Make sure your houseplants are not situated too close to hot air from a heating duct, or near doors that open to the outside—the rapid temperature changes can injure them. Be sure to move your plants away from the fireplace whenever you have a fire burning during the winter. If you have a plant sitting on a windowsill, move it to a different location during cold weather, lest the cold glass damage it.

It is a good practice to turn your plants on a regular basis, half a turn every three or four days, so the entire plant gets even light throughout the fall and winter. Most plants will take a brighter exposure during the winter season than they do during the summer months. Plants with bright-colored foliage, particularly, should be placed where they can get more light during the fall and winter. If they receive insufficient light, a certain amount of foliage color will be lost. As a general rule, most houseplants prefer room temperatures of 65 to 70 degrees and slightly cooler at night during the fall season.

Of course, specific houseplants require specific care, so here is a list of some popular houseplants and their basic requirements:

African violets. By far the most popular of all indoor flowering plants, African violets need a location where they receive bright, indirect sunlight. They will benefit from monthly fertilizing with an all-purpose houseplant fertilizer even during the fall months. Ideal room temperatures are 70 to 72 degrees and slightly cooler at night. African violets require plenty of humidity. Keep the soil moist but not continually wet, and allow the top half inch of soil to dry to the touch between waterings.

Aphelandra. Because the large green leaves of this plant are striped with white, its common name is zebra plant. Its basic needs in the fall are plenty of humidity and filtered light. It is also important to avoid overwatering and allow the soil to dry between waterings. There is a natural tendency for the lower leaves to drop; don't be alarmed when this happens. If it becomes severe, simply cut the plant back to 3 or 4 inches from soil level to encourage a new branching habit. The problem is accelerated when the air is hot and dry or when the soil is kept too moist. New plants can be started from cuttings taken when the plant is not in flower. When an old plant becomes leggy and unsightly, it is sometimes best to replace it with a new plant started in this way.

Azalea. It will grow and flower best when kept in room temperatures in the high 60s or low 70s. Keep the soil cool and moist but not continually wet. Azaleas should have a bright light exposure and should not be fertilized during their flowering season. Immediately after flowering, the plant should be repotted in a container one size larger. Azaleas can be set outdoors in the spring after all danger of frost has passed.

Caladium. In recent years this plant has gained tremendous popularity. Its large colorful leaves provide a bold texture that is a nice change from most houseplants. It is important to understand that this plant grows from a tuber and has a dormant period. This means it requires a rest. When a plant gets straggly and limp, simply withhold water gradually until all the leaves have died, then place the tuber on a dry shelf to rest for two or three months. After that time, replant it in fresh soil, and it will start to grow again. When the plant is in a healthy growing state, it will need indirect sunlight and warm room temperature. Keep it moist but never overwet. Humidity is important too, and a glass of water nearby or a humidity tray will help provide this.

Chrysanthemum. This can be grown anywhere in the home in bright light. Water thoroughly and check watering every three or four days. Fertilize monthly while plants are in bloom. After they are finished flowering, cut them back to within 3 or 4 inches of ground level. Plants can be set into the garden in the spring after all danger of frost has passed.

Citrus. Many types of citrus plants can be grown as houseplants. Among the most popular are dwarf lemons, oranges, limes, and grapefruit. Attractive leaves, fragrant flowers, and fruit make them especially nice for home use. Exposure, humidity, and watering are the prime cultural concerns. Place where there is plenty of humidity and at least four hours of bright light. Good air circulation is also important. They do best if the soil is kept moist but not overwet. Problems can be encountered when the plant is placed where the air is too hot and dry, when air circulation is poor, or when a plant is kept too moist.

Coleus. An outstanding characteristic of this plant is its multicolored leaves. During the fall it goes into a semidormant stage, requiring different care from that of the rest of the year. Actually fall and winter can be a difficult time to grow this colorful plant. It prefers indirect light such as a north or east window. The soil should be kept moist but never overwet. Repotting may be needed. A few leaves will likely drop naturally; however, extensive leaf drop is caused by too much light or extremes in watering. Small leaves can be caused by lack of sufficient light or by watering extremes. Plants grown outside in the summer months can be brought in during the fall season to be grown as houseplants.

Crossandra. This tropical flowering plant is sometimes known as the firecracker flower. The orange flowers and glossy, dark green leaves make an interesting color combination in the home. Fertilize monthly when in bloom. Place it in an area where it gets bright indirect light. Provide humidity, and keep the soil moist but not continually wet.

Gloxinia. Keep gloxinia in a cool room where temperatures range between the high 50s and low 60s. Remove some of the inner growth to encourage the buds to fully develop. They require lots of humidity, which can often be provided by placing a glass or vase of water near the plant. Never mist the foliage. Their care is similar to that of tuberous begonias. Keep the soil moist but not continually wet, and never water into the center of the plant. Gloxinias should be fertilized every three to four weeks with an all-purpose houseplant fertilizer. Plants kept in the house more than nine months should be allowed to die back naturally and rest before starting them over again.

Jade plant. This plant thrives on a certain amount of neglect. Possibly the most common mistake made during this time of year is to overwater the plant. In most homes it should not be watered more than once every three to six weeks during the winter dormant season. Fertilize only once in an entire year and never during the fall or winter. Minimum humidity is required, bright light is needed, and for best growing results the plant should be kept root-bound.

Palms. It is quite easy to grow palms. Their main requirements are protection from drafts and plenty of light and humidity. If a plant is exposed to drafts, the tips of the leaves will likely turn brown. This problem can also be caused by insufficient humidity or by watering extremes. Keep the plant root-bound in well-drained soil.

Peppers. Provide ample humidity and bright light for them. Temperatures should be on the cool side, in the high 50s or low 60s. Fertilize every three to four weeks with an all-purpose houseplant fertilizer. Water thoroughly and then allow the soil to dry between waterings. Peppers suffer from rapid temperature changes, overwatering, and lack of humidity.

Prayer plant. This old-time favorite is once again becoming popular because of its interesting leaves. The most common mistake made in growing it is exposure to too much light. For brighter leaf color, provide indirect light; a north window is excellent. To grow at its best, it also requires room temperatures above 65 degrees. Like most tropical houseplants, this one also needs plenty of humidity.

Rieger begonia. These plants will flower for a long period of time during the winter if kept in bright light. Place them in a room where the temperatures vary between 55 and 70 degrees. Provide humidity for them. They should be fertilized monthly with an all-purpose houseplant fertilizer. As a rule, keep the soil moist but not continually wet, allowing ½ inch soil to dry to the touch between waterings.

Spider plant. New plants are quite easy to start from offshoots of the mother plant, making it a rather inexpensive plant to grow. This, no doubt, has contributed to its popularity. It grows and produces offshoots best when it is kept pot-bound. Water

thoroughly and then allow the soil to dry before rewatering. Provide plenty of humidity and bright light. Average room temperatures are ideal, and a north or east window is best.

Wandering Jew. There are many varieties of this plant, and most have very attractive leaf color. The most common problem encountered during the fall is loss of leaf color caused by too much shade. Bright indirect sunlight is needed. Be sure the soil is well drained; keep it moist, but not overwet. Lack of humidity or stagnant air can cause the inner leaves to turn brown and drop. This is especially true of the varieties grown in hanging baskets. Problems with this plant are greatly increased during the months when the thermostat is turned up, causing room temperatures to become too hot and dry.

TERRARIUMS

In recent years the terrarium has become a very popular way to grow and display houseplants. It is also one of the easiest ways, because the plants require only sparse amounts of water and occasional pinching back.

The true terrarium has a cover or plug to seal it off from the air outside. Large bottles, jugs, glass canisters, and candy jars often are used. The result is a self-contained unit, capable of recycling air, water, nutrients, and fertilizer in balance to sustain plant life almost indefinitely.

Containers that are not completely closed have

also been used successfully for this type of gardening. Brandy snifters, wineglasses, fish tanks, and clear bubble containers are most often used. Although these are not true terrariums, they are treated similarly; but they will need some extra care.

The narrow-neck type of container presents quite a challenge because of the difficulty of getting plants inside. Professionals have special tools to do this, but the home gardener must improvise. Two tall matchsticks or a pair of chopsticks can be used, but not everyone has the patience for this. If you do not think you want to tackle this task, have your terrarium professionally planted. Another alternative is to use one of the new two-piece containers that permit easy access for planting.

One of the biggest problems when planting a terrarium is the selection of plants. Too often plants are chosen that grow too rapidly for the space available. Be sure you select only slow-growing plants. A second consideration in choosing plants is compatibility: Select plants that grow at about the same rate in height and width, and have similar cultural needs. Third, choose some plants that have different heights and shapes—just as you would in the outdoor landscape. Finally, since a terrarium is actually an indoor miniature landscape, be sure to consider foliage texture and color when making your selections.

If you are planting a terrarium for the first time, the following are some pointers on how to proceed. If you have a terrarium that did not succeed the first time, why not try again? Simply discard the old soil and start over, following the steps outlined below.

1. Clean the container thoroughly.

2. Cover the bottom ½ inch with charcoal granules. This helps provide drainage and prevents any unpleasant odor.

3. Add a sterilized potting soil. As a rule the soil should take up no more than one-fourth to one-third of the space in the container. For example, if the container is 12 inches deep, soil should cover 3 or 4 inches of this depth. This proportion keeps the entire planting in balance.

4. Now you are ready to plant. Arrange the plants on a table before you place them in the terrarium. Plan the arrangement that will look best in the container.

5. Before removing the plants from their pots, water them thoroughly so the dirt will cling to the roots. This will help reduce transplanting shock. If the roots are densely matted, gently loosen them so they will be able to grow out into the surrounding soil.

6. Place the plants in the container according to your plan. Then lightly moisten the soil. For added interest, shells, rocks, moss, small pieces of driftwood, or a small container of water resembling a pool or pond can become part of the arrangement. Use your imagination to individualize your design and make it more interesting.

As mentioned earlier, watering is one of the few concerns in growing terrariums. There is a tendency to overwater. A closed container seldom needs watering at all; it may go as long as a year without needing additional moisture. The open container will need watering occasionally. Location and temperature in the home will dictate the frequency of watering. With a little experimentation, you will know very soon how often water is needed in your home situation. Often you can determine the amount of moisture in the container by visually examining the terrarium soil. Above all, never overwater.

Location of the terrarium in the home is important too. Choose a bright spot, but avoid direct sunlight or close proximity to a heating duct, fireplace, or the like. If condensation forms on the inside of a closed container, simply remove the top part until it has dissipated.

If the plants tend to lean toward the light, turn the container regularly to encourage upright, bushy growth. Turning a quarter-turn every few days will solve the problem quite well.

Should the plants become spindly or too large for their surroundings, simply pinch or prune them back as necessary. This can be done with your fingers, a pair of scissors, or small pruning shears.

Should mold form in the container, it could be the result of overwatering, a disease on one of the plants, or too much fertilizer. If it forms on the soil, simply remove it with a fork. If it is on the leaves of a plant, it could be a funguslike mildew, and a fungicide should be used, sparingly.

If you realize you have overwatered your terrarium, move it closer to heat so it will dry out more quickly, reducing the chance of mildew or mold forming. Because terrariums create a recyclable atmosphere, fertilizer seldom is needed. A light application once a year usually is considered adequate. Terrariums seem to thrive on a certain amount of neglect, and this is one of their greatest assets. They can provide much enjoyment with a minimum amount of effort on your part.

LIGHT-SENSITIVE HOUSEPLANTS

Early September is the time to begin giving special attention to poinsettias, Christmas cactus, and other specialty houseplants. Each of these houseplants requires the same type of care that other houseplants require in the fall, but they also have some special light requirements.

All of these plants are considered light-sensitive, and in order for them to flower they must have fourteen hours of total darkness and ten hours of bright light in each twenty-four-hour day.

Between the first and fifteenth of October, the plants will need to be moved to a new location. It will be necessary to provide uninterrupted night-time darkness if the plants are to set flowers. Light is needed during the daytime, then total darkness at night. This requirement is very often misunderstood. These plants are very sensitive to light, and flowering will be delayed if a plant is exposed to any type of light during nighttime hours, even if for only a few seconds. It is best to place the plant in a room where there is normal light during the daytime but where there is no chance of light entering at night. A utility room, unused bedroom, or heated basement is ideal. As an extra precaution, it is wise to unscrew the light bulb in the room so there is no chance it will be turned on by accident.

Another way to provide uninterrupted darkness at night is to cover the plant with black plas-

Poinsettias need 10 hours of light and 14 hours of darkness in order for them to flower in time for the holidays.

tic or a cardboard box. If you use this method, cover the plant as the sun goes down in the evening, and remove the cover when the sun comes up in the morning. Once the fat little flower buds begin to form on the tips of the stems, the plants can be returned to their regular spots in the home. This process will take from six to eight weeks or longer.

It has often been recommended that poinsettias be placed in the closet. That is all right provided they are brought out for eight to ten hours each day for exposure to bright light. In other words, the plant cannot be left in the closet twenty-four hours a day.

Fall is the wrong time of year for repotting or pruning any of the Christmas plants. These jobs should be done in early spring after the normal flowering season.

It may not be easy to get your plants to bloom for the holidays, but you will have fun trying. I have had reports that flowers on such plants often appear in late January instead of at Christmas, but if you follow directions carefully, perhaps you will succeed in getting blooms at the earlier time.

Give your houseplants adequate care during the fall months; but remember, do not become a slave to them. Also, give your Christmas plants the uninterrupted darkness and light requirements that they need, and enjoy their beauty during the holidays.

Bringing Tender Plants Indoors Before Winter

Fall is the time of year to give some thought to what you plan to do with the fuchsias, geraniums, begonias, dahlias, and other tender plants in your garden to protect them over the winter months. You can enjoy their beauty in the garden as long as the winter stays mild; but when cold weather threatens, at least some plants should be moved to their winter resting places immediately, because even a light frost will ruin them. Fuchsias are a bit hardier than most tender plants and can withstand a light frost, but it is best not to wait too long.

There are several places to store your tender plants. Your choice will depend on the space you have available. Among the most popular places are the basement, garage, utility room, storage room, and crawl space under the home or mobile home. Apartment dwellers often find a downstairs storage room suitable. If you have a greenhouse, tender plants can be stored either on or under a bench.

Following are a few suggestions for wintering the plants mentioned.

Tuberous begonias. Bring the plants into a heated room and begin withholding water. Allow the foliage to die back naturally. Once this has occurred and the stems separate easily, the tubers can be taken from the soil and stored on a shelf until February or March. At that time they should be repotted and the growing process will begin again.

Geraniums. These plants can be wintered as houseplants. Prune them severely and place them in a semiheated basement, garage, or utility room. The temperature should be in the high 50s or 60s. Keep watering at a minimum; once or twice a month is adequate. Leggy growth that develops should be cut off as it appears. Some gardeners report excellent results by digging the plants, bare-rooting them, and hanging them upside down in the basement or garage where the temperature is between 50 and 60 degrees and where there is no chance of freeze damage. The bare-rooted plants can also be placed in a plastic bag with a little moist peat moss or sphagnum moss. Again, hang them upside down. Although this method has not worked well for me, many gardeners report excellent results using this technique.

Fuchsias. These plants can be buried in the ground. Many hobbyists prefer this method over all others. Simply dig a hole 2 to 3 feet deep, placing drainage materials such as gravel, sand, or straw at the bottom. Lay each plant on its side, covering it with a mulch of peat moss, bark, sawdust, or straw. Dig up the plants in February or March, repot in fresh soil, and the growing process will begin again. Fuchsias can be wintered in the same ways as geraniums.

Dahlias. The most successful way to winter dahlias is to mulch the soil over the tubers with 3 to 6 inches of bark, sawdust, peat moss, or straw. Make sure the tubers are in well-drained soil. If it tends to be clay, hardpan, or remains wet all winter, the tubers should be dug and stored in a dry place such as a basement or garage. Use dry vermiculite, shredded newspapers, or similar materials to store them.

Impatiens and wax begonias. The easiest way to winter these is to pot them and treat them as houseplants for the winter. They make excellent indoor flowering plants when placed in indirect sunlight. In such locations they will usually flower sparingly all winter long. When all danger of frost has passed in spring, the plants can be returned to the garden.

Any of the annuals that you are going to try to save as houseplants should be potted in a regular houseplant potting soil to avoid introducing soil-borne insects or diseases from the garden. The size of the rootball will be the determining factor in establishing what size pot you need for each plant. If the rootball is too large, you can often reduce its size by carefully shaving away some of the excess soil.

Since these plants are now accustomed to rather cool evening hours and varying temperatures, it's a good idea to make the transition from outdoors into the home quite gradually. This gradual transition can be achieved by first moving the plants into a cool room, unheated basement, or covered porch; then, after three or four days, moving them into their permanent place in the home. When the plants are first moved into the home, they will suffer from the hot, dry air unless ample humidity is provided for them.

Select a spot similar to the location these plants had in the garden. Since impatiens and coleus are generally grown in a fairly shaded spot, it is important to keep them out of bright direct sunlight, at least until they become established. Bright indirect light would be ideal for them.

At first there is a tendency to overwater these plants, so you may have to experiment a little to determine their watering needs. It is generally a good practice to water thoroughly and then allow the soil to dry moderately before rewatering. Location, temperature, soil, pot size, and type of heat will all be factors in determining how frequently each plant will need to be watered.

After three or four weeks, you can treat these tender plants like ordinary houseplants. Feed them with an all-purpose houseplant fertilizer, and pinch or prune back any leggy growth that develops. The best varieties and their special care follow.

Wax begonias. Low-growing fibrous wax begonias are often grown and sold as houseplants. If you have a few of them in the garden, fall is the time to dig, pot, and bring them indoors, before they are touched by the first light frost. The wax begonias and other types of fibrous begonias can be used as indoor winter houseplants.

Impatiens. The common impatiens, bizzy-lizzy, and the New Guinea impatiens can be potted and brought indoors as houseplants for the winter. Impatiens are apt to lose quite a few of their flowers in the transition from the garden to your home; even a few leaves may drop. New Guinea-type impatiens are hardier and will take the transition quite easily. They are best known for their attractive, variegated foliage and distinctive flowers.

Coleus. This is another plant that makes the transition from outdoors to indoors quite easily. They tend to get a little spindly in the garden during the summer, so it may be necessary to pinch them back to create a bushier, denser habit of growth. They are frost-sensitive and must be potted and brought indoors before the first frost if you want to keep them as houseplants.

In the spring, after all danger of frost has passed, these plants can once again be moved into the garden to provide seasonal color outdoors.

Propagating Plants

Although summer is considered a good time to take cuttings, I seem to have better results if I take my cuttings in November, December, January, or February. Additionally, I find it easier to take care of the cuttings; they are less likely to be neglected, since more time is spent indoors. Keep in mind that although it is fun to produce plants from cuttings, it will take time to do it properly. They need regular watering, proper light, and adequate heat in order to root and grow properly.

Take cuttings from mature tip growth. If the tip growth is too new and tender, the cuttings will simply wilt; so select growth that has matured for at least thirty to sixty days. You can recognize mature growth because it is usually a darker green color, sturdier, and more rigid. Early morning or late afternoon is the best time to take cuttings.

Take your cuttings with a sharp knife or pruning shears, cutting at a slight slant. Pick off the lower leaves of the cutting, leaving just the tip ring of foliage. If it is a large-leaf plant like a rhododendron, it is a good practice to snip off about one-third to one-half of the tip growth; otherwise there is apt to be a certain amount of water loss through the leaves in the form of evaporation.

If you are taking just a few cuttings, you can start them in a pot, tray, flat, or cut-off milk carton. The important thing is to be sure the chosen container is clean and provides proper drainage. The starting medium should be 3 or 4 inches deep, so the new starts will have sufficient room to establish a good root structure. Dip 1 inch of

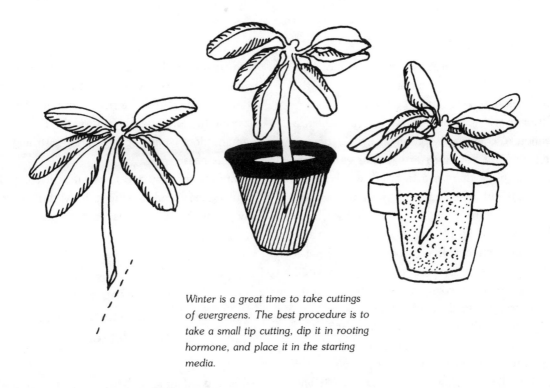

Winter is a great time to take cuttings of evergreens. The best procedure is to take a small tip cutting, dip it in rooting hormone, and place it in the starting media.

the cut end into a rooting hormone powder or solution, then tap the cutting with your finger to knock off any excess.

The most common growing mediums are vermiculite, perlite, sponge rock, peat moss, and sand. Different kinds of cuttings root better in various rooting mediums. I've had good results by rooting most cuttings in a combination of 50 percent peat moss and 50 percent fresh water sand.

The size of the cutting will depend upon the particular type and variety of plant. Take small cuttings from low, slow-growing plants; larger cuttings from large-leafed, taller-growing plants. Most cuttings should not exceed a length of 2 to 6 inches. Heathers, evergreens, azaleas, and dwarf rhododendrons can be started from 2-inch cuttings; while large-leaf rhododendrons and camellias may require cuttings of 4 to 6 inches. Professionals often take their cuttings just below the second or third leaf node.

In planting them, the amount of space between cuttings will depend on their size. Small cuttings can be placed quite close together; larger ones may need up to an inch or two for proper root development. Press the cutting firmly into the rooting medium so it stands by itself.

Cuttings will root best if they are placed in a greenhouse, cold frame, or bright light exposure in the home. If you are starting your cuttings in the home, place them near a bright window, but keep them out of direct sunlight. They will do better in the home if they have bottom heat. This can be provided by placing them on a hot-water tank, or on a clothes dryer, where they will get a lot of heat when it is operating. Cuttings started in a greenhouse or cold frame will benefit from bottom heat provided by a heating cable.

Throughout the rooting period, keep the starting medium moist but never continually wet. Temperature, container size, cutting size, and rooting medium will determine how often it will be necessary to water.

Different types and varieties of plants will take varying lengths of time to develop new roots. As a rule, most cuttings will take 60 to 120 days to root in the home. Cuttings started in a cold frame or greenhouse will usually take even less time.

Newly rooted cuttings can be planted in individual containers as soon as they have developed sturdy root systems. Cuttings taken in the summer are ready to be potted around the first of November. A commercial potting soil can be used. If you prefer to mix your own soil, you can use equal parts of sandy loam, peat moss, and fresh water sand. Treat the cuttings gently because the tender new roots are easily damaged. After potting, return the new plants to the same location to continue their growth. Do not set them outdoors until spring, after all danger of frost has passed.

Cuttings are easy and fun to take if you follow these few basic rules. Why not try starting some new plants this way for use in your garden?

Mulching for Low Maintenance and Winter Protection

Fall is a good time to begin getting your flower and shrub beds ready for the cold months ahead. By mulching, you can cut down on the growth of weeds and grasses over winter, plus provide a protective blanket for the roots of your favorite trees and shrubs. Mulching also improves the appearance of your landscape beds and at the same time helps prevent soil erosion.

The most popular mulching materials are bark, sawdust, straw, peat moss, and leaves. Evergreen boughs, grass clippings, and shredded newspapers are also sometimes used. Bark is probably the most popular: It looks nice because it blends well with garden plants, and it is relatively easy to apply. In the past, sawdust was used quite extensively because it was cheap and readily available. However, its color is not as attractive in the garden, and it leaches nitrogen as it decomposes. Bark also leaches nitrogen in the process of decomposition, so if either of these materials are used, added nitrogen will be needed following the spring.

One of the most attractive of all mulching materials is peat moss. It also has many benefits. After being used as a winter mulch, it can be spaded into the soil, where it will benefit the plants by supplying excellent humus, permitting better drainage, and aerating the soil. It would be used more often if not for the cost involved.

Straw, leaves, and grass clippings are not nearly as popular as bark, sawdust, or peat moss, mostly because they are not very attractive in the garden. I personally do not use them because they can be incubators for many overwintering insects and diseases.

When mulching, it is important that the material not be spread too deeply in some areas. It should be spread only about an inch or two in depth directly under trees and shrubs. In open spaces between plants, mulch can be spread much deeper, to a depth of 4 to 6 inches or more if desired. Keep in mind that surface-feeder plants like camellias, azaleas, or rhododendrons should be mulched to a depth of only an inch or less; if the mulch is spread deeper than that, it should be removed in the spring. It is especially important that the mulch not be mounded up

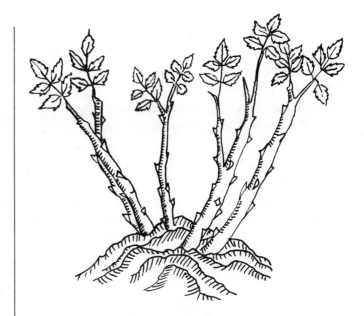

Safeguard your roses during wintertime by mounding peat moss or bark up around the base of the rose canes.

around the crown of any plant; otherwise the mulch may cause a rot affecting the bark and cambium layer of the stem or trunk, which could eventually have serious effects on the plant's vitality. Roses, cane berries, and some perennials are exceptions to this rule. In fact, in the case of roses, it is often a good practice to cover the lower 4 to 6 inches of stem with a layer of peat moss, bark, or sawdust for added winter protection. In the spring, this mulch should be pulled away from the lower canes.

Keep in mind that watering needs can be affected by mulches applied on shrub beds. Mulching usually helps to reduce evaporation of moisture from the soil, but not always. Sometimes the mulch absorbs the moisture, and the natural rainfall may not get down to the soil or the roots of your plant where it will do some good. It's a good idea to pull the mulch material back every now and then to see whether the soil below has sufficient moisture. If the soil is dry, bring out the garden hose and water those areas thoroughly. Water at a time when the temperature is above freezing.

HERBICIDES

Before applying any mulch to your flower beds, it is important to pull all weeds and nuisance grasses. Once this is done, there are several herbicides that can be used to help control their regrowth. Fall is one of the best times to apply most of these herbicides.

A preemergent herbicide, as the name implies, kills weeds before they emerge from the soil. Apply the herbicide, then mulch, and forget about weeds for several months.

Keep in mind that there are several different kinds of herbicides on the market, and each has its advantages and limitations. Some can be used in ornamental tree and shrub beds only. Others can be used where flowers and bulbs are planted.

Still others are safe to use in the vegetable garden. Do not try to substitute one for the other or you will probably kill desirable plants. Choose the right one for the job you have in mind and then follow directions carefully.

The various herbicides are also limited as to the weeds they will control. You may not be able to get 100 percent control of all the weeds growing in a specific area. Refer to the label to determine which types of weeds a particular product will control.

A third limitation of herbicides has to do with timing. You must understand how soon a particular product can be used around newly planted trees and shrubs, flowers, bulbs, or vegetables. For example, Casoron should not be used near trees and shrubs until the plants have been established for three months or more; nor should new plants be placed in Casoron-treated areas until three months after an application has been made. The label will indicate when and around which crops it can be used.

Special precautions need to be taken when using herbicides during warm weather, because evaporation and the volatile action upward can reduce their effectiveness. Furthermore, if improperly applied, the volatile action into the air can burn the foliage of nearby plants. To avoid these problems, it is important to water in the material when it is used during warm weather. Moisten the soil, but avoid puddling and washing the area, which could concentrate the material in one location or wash it into an undesirable location.

Particular care must be taken when an herbicide is used in a sloping area. The material could be washed away by rain or watering, resulting in heavy concentrations at the base of a slope and injury to plants in that area.

If the number of do's and don'ts I have mentioned here makes the use of herbicides seem too complicated to be practical, let me assure you that they are actually very easy to use and can save many hours of work. It is important, however, that you understand the necessity of reading the label and following instructions to the letter. If you do, you will have good results in controlling weeds without doing damage to surrounding plants. Success is affected by soil cultivation, method of application, and watering technique. All of these things are explained on the label of the product you use.

The following are two of the herbicides generally available at local nurseries and garden centers:

Casoron. This is one of the most popular herbicides. It can be used only in ornamental tree and shrub beds. The label lists the individual plants around which it can be safely used. It does an excellent job of controlling nuisance weeds like horsetail, quack grass, chickweed, and many others that are difficult to kill. Remember that it has limitations, so follow instructions carefully.

Dachtal. This herbicide is gaining in popularity. Used properly, it will control weeds and grasses in the vegetable garden area and around annuals, shrubs, and trees. In commercial grades it has additional uses. It is often used to get rid of annual grasses in the lawn. It is also used to control veronica (a blue-flowering annual) that is a nuisance in most lawns. Read the entire label before using Dachtal.

You can cut down on garden maintenance, improve the appearance of your flower and shrub beds, help prevent soil erosion, and protect the root systems of your favorite trees and shrubs by mulching your flower and shrub beds in the fall.

Leaves, Grass Clippings, and Compost

Fall is an excellent time to begin recycling garden waste by composting. The fallen leaves, grass clippings, and unused plant parts that are sometimes discarded can be put to work for you by the simple process of composting.

As the leaves begin to fall from the trees, and as you are mowing the grass for the last time, collect this garden refuse and start building a compost pile. Unused plant parts from the vegetable garden and from annual flowers can also be collected and used. Composting produces humus, which can be used to help build up your soil with organic matter.

Many people think composting is a tedious task, but it actually takes less time than burning the waste material or hauling it away. There are so many misconceptions about composting, it is a miracle that even a few gardeners do it. It is, as I said, simply the recycling of garden refuse. You don't have to go to all the trouble and expense of building a compost bin or buying complicated, expensive equipment. It can be easily done in a garbage can, garbage bag, a hole in the ground, or a pile aboveground. Simply build the compost heap in layers and place it out of sight for appearance's sake. It should be accessible to water and easy to get to. Behind a garage, fence, or a few trees or shrubs would be an ideal spot for a compost pile.

The dimensions of the compost pile can vary. You will find it a good practice to keep the pile at a convenient working height of 4 or 5 feet. Other dimensions are optional; but if you decide to build a compost bin, I'd suggest the area be 4 or 5 feet wide and somewhat longer. My own property is about three-fourths of an acre, so there is considerable waste material available for composting. My compost pile is about 5 feet wide, 8 feet long, and 3½ feet tall. Many city gardeners will find they can get by with a much smaller enclosure than this.

The most important part of composting is to build the compost pile properly. It should be done in layers. Make a 4- to 6-inch layer of garden refuse to start. This would include your leaves, unused plant parts, and grass clippings. Next, cover with 2 inches of soil or manure. If you use manure, it is best to lightly cover it with soil so rodents and insects—particularly flies—are not attracted to the compost area. The entire compost pile is made by repeating these two layers until the pile is at a convenient height. It is also a good idea to add a complete fertilizer like 5-10-10 unless you have already used manure. You can speed up the composting action by adding a commercial composting product to each layer.

It is important that the last layer be concave to collect water. Punch holes in the compost pile with a crowbar, shovel handle, or similar tool. This helps speed the process of decomposition. It is also important to occasionally add water to the compost pile; decomposition is faster when the pile is kept moist—but never wet.

For years it has been recommended that the compost pile be turned—in effect reconstructing the original pile by putting the top material on the bottom. I do not do this; instead, I recommend that if, when you start to use your compost, you find that your top layer is not thoroughly decomposed, you simply use that material to begin your next compost pile.

When you think your compost is about ready to be used, it is a good idea to screen it through a 1-inch wire mesh to sift out the coarse material, which can be returned to the pile for further composting.

Always cover the top of the pile with soil to avoid attracting flies or rodents. Also, avoid using twigs or branches, mature weeds, bones, madrona or walnut leaves, or similar materials that would decompose too slowly. Some of these materials can be used if they are put through a composting shredder first. Shredders are available at many rental agencies. Using one will save you the time it takes to get rid of the unusable waste.

In my own compost pile, I never use any plant parts that are diseased or insect-infested. They are sent away with the garbageman. This is especially true of leaves from rosebushes, because mildew, aphids, and other rose problems can spread throughout the pile; it is not worth the risk.

Grass clippings—providing you have not used a combination lawn food and weed killer on your lawn within one year—and fallen leaves can also be spread over the garden area and tilled or spaded in with your existing soil to decay naturally over the winter without composting. The spading or tilling should be done when the soil is clearly dry and workable.

Instead of getting rid of the waste materials in your garden, start to recycle them this fall. They can become valuable humus that will add nutrients, retain moisture, and aerate the soil in future years.

A Child's Indoor Garden

There are some fascinating indoor gardening projects for children to try in the fall. When weather conditions limit playing activities to the home, indoor gardening projects become exciting and educational pastimes—providing the plants you choose are easy to grow, fast-growing, and hold the child's interest.

One of the all-time favorite plants for children to grow is the cactus. This plant thrives on minimal care in the home, yet continual growth and attractive flowers make it an exciting plant for children.

The coleus plant with its bright-colored foliage is another popular choice for children to grow.

An inexpensive project that kids enjoy is growing orange, lemon, grapefruit, and tangerine plants from seed. Save the seeds from the fruit you eat and allow them to sit for a couple of days, then plant them in a pot of soil, using three or more seeds per pot. When the seedlings begin to grow, thin them and transplant to individual pots. Children enjoy the bright glossy foliage, which is very attractive in the home. At the same time, they have the satisfaction of knowing a plant has developed from a seed they started on their own. Don't disillusion them, though: Explain that the plants will not produce fruit, as this seldom happens.

One of my favorite projects for children is

growing the top of a pineapple. Supermarkets often feature them in the fall and winter. Use the top growth with an inch or two of the fruit attached; the rest of the fruit can be enjoyed at the dinner table. Set the pineapple top on a bed of moist sand or soil, fruit side down, and firm it in place with two toothpicks, penetrating through the meat of the fruit into the soil below. Once the plant has rooted, transfer it to a soil-filled pot.

A similar project can be undertaken using the tops of carrots, turnips, parsnips, or beets. Simply cut off the foliage and about an inch of the vegetable and proceed as you did with the pineapple.

An avocado seed can be forced into growth in about a month when it is grown in a glass of water. Place toothpicks in the sides of the avocado seed about 1 inch above the base (the flat end). Rest the toothpicks on the top of the glass, with the base of the seed actually touching the water. Cover the glass with foil until the roots begin to grow, because daylight is apt to spoil the growth. When the roots begin to grow down into the water and the top has grown 6 to 8 inches, begin mixing soil with the water. After a couple of weeks in this combination of water and soil, the avocado plant should be carefully potted in a container of soil. This can be an exciting project for children, as these seeds will eventually develop into trees and attain a height of up to 5 feet or more. They can be set out in the garden in their containers in the warm summer months

Children really enjoy starting pineapple plants by cutting off the top portion, firming it into the soil until it's rooted, and then transplanting it to the pot.

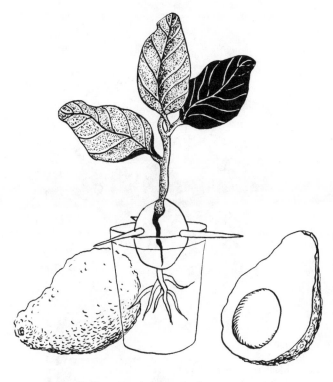

Avocado plants are fun to grow for children of any age, but be patient. The method does not always produce roots, and the foliage may take some time.

and should be brought back inside in the fall. While indoors, keep them where the air is rather humid.

Sweet potato tubers can also be grown by the toothpick method. The tapered end of the tuber should be down, with about one-fourth of the tuber actually in the water. Once the vine has developed, the tuber can be transplanted into soil if you wish.

One of the most fascinating bulbs to start as a winter or fall indoor project is the hyacinth. Use a hyacinth glass or any plastic or glass container with a narrow top opening. Fill with water to about one-fourth to one-eighth inch from the top, then rest the bulb on the opening. In a short time the roots will develop into the water and the top growth and flowers will appear. With this project, the child is able to observe the roots and the top growth right up to flowering time. As a bonus, their flowers are bright and fragrant, making them especially noticeable. Many varieties of hyacinth, tulip, and daffodil bulbs may be started in soil in pots.

The key to keeping children interested in gardening, whether inside or outdoors, is to keep the projects simple, let them have most of the responsibility, and choose only plants that will give rather rapid results. As they progress in gardening, there are all kinds of bulbs, seeds, cuttings, grafts, and other gardening projects to explore.

Slugs

Among the many possible fall projects, perhaps one of the most important is slug control. With the cooler weather that usually arrives in late September and October, slugs become quite active. Steps should be taken to control them before they devour the foliage of your favorite flowers, vegetables, and shrubs.

When tender new growth disappears overnight, slugs are usually responsible. Another telltale sign of their presence is the trail of slime they leave behind. They don't have a natural enemy; and as far as I have been able to discover, they do not have one beneficial characteristic. Snakes, ducks, geese, toads, and some birds do eat them, but that does not help most of us very much. They are truly pests and should be eliminated before they raise havoc in the garden.

Fall is a particularly important time of the year to control slugs because it is one of their major egg-laying times. It is said that they are bisexual and can lay an average of twenty to fifty eggs in each cluster. The clusters look somewhat like little BB-size balls of colorless jelly. Destroy them wherever you find them. Depending on the temperature and humidity, they hatch in ten days to three weeks from the time they are laid, and the slugs can mature to adulthood in as little as six weeks, although generally this takes three to twelve months.

When you are working in your garden during the fall, look for slugs in several different locations. Most often they are found along the edge of the lawn and flower bed area where it is cool and moist, but you will also find them under boards, rocks, and at the bases of low-growing plants.

The true garden slug, the spotted garden slug, and the tawny garden slug are the most common

Get as many slugs as you can before winter so they will not be such a problem in the spring.

species in this region. Although they extend up to 4 inches or more when they are on the move, their average size is about 2 to 3½ inches in length. These slugs range in shades of orange, brown, and tan, while some are black, spotted, or two-toned.

During the winter, slugs hibernate and seldom put in an appearance. During this time, they burrow several inches into the soil or disappear under rocks, large clumps of grass, or boards.

People have tried all kinds of different ways to control slugs in their gardens. It seems like every time I mention this subject at least half a dozen readers write in to suggest methods they use. One such method is a neighborhood competition to see who can collect the most slugs at night. To use this method, all you need is a flashlight, a stick, and a bucket to collect them. The next morning you can compare notes with the neighbors over the back fence.

Another popular method is to go after the slugs with a salt shaker. In recent years it has also been very popular to trap the slugs with beer. This is done by filling a small bowl with stale beer and putting it in the areas where the slugs are active. Stale beer attracts the slugs and they drown.

A new product called Slugfence, developed in Washington State, does an excellent job of keeping slugs out of areas where the fence is installed. Still, probably the most popular method of controlling slugs today is by using commercial slug-bait products. Available in meal, pellets, powder, liquid, granules, and gels, their effectiveness depends primarily on the frequency of application and the way in which they are applied. It is important that all types of slug baits be applied only as directed on the label. Special attention should be given to any cautions on the label, especially where they pertain to children and pets.

Weather is also a factor in the effectiveness of baits; if the bait can be covered and protected from sprinklers or rainwater, it will last much longer. You can cover the bait with a shingle or a piece of wood to keep it dry.

Whatever method you use, fall is the time to begin a regular slug control program, before they ruin your plants.

Miscellaneous Fall Projects

Fall is also an excellent time to lime the lawn and some of your garden plants with dolomite or agricultural lime. Lilacs, roses, clematis, and other alkaline-loving plants should be limed.

There are also many greenhouse projects you can undertake during the fall months. Besides propagating plants, you can seed many plants—snapdragons, dusty miller, foliage houseplants, cyclamen, coleus, calendulas, African violets, and others. Fall is also a good time to pot many plants in the greenhouse, such as spring-flowering bulbs, greenhouse varieties of primroses, amaryllis bulbs, tulips, daffodils, hyacinths, crocuses, geraniums, fuchsias, begonias, and other tender plants.

Finally, fall is a good time to take care of any and all outside chores that must be done before the first frosts. Take advantage of the nice weather in September and October to accomplish important projects before winter sets in.

WINTER

Winter weather can be discouraging at times. However, it's a great time to do indoor gardening, and there are many other projects that can be undertaken, very few of which depend on good weather.

Three projects that do depend on good weather are pruning, getting your soil into shape, and planting roses. Many trees and shrubs need to be pruned during this time, their dormant season. A heavy snow could do this for you, but probably not the way you want it done. Working on your soil is more dependent on weather than pruning is; a freeze or too much rain can make soil unworkable. Weather permitting, however, this is a great time of year to get your beds ready for spring planting, and roses should be planted during their winter dormant season.

A couple of outdoor jobs that aren't so weather-dependent are winterizing tender plants and giving your lawn winter care. These are both minor winter jobs and thus won't require too much time.

The most enjoyable winter projects are the ones accomplished indoors. Starting vegetables like tomatoes, potatoes, and even peas, gives you a large jump on the spring planting season. Houseplants are also fun to work with at this time of year.

Some of the mental projects are equally enjoyable. Planning your landscaping, whether you live inland or by the sea, is a great winter project. Choosing Christmas presents in the gardening line is also a neat mental activity. A nice project that blends the physical and mental, with a touch of artistic ability thrown in, is choosing a Christmas tree.

Don't let the winter weather discourage you. Many garden projects can be done regardless of weather. Most of all, don't become a slave to your garden. Winter is the dormant season for most plants, and you deserve a bit of dormancy, too.

Vegetables

Just because winter comes doesn't mean you cannot grow a few vegetables. There are two ways of growing vegetables in the fall and winter so that you will have fresh vegetables for a longer period of time. When fall and winter weather is unsuitable for growing vegetables outdoors, it's time to consider growing a few indoors.

Many vegetables, of course, cannot be grown indoors—their light and temperature requirements are not suitable for indoor culture—so concentrate instead on those that can. Among the best vegetables to grow in the home are salad vegetables—lettuce, spinach, chard, radishes, carrots, beets, and cherry tomatoes. (It should also be noted that these can be grown outdoors in a cold frame, hot bed, or similar cover.)

To get started, you will need pots and containers, soil, fluorescent lights, and a little space.

For soil, you can either use commercial potting soil or mix your own. If you use soil from the garden, it should be sterilized.

For containers, you can use pots, gallon containers, tubs, flats, or other similar containers. Be certain they are clean and have adequate drainage. If you are going to grow carrots or beets, the container should be at least 6 inches deep—and, of course, be sure to grow the smaller varieties of carrots. To provide additional drainage, add some pot shards or gravel to the bottom of each of your containers.

A basement, utility room, or unused bedroom is ideal for growing your winter vegetables. Maybe you have a more suitable place in the corner of your kitchen, dining room, or heated garage. Whatever spot you select, be sure to provide a waterproof base so that excess water does not do any damage to your home. This protection can be provided by waterproof plastics or a waterproof tray filled with fine gravel; the excess moisture will drain onto the gravel, providing the extra benefit of increased humidity.

It is important to provide adequate light for your vegetables. Unless you have a greenhouse or an equally bright spot in your home, you'll need to rely on artificial light from fluorescent tubes. Arrange these lights so they can be moved as your vegetables begin to grow. Keep your lights about 8 inches above your crops and leave them on for fourteen to fifteen hours each day.

It is a good idea to keep the room temperature at about 70 degrees until your seeds germinate, and then keep the temperature between 65 and 70 degrees.

Lettuce is one of the easiest crops to grow in the home. The loose-leaf types are the best ones. If you stagger the seeding dates by a couple of weeks, they will reach maturity over a longer period of time. Keep in mind that lettuce needs a warmer temperature than some crops, like spinach, which will do better if the temperature is about 15 degrees cooler.

Radishes will be the first to mature; in fact, you can count on them to be ready for harvest in about thirty days. Lettuce, beets, and carrots take about sixty days; and tomatoes a little longer.

Your vegetables will need supplemental feeding with an all-purpose liquid plant fertilizer. Follow label directions and be sure the product is safe to use on edible crops.

You will have to experiment a little with water. Room temperature, location, light, and soil will determine how often the plants need to be watered.

If you want to save a little money and at the same time enjoy fresh vegetables, grow a few in your home during the fall and winter.

Roses Need Special Care—Even in Wintertime

The Pacific Northwest winter dormant season, December through February, is the time to plant or transplant roses. The main reason for planting roses in the dormant season is to allow time for root development before the growing season begins. In addition, this is when the best selection of varieties is available.

Probably the single most important factor in growing roses is to choose the right planting location. Roses have three prime requirements in this regard: First, they need a bright, sunny location to perform at their best; second, they need soil that is well drained; third, they need a spot where there is air circulation. In the shade, roses tend to grow leggy and flower rather sparsely. If the soil is not well drained, the roots are apt to suffocate because air is cut off and the soil remains too wet. Under such conditions they are also more susceptible to winter freeze damage. If the air is stagnant, roses are susceptible to diseases like mildew.

Transplanting may be called for if a bush has outgrown its present location or if it is in the wrong spot. Roses in shady locations or in areas where air circulation is poor should be moved to a more suitable location.

If you are buying a new rosebush, first select a husky, top-quality bush; second, select one that has three to five sturdy canes and a nice fibrous root structure. Be sure to select a variety that does especially well in your location. If in doubt, consult your local nursery, a neighbor, or one of the local rose societies. Nothing is more discouraging than trying to grow a rose that is not suited to your climate.

Rose planting is really very easy and can be done with minimal preparation; but if you want to give your bushes a head start, take the time to properly prepare the soil. Dig a planting hole at least twice as wide and deep as the root system. In most cases it will need to be 2 feet wide and about 2 feet deep. An even larger hole may be necessary for transplanting established plants. Always prepare the hole prior to digging up an established bush, so roots will be exposed to the drying air for the shortest possible time.

Roses are robust growers, providing abundant flowers and foliage over a relatively short season, so it is important that the soil be fertile. Add ample amounts of peat moss, compost (if available), processed manure, and an all-purpose, nonburning transplanting fertilizer to the existing soil. Mix together thoroughly.

After digging a new hole, check soil drainage by pouring a gallon or two of water into the hole and observing how long it takes to drain away. If it stays in the hole for five minutes or more, it will be necessary to provide adequate drainage.

As you set the rosebush into the hole, spread the roots over the cone and be certain that the bud union—the knobby swelling at the base of the canes—is level with the ground. Fill in the hole with the prepared soil and firm it around the bush with your feet. Then soak with water.

To finish off the planting area, you can spread a light layer of mulch around the plant. Bark, sawdust, and peat moss are the best materials to use. The mulch will protect the roots during the cold winter weather and help cut down on the growth of weeds. Avoid pruning your rosebushes until at least mid-March, although it is possible to do very light tip trimming during the winter.

Roses will require more plant food than most garden plants because they are such robust growers. The first feeding should be March, using a rose or all-purpose garden food. Monthly feedings should continue until July. Thoroughly water in the plant food immediately after application.

MINIATURE ROSES

If you have never tried them, you might enjoy growing miniature roses. There are many beautiful varieties in a wide range of colors, including white and shades of pink, rose, and red. It is impossible to list even the most popular ones without overlooking some of the outstanding varieties. Many nurseries and garden outlets around the Northwest feature miniature roses in the springtime, and you can see for yourself what is available. They are usually available in 4-inch pots, ready for indoor or outdoor planting.

Miniature roses grown outdoors are treated like other types of roses. They should be placed in the same type of soil used for regular rosebushes—a well-drained sandy loam type is ideal. Peat moss, compost, or vermiculite can be combined with most Northwest soils to improve their makeup. Plant miniature roses in full sun, either in open soil or in containers on the patio, lanai, or deck. Prepare an extra-large hole, mixing the soil thoroughly to a depth of 8 to 12 inches. The roots need well-worked soil in which to become established. Keep them well watered and feed them every three to four weeks from March to October. Fish fertilizer works great.

Miniature roses are treated much the same indoors. To make sure they get plenty of humidity, a saucer full of gravel and water under the pot works well. Keep plants groomed by pinching off leggy growth; and if insects or diseases become a problem, take them outside to spray them.

When a plant outgrows its container, repot it in a container one size larger. A good, all-purpose houseplant potting soil is recommended. If you use soil from your garden, sterilize it first.

If you are going to plant or transplant roses, winter is the best time to do it.

Lawn Care

Not much can be done in the lawn area during the winter. If the grass is uneven, it is wise to mow it on a nice day to keep it looking better the rest of the winter. And if you have not applied a fall or winter lawn fertilizer, it is all right to do so on a warm day; but you must do it when the grass is not frozen—otherwise, your footprints and the wheel tracks of the spreader might remain on the lawn until new growth begins in springtime.

Late February is a good time to apply a spring-type lawn fertilizer. (If moss is a problem, you may want to select a brand of fertilizer that also contains a moss killer.) Late February is also a good time to apply dolomite lime to the lawn. It is wise to give the lawn a mowing before spring arrives.

Winter is a good time of the year to observe the grass growing under your tall trees. This is one of the most difficult places to grow a nice-looking lawn. If you have a few tall trees in your garden and you want to keep your lawn looking nice under them, there are a few basic procedures you will have to follow each year. Proper feeding, liming, adequate watering, and yearly overseeding are prime factors in successfully growing lawn under trees.

The shade from overspreading branches and the encroachment of roots into the soil area of your lawn are the two major factors that make it difficult to grow lawn under trees. Heavy shade, soil acidity, and insufficient nutrients are the main reasons why moss is so prevalent in the lawn areas under the taller trees.

It is common to find surface tree roots right in the lawn area. They grow toward the surface because that's where they can get the water and nutrients you are applying on the lawn. One of the easiest ways to help correct this condition is to perforate the area with a crowbar, root feeder, or piece of pipe to a depth of 12 to 18 inches or more. Next, put a tree fertilizer down the holes to encourage tree roots to grow deeper. Additional benefits of this procedure are that it helps to anchor the tree by getting the roots deeper into the soil.

Since grass roots are competing with the feeder roots of your taller trees, the grass under the trees will require more frequent feeding—preferably every six weeks. It is recommended that a fertilizer with a ratio of 3-1-2 be used to feed the lawn under trees. To make this simpler, a 12-4-8, 9-3-6, or similar formula would conform to the 3-1-2 ratio. Apply the fertilizer according to the label instructions, watering thoroughly after application.

Since the soil under tall trees tends to be quite acid, you should apply agricultural or dolomite lime at least once a year in either the spring or the fall. The growth of moss in any of these areas will indicate the need for lime. If moss is present, a lawn moss killer can be applied.

Because tree roots rob both water and nutrients from the grass, the lawn area under tall trees may require more water than the rest of the lawn, and it may even be necessary to water occasionally in the winter. Use of a lawn perforating tool will help get the moisture down to the grass roots quicker.

One of the most important steps in establishing a thicker, greener turf under trees is that of reseeding each year. Actually, the process is called "overseeding," for you simply broadcast new seed over the established lawn. The best time to do this is between mid-March and late October. For overseeding, use a seed mix that blends with the rest of your lawn area. A fescue blend of grass seed will do best in the shady locations of your lawn. Use approximately one pound of seed per 1,000 square feet of lawn area, and keep the soil moist until the seed germinates.

Needles or leaves that fall from tall trees should be removed periodically so they do not smother the grass. Simply rake them off and add them to the compost pile.

Finally, avoid walking on the grass during freezing or frosting weather; grass blades break easily when they are frozen. Yellow spots will appear where you have stepped, and they will not go away until new growth begins in the spring. Needless to say, this can ruin the appearance of an otherwise attractive lawn. Accomplish any lawn renovation projects when the weather is moderate.

Trees and Shrubs

PRUNING

Winter is an excellent time to prune many of the deciduous trees and shrubs in the garden, including fruit, flower, and shade trees. These types of plants are pruned during their winter dormant season in December, January, or February.

Pruning is sometimes neglected because it is believed to be a difficult task. Actually pruning is quite simple providing you use good common sense. Never prune a tree or shrub just for the sake of pruning. Many trees and shrubs may grow for years without needing to be pruned; others need yearly pruning to keep them in top shape. Proper pruning can help determine the ultimate size, bushiness, and vitality of the latter.

Keep in mind that winter is not the time to prune *all* trees and shrubs. For example, in this region it is generally recommended that roses be pruned around mid-March; and spring-flowering deciduous plants like quince, forsythia, and spirea should be pruned after they have finished flowering. Evergreens like junipers, conifers, and broad-leaf types are pruned a little later in the season, in March, April, or May. So the primary pruning concern during winter will be deciduous trees.

Study the size, shape, and branching pattern of any tree or shrub before you begin pruning; then begin your pruning to enhance the beauty and shape of the plant. Remember, Mother Nature has an intended growth habit for each tree and shrub, and you should keep this in mind in judging how to prune it. Improper pruning can completely ruin the shape of any tree or shrub.

How you prune will depend upon the particular type of plant. For example, strong, sturdy pruning is required for fruit trees; in fact, it is generally recommended that one-third to one-half of last year's growth be removed so that only one or two new branches develop, sturdy enough to support fruit. On the other hand, light tip pruning, which results in the development of several small shorter branches, is often done on flowering trees to encourage a bushier, more prolific plant.

The initial pruning of any tree or shrub should include the removal of certain types of growth. Start by removing all dead, decayed, and weak branches. Be certain to cut back until you reach healthy, live wood.

Branches that rub together or crisscross need pruning attention. Remove the weaker of the two branches unless the weaker one will eventually help to make a better branching pattern. Remov-

al of this type of growth opens up the tree and allows for better air circulation and sunlight exposure.

Next remove long, upright water sprouts that grow completely out of proportion to the rest of the tree. Also remove any sucker growth that develops around the base of the trunk. These growths must be removed flush with the branch or trunk from which they originate; otherwise they will grow right back again.

Remove the weak branch of a V-shaped crotch in your tree because heavy winds or an accumulation of snow could break it off, possibly causing injury to surrounding plants. Leave one single leader or header on trees that should only have a single stem. Remove all others.

Branches that are too low, making it difficult to mow or work around the base of the tree, should be cut and removed. Lower limbs not only are a nuisance but also tend to provide too much shade on the turf or soil around the base of the tree.

Once you have removed the above-mentioned growths, you are ready to begin pruning the tree. Here are a few basics to observe.

1. Use common sense in determining which branches need pruning and how much they are to be pruned. Remember, prune as Mother Nature intended the tree to grow. In other words, don't try to make a spreading tree out of one whose natural tendency is to grow upright.

2. An effective job of pruning requires two people. One should be in the tree doing the pruning, while the other stands away from the tree and advises which branches to cut and how much.

3. If you are totally unfamiliar with pruning, seek the advice of a knowledgeable neighbor, nurseryman, or master gardener, or refer to an illustrated pruning manual. Pruning books or manuals are for sale at most garden outlets, or you can check one out from your local library.

4. Most important of all, never prune for the sake of pruning. Prune only those trees and shrubs that need to be pruned. Many of the flowering and shade trees may go an entire lifetime without needing pruning of any kind.

As a rule of thumb, make your pruning cuts just above an outside growth bud. This forces the new growth outward, which tends to open up the tree and allow for better air circulation and sunlight exposure.

Have the proper pruning tools on hand before you start. Small hand pruners are ideal for cutting small branches. A pair of lopping shears is needed for medium-size branches, and pole pruners for reaching high branches. A pruning saw is handy for cutting medium to large branches. Be sure you use good, sharp, clean equipment, and always sterilize your pruning shears after cutting back any dead or decayed branches; otherwise, you are apt to spread the decay to your next pruning cut. To sterilize, simply dip the shears in a solution of chlorine bleach. Treat your pruning cuts with a pruning healing compound—especially important here in the Pacific Northwest where we have problems with moss and various types of fungus growth.

The main reasons for pruning are to enhance the beauty of a plant, help maintain its size, and help increase the production of flowers or fruit. Regular pruning encourages maximum fruit production, and produces a sturdy structured tree that can support the fruit. This is why fruit trees definitely need to be pruned yearly.

Don't let the trees in your garden get out of control, ruin your neighbors' view, or become a wind hazard. Keep them looking their best and performing their best by giving them the pruning attention they need during the winter dormant season.

DORMANT SPRAYING

Another important task to accomplish with your deciduous trees and shrubs is dormant spraying. Dormant spraying is especially effective for deciduous trees and shrubs. Fruit trees, flowering trees, roses, forsythia, lilacs, raspberries, blackberries, and quince are a few typical examples. Many insect and disease problems on deciduous trees and shrubs can be eliminated by adopting a simple winter dormant spraying program.

The best time for dormant spraying is from

just after the last leaves have fallen until a couple of weeks before new growth buds begin to open in early spring. During normal winter weather, this usually means a first application in December, the second in January, and the third in February. The three sprayings are recommended to ensure the best control of overwintering pests and diseases. Peach-leaf curl is especially hard to control, and I suggest an earlier spraying on about November 15 for this problem.

I am often asked the question: "Our commercial sprayer only sprayed once or twice this winter—is this enough to control overwintering insects and diseases?"

Since licensed professionals are permitted to use more potent sprays than are available to you, they may determine that fewer applications are needed. They are specialists; and after an on-site inspection, they can determine a spray program that best suits your particular garden needs.

Before you start to spray, it is a good practice to check for dead, decayed, or damaged areas on branches or trunks of your trees. These areas offer winter protection for insects and diseases, and should be cleaned out with a sharp sterile knife or pruning shears. Be sure to treat the cut surfaces with a pruning healing compound, sometimes called "pruning paint." This will also help to avoid future infestations.

Weather conditions must be considered in deciding when to winter-spray. Try to select a day when there is no chance of rain for a period of at least twenty-four hours, and avoid spraying during freezing weather or when a strong wind is blowing; the mist is apt to carry to surfaces where the spray is not wanted. Sometimes these weather conditions are hard to predict, so this chore may become quite a challenge to complete.

Select a type of sprayer that will be convenient for you. The tank sprayers that can be slung over one's back are often used. A trombone-type sprayer is also handy and easy to operate. If you adjust the knob on these two types, the spray will reach up to 15 or 25 feet into the trees. Sprayers that fit on your garden hose are also sometimes used for dormant spraying, but many do not have the capacity to hold the dilution quantities recommended.

For years the most popular type of dormant spray has probably been the liquid-lime-sulfur-oil combination. It is often used on deciduous fruit, flowering, and shade trees, roses and deciduous shrubs; however, it should not be used on apricots nor on broad-leaf or conifer-type evergreens, as it will burn and damage them. Some major chemical firms now have dormant spray materials simply labeled "dormant spray."

Since many types of dormant sprays stain painted surfaces, you will need to take steps to protect such surfaces. Likewise, both broad-leaf and conifer evergreens should be given a protective covering so they are not damaged by the spray. To protect painted surfaces, simply tack up polyethylene, newspaper, or a similar material. Cover evergreens with similar materials.

When spraying, be sure to thoroughly cover the new tip growth, the old growth, and the trunk of your deciduous trees and shrubs. Properly applied, these dormant sprays will help control overwintering scale, aphid eggs, spider mites, scab, powdery mildew, and several types of moss. However, they will not control spruce aphid—a common problem in the Pacific Northwest in January or early February. To control this insect, found only on spruce trees, use an all-purpose summertime insect spray that specifies aphid control on the label. Diazinon, Isotox, and other aphid sprays are generally used to control the spruce aphid. Be sure to follow directions on the label of the spray you choose.

If insects and diseases have been a problem on your fruit, flowering, and shade trees or deciduous shrubs and berries over the past year, begin a winter dormant spraying program as soon as possible.

Houseplants

Because of the cold weather in December, January, and February, there are a few things to think about in caring for houseplants. These reminders may save your plants from damage.

Plants on windowsills can be frostburned in a cold snap—either by very cold air penetrating through the window sash or by contact with the frosted glass—so plants should be moved back a foot or two from the window in winter.

During extremely cold weather the furnace runs more, creating even drier air than usual. Adequate humidity becomes more of a problem for plants. You will find that when plants are grouped together a more favorable environment is created and humidity problems are lessened. Keep houseplants away from the blast of hot air from heating ducts or the fireplace, and it is best if plants are kept off the television set and similar appliances.

Because conditions in the home change quite a bit during very cold weather, it may be necessary to change your whole system of care. Check frequently to be sure your plants are receiving enough water. This can be done in one of several ways. Some use a water meter; others lift the pot to test its weight; and still others use the toothpick method (see p. 117). It is important to keep a close watch on watering. There is a tendency to overwater in the wintertime, and this should be avoided.

At this time of year, the sun is much lower in the sky so there is not as much light available for houseplants. Yet African violets and other flowering plants need brighter light in winter than during the rest of the year. African violets will flower best if they are placed 2 or 3 feet from a south or west window. It may become necessary to move some to locations where more light is available.

If you have a spot in your home where you would like to grow a houseplant but have only limited light, there are quite a few different plants that will survive, look nice, and require very little special care.

It will generally take about a month to six weeks for most plants to become acclimatized to your home. The low-light plants are no exception, and most of the plants that are placed in low-light areas of the home will not grow quite as lavishly as they would in moderate light exposure.

The natural habitat of most houseplants is tropical jungles. A few species grow on the jungle floor, where they are shaded by overhead trees and get only filtered light. They are the ones that will grow best in low-light conditions in your home.

Since most of the tropical houseplants we buy are grown in greenhouses where light conditions are quite bright, you will have to acclimatize them to your home. With limited light, most tropical houseplants, like most other houseplants, will not require as much food and water as they would in moderate to bright light exposure, but they will need as much humidity as your other plants. You will have to experiment a little to determine how frequently to water each type.

Following are some of the best low-light plants:

Grape ivy. One of the really outstanding plants to use in a low-light area. This plant makes an especially nice hanging basket plant. Actually, it is a very versatile plant. It has holdfasts, so it can even be trained upon a trellis. It's also a very nice plant to use on a shelf or table. It will need to be pinched back occasionally to keep it bushy.

Chinese evergreens. These come in several varieties, some with very attractive variegated leaves. One of the best-known is Silver Queen, which has margins of silver and cream on the gray-green leaves. Its lighter foliage color adds a bright spot to a low-light area in the home, and the multileaf stalks eventually make it a very bushy, attractive plant. Eventual growing height is 18 inches, making it an excellent plant to use on the floor or on end tables, coffee tables, and similar low places.

Pothos. There are several varieties of this plant. They make great hanging baskets and upright plants for low-light areas in your home. The varieties that have variegated green, yellow, and white foliage are especially nice for adding a spot of color. These are easy plants to grow—they thrive on a certain amount of neglect.

Prayer plant. This is another ideal plant to grow in low- to medium-light exposure. In fact, if this plant is grown in too much light, the leaves will form brown edges. In recent years many new varieties have been added, some with attractive markings in shades of red, cream, various greens, and brown. Although these plants are generally grown as upright plants in pots, they also make beautiful hanging baskets.

Rubber plant. Another super selection for low-light exposures. There are several different varieties that are suitable as houseplants. They can eventually grow up to 10 feet in height or more, so give them plenty of room. The variegated cream and green leaf varieties are especially bright in a low-light area.

Fatsia. The big, bold foliage of this plant provides an interesting tropical spot in moderate- to low-light areas in the home. It can eventually grow to 4 or more feet in height, so it should be given plenty of room. The large, maplelike leaves are often up to a foot across. Wipe the leaves every few months with a damp cloth to keep them clean.

If some of your favorite plants are getting a little leggy or spindly and need to be pinched or pruned back, winter is an excellent time to do it. In fact, the best time of the entire year for pinching and pruning back houseplants is just before they go into their spring growth cycle.

Winter is also a good time to take cuttings of your favorite houseplants. Leggy, spindly, or uneven growth can be cut just below a leaf node, dipped in a rooting hormone, and then started in a combination of 50 percent sand and 50 percent peat moss. Keep the cuttings in a bright light area where temperatures range from 55 to 70 degrees day and night. Once the cuttings have rooted, they can be individually potted in small containers. Tip cuttings of most houseplants should be only 2 to 5 inches in length, depending upon the growth habit of the parent plant.

Insects and diseases seem more prevalent in the winter. If you find discolored or mottled leaves, examine their undersides with a magnifying glass for insects. A white, powdery substance on the outsides of the leaves can be mildew or some other disease. Use the proper houseplant spray when you detect a problem.

Most houseplants are in their dormant season during the winter and do not need as much fertilizer as during the rest of the year. Do not feed more than once during the winter.

If roots are protruding from the drainage hole or over the surface soil of a houseplant, winter is a good time to repot it. Choose a pot only one or two sizes larger than the original, and use a good grade of potting soil. Loosen dense and matted roots carefully so they can grow into the new soil.

After Christmas, poinsettias that have lost their lower leaves and are beginning to look quite ugly can be pruned back. Cut the stems at least halfway to the ground. Continue to water and fertilize the plant as you normally would, and keep in a bright location.

If you received an azalea or chrysanthemum at Christmastime, these plants will need special attention in the late winter. When they have completed their blooming cycle, place them in the basement or heated garage where the temperature ranges between 45 and 65 degrees. Cut the chrysanthemums back to about 4 inches from the soil level once they have finished flowering. Do not prune the azaleas; simply remove the old flowers. Neither of these plants should be set out in the garden until all danger of frost has passed. At that time the azaleas should be placed in a shaded, cool location, and the chrysanthemums should be placed in a hot, sunny location. There are usually four to six chrysanthemum plants per pot; separate them and plant individually in the garden.

Do you need more information on how to grow houseplants? Many houseplant books are on the market—but before you buy one, check to see if the author is pictured in a greenhouse. If so, you probably do not want that book, because in many cases he is telling you how to grow houseplants in a greenhouse environment, not how to grow them in your home.

Wintering Tender and Flowering Plants

When cold weather arrives in the winter months, it is important to know how to provide winter protection for early-flowering and other tender plants. With a little extra care, you can avoid damage from heavy frost or freezing weather.

Keep in mind that most of the plants grown in the Pacific Northwest are completely hardy and seldom require any special protection. However, the early-flowering rhododendrons, camellias, azaleas, and others do need special care during any exceptionally cold spells. Plants like fatsia, japonica, ceanothus, *Daphne odora*, bottlebrush, and other specialty plants will also need special care whenever the temperature goes below 20 degrees or when a sudden frost occurs.

If you have tender perennial plants or low-growing shrubs that need protection, straw or cut evergreen boughs can be used. Tender plants like geraniums, fuchsias, and begonias should be moved inside before the first frost. Winter them in a basement, garage, or crawl space under the house where the temperature remains above freezing and averages between 40 and 50 degrees throughout the winter.

Plants like wax begonias, impatiens, and fibrous begonias can be dug, potted, and taken indoors for use as houseplants during the winter season. Next spring, after all danger of frost has passed, plants can be set outdoors once again.

Burlap, sheets, blankets, or large towels can be used to cover plants. Use enough to completely cover the top and the sides of each plant. If you use sheets or blankets, you can often cover several plants at one time. Cloth is best because it allows the air to circulate and light can reach the plant at the same time as it is getting warmth. Without good air circulation and light, plants suffer in a very short time. For this reason, covering material should be placed on the plant only during a cold spell; as soon as the weather moderates, it should be removed. Do not leave it on any longer than necessary.

It is a good idea to support the covering material with stakes so the weight of the material is not resting on the plants. Place a stake on each side of the plant, then drape the cover over them. This technique has the added advantage of providing air space above the foliage and below the covering material.

I have found it best to avoid using clear polyethylene to cover plants. It acts much like an unheated greenhouse: As the sun rises in the morning, the temperature under the plastic also rises, and this rapid change from nighttime lows can be damaging to plants. In addition, most clear materials do not have breathing holes; consequently, there is poor air circulation.

This doesn't mean that no polyethylene can be used. Green or black plastic with breathing holes is satisfactory. Be sure to remove it as soon as possible though. If clear plastic is all that is available when a cold spell hits, it is better than nothing at all; but be sure it is draped over stakes so there is a 12- to 18-inch space between the plastic and the top of the plant.

Snow is Mother Nature's winter protection, so it should be left around the plant. It can also be left *on* the plants if it is not so heavy that it will break the branches. If heavy wet snow falls, simply brush some away and leave the rest for protection.

A light covering of snow provides a natural protection for plants in wintertime, but too much snow will break branches and needs to be brushed off.

A Few Ideas on How to Start or Finish Your Landscaping

Attractive landscaping is one of the best investments you can make around your home. Most things you purchase for the home begin to decrease in value as soon as you buy them—the car in the carport, the rugs on the floor, and the draperies at the window. However, trees and shrubs grow and increase in value as the years go by.

In order to save time, money, and effort, it is best to start with a basic landscaping plan; otherwise, you are apt to end up with a hodgepodge design that never really suits your taste or needs. So often a plant is purchased simply because it is appealing; no consideration is given to how it will grow, the exposure it needs, its hardiness, or the amount of care it will require. An overall landscape design will help you choose plants that are suited to the particular locations and uses you have in mind. But don't expect to complete the entire project overnight. Unless you have countless hours of spare time and a sizable budget, expect to carry out your plan gradually.

The most important consideration in basic landscaping is a clear idea of what you want to accomplish. To get started, simply lay out on a piece of paper the location of property lines; where the house is situated on the property; where walkways, driveways, and patio are located; and where existing trees and shrubs are situated. Do this to scale if possible so you can keep everything in perspective. If that is too difficult, simply sketch your place as you see it.

Some of the most interesting landscaping I have ever seen has been accomplished by home-

owners who have a little creative ability and a good imagination. Sometimes an idea used in another landscape can provide inspiration. A few changes can turn someone else's idea into a new design that may be better than the original.

After you have made a sketch of your property, divide it into areas. If you have small children,

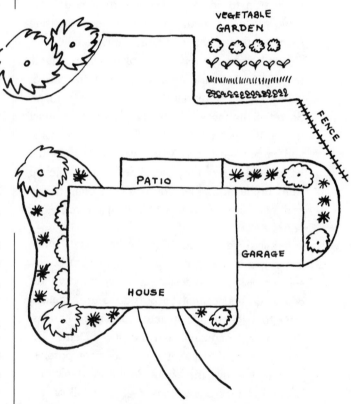

Take time to plant your garden so you'll end up with a layout that suits the needs of your entire family.

you may want a play area for a sandbox or swing. For older children, a badminton area or basketball court may be desired. If you want to be able to hang out the wash, you will need a utility area. You will probably need a place for garbage cans, too. Plan for an entry area, patio area, and maybe a vegetable garden. If you eventually plan to add a toolshed or greenhouse, reserve space for them. In other words, set aside room for the activities of your entire family.

Don't make the mistake of planning your landscaping to appeal to your neighbors instead of yourself. Plan primarily for your own enjoyment. So often the nicest plants are placed up against the house, yet most of the time you are inside and cannot see them. Attractive plantings should be located where they can be seen and enjoyed from inside also. Plan for you and your family and include plants that are particular favorites of yours.

It might be a good idea to check your entry landscape and see if it might be improved by some revision or redesign. If so, a rainy winter day when you cannot be outside is an excellent time to begin thinking about possible changes. First of all, roughly sketch the present entry design on a piece of paper. Then consider possible ways to improve the layout. You may think of a dozen or more possibilities. Get them all on paper. This is a good way to organize your thoughts and get the project under way.

Some of your ideas may come from entry plantings you have observed around other homes. Such plantings can be adapted for use in an entirely different situation with just a little imagination. Garden catalogs and landscape books are other sources of ideas. By adding a personal touch to something you see, the final design can be more interesting than the original.

It is a mistake to try to design an entry area around an existing walkway that you do not like. Perhaps that walkway was installed many years ago by the builder and it does not meet your needs or taste at all. There are many possibilities for redesign, and not all of them are expensive.

In many cases, the concrete can be broken up with a sledgehammer so you can start from the beginning. Often the broken pieces can be used in the new design, new concrete can be poured, or some other material can be used to give the desired effect; your budget may be the determining factor in your choice. Complete revision is often the simplest solution in the long run.

The entry area is a good place to incorporate a special feature in your landscaping. Perhaps you would like a waterfall or reflecting pool in your garden; or you may have a lantern, a figurine, or a decorative container you would like to display in some way. Any one of these things would provide an excellent focal point in the revised entry design. The use of such objects or features can completely change the character of the area.

Plan to have something in bloom in the entry area at all times. Annuals and perennials can be used during the summer; flowering and berried plants are very colorful in fall and winter; and bulbs can be combined with spring-flowering plants that grow so well here in the Northwest. Try to include one or two plants that have a pleasant fragrance, too.

Flower colors are only one way to add interest to the entry area. The design often can be highlighted with plants that have contrasting leaf color. One of the various shades of green, gold, silver, blue, or red might supply just the right touch.

Bold, medium, and fine leaf textures are available, and this is still another way to add interest to such plantings. How well the plants you choose fit together will determine the effectiveness of the design.

Yet another important dimension in good landscape design is plant shape. There are low spreading plants, bushy plants, upright plants, and columnar types from which to choose. A pleasant mixture will give the most attractive design.

Should you desire privacy around your front door, there are many ways to achieve it. You may need a decorative panel or fence, but quite often you can create a more effective visual barrier with shrubs and small trees.

If you decide after doing the preliminary sketching that redesigning the entryway is more than you can handle alone, consult a landscape architect or designer. Of course, there will be a charge for this service, but it many be a good investment—you will get a workable, attractive plan using plants you like, placed properly in the planting area.

Landscaping the shady north side of your home may seem difficult, but if you plan your design using shade-loving plants and attractive combinations of foliage textures, leaf colors, flower colors, and fragrances, it is possible to create an outstanding landscape setting on the north side.

Spend some time planning which shade-loving plants you would best like to use in the shaded portion of the garden. Once you have made up your mind, winter is an excellent time of the year to select and plant them. We are fortunate here in the Northwest to have many plants that grow well in the shade. Indeed, one of the biggest problems may be deciding which ones to use. With planning and a little imagination, it is possible to design some very interesting shade plantings.

Shade plants have four basic cultural needs that should be kept in mind when planning a landscape arrangement for a shaded area.

1. They need as much indirect light as possible. Place plants out away from the object providing the shade, whenever this is feasible. Sometimes a few of the lower branches of a tree can be removed to open up an area, allowing more light to enter and improving air circulation.

2. Good air circulation is essential. If the air is stagnant, the plants will very often grow poorly and be more susceptible to fungus problems.

3. Soil must be properly prepared before planting. Soil in shaded areas tends to be sour and more compacted than in other parts of the garden. Dampness and moss can be other problems. Take time to provide proper drainage. Vermiculite, sponge rock, peat moss, and similar soil additives help improve drainage, and they all assist in aerating the soil. Charcoal or dolomite lime will help sweeten the soil.

4. Give special consideration to feeding and pruning. Plants in the shade tend to grow more lush and develop spindly or leggy branches. Tip pinching or pruning this growth may be necessary to keep plants bushy.

Select plants with interesting shapes. If varying shapes are used indiscriminately, you often end up with a hodgepodge of plants and an uninteresting landscape. On the other hand if you combine the various plant shapes in a pleasing way, they blend nicely together and accent each other. Taller plants are used in the background, medium plants in the center planting, and lower-growing plants in the foreground. Conical or roundish plants are generally used in midbed planting spots, spreading plants are used in the foreground, and the upright plants in the background.

The south and west sides of the house are often considered the most difficult areas for selecting landscape plants, because of the sunny exposure. It is the combination of direct sun and reflected sunlight from the house that narrows the choice of plant types that can be grown successfully in this exposure. But don't fret—there are many beautiful plants that will grow on the south and west sides of your home.

One of the biggest errors in landscaping the sunny south or west side of the house is the use of the wrong types of plants. For example, rhododendrons, camellias, azaleas, and even skimmia are often planted in this exposure, but none of these plants does well in full sun, especially with the reflected sunlight from the house. So avoid the use of these plants and use sun-loving plants instead. Before deciding which ones to use, ask yourself the following questions:

1. Should the plants be evergreen or deciduous?

2. Should they be flowering types, and, if so, what colors?

3. What color should the foliage be?

4. What leaf texture would be most desirable—fine, medium, or bold?

5. How tall can the plants grow?

6. Are soil conditions adequate for the desired plants?

The answers to these questions will help you decide which plants to choose.

Keep in mind that plants grown in a sunny location will need more water than those grown in most other parts of the garden. The combination of sun exposure, sun reflection, and wind tends to dry them out much more quickly than those grown in more protected areas. Moreover, these plants are often grown under the eaves of the house or under tall evergreens where the soil tends to dry more quickly and where rainwater seldom reaches. Frequent watering will therefore be necessary to keep plants growing at their best on the sunny side of the house.

All varieties of conifers and junipers do well in full sun. They are available in a wide range of foliage colors, including the various shades of green, gold, silver-blue, and gray. The various growing heights and shapes available make them versatile plants for sunny locations. However, they do not flower, and in most cases the leaf textures are very similar, so other types of plants will be needed to provide variety and a pleasing overall effect.

Going to the other extreme, there are quite a few colorful plants—like quince, roses, lilacs, beauty bush, forsythia, and spirea—that do well in full sun. The problem with this group is that they all lose their leaves in the winter, so you probably will not want to use them exclusively in a planting. Some evergreens will be needed to help conceal their bareness and create interest in the winter season.

You will probably come to the conclusion that at least some of the plants chosen should be evergreen, have textural variety, and provide flower color. What you are looking for are broad-leaf evergreens. The following are some of the ones that will do well on the hot south or west side of the house:

Stranvaesia. Two varieties are commonly grown here. Undulata, which grows to about 5 feet, and Davidiana, which may reach 10 or 20 feet at maturity. Either one can be kept lower by pruning. Late spring flowers appear in whitish clusters followed by red berries. New leaves are a light bronze color.

Abelia. The variety Edward Goucher is one of the most popular. Its pinkish purple flowers appear from July through October. It reaches approximately 5 to 6 feet at maturity, but can be kept lower with simple pruning. Semi-evergreen, it loses some leaves during winter.

Ceanothus. This is one of the beautiful blue-flowering evergreens. Upright varieties like Puget Beauty and Mount Haze are very colorful. This plant tends to winterkill or freeze back if it is watered in late summer, so withhold water after about August 15.

Escallonia. This summer-flowering plant provides a lot of color in the hot bright sun. Several varieties are popular here, ranging in shades of light pink to rose or red. Some varieties may attain a height of 7 feet at maturity. This can be controlled by pruning.

Laurestinus. This is an excellent plant to use for color during the winter and early spring. It blooms sporadically from November on. Flowers appear in pinkish white clusters. This is another tall shrub that may reach 12 feet, but it can be kept lower by pruning.

Cotoneaster. From the low-growing varieties to the tall upright ones, this is an excellent plant for hot sun. Flowers are generally whitish in color, followed by fall and winter berries that are either red or orange. Berries are an excellent source of food for the birds. The upright varieties have a graceful spreading habit, which can be confined with pruning.

Firethorn. Covered with clusters of white flowers in the springtime, red or orange berries follow, depending upon varieties. They are ideal for espaliering against a wall, or can be grown free-form. Prune to control height.

Choisya ternata. Commonly called Mexican orange, this plant has glossy dark green leaves, clusters of white spring flowers that look and smell somewhat like orange blossoms. It may attain a height of 6 to 8 feet unless pruned.

Heather. There are dozens of varieties that can be used on the south or west side of the house. By careful selection, it is possible to have some varieties in bloom all twelve months of the year. Flower and leaf colors vary considerably by variety.

Veronica (Hebe). Two of the most popular varieties in this region are Autumn Glory and Buxifolia. Autumn Glory flowers from June until the first frost with light lavender-blue blossoms. Buxifolia has rather insignificant white flowers. Both have bushy habits

of growth to about 2 feet at maturity. They need pinching or pruning to keep them bushy.

You can also use annuals and bulbs on the sunny sides of the house. Marigolds, snapdragons, zinnias, verbena, petunias, lobelia, sweet peas, stock, and Livingston daisies are a few of the outstanding annuals that grow well in the sunny part of the garden. Godetia, cosmos, alyssum, and nasturtiums are excellent annuals to grow from seed in the sunny garden.

Among the best bulbs and tubers to grow in the sun are dahlias, cannas, tulips, daffodils, hyacinths, and crocuses. All of these do well in full, bright sunlight.

GARDEN COLOR IDEAS

While mulling over ideas for your landscape, give some thought to planning colors for the spring and summer garden. You will want to choose colors that suit your taste and complement your interior decor. A little planning can transform a mediocre garden design into an outstanding floral display.

First decide which colors you want to include in the garden. Then decide which types and varieties of annuals will accomplish what you want to do. Keep in mind that the best displays are achieved when a single color is used in one grouping. Whether you plant in small groups or one large mass planting, each group should be all the same color. The random use of color is not nearly as showy and interesting.

It is a good idea to include some white flowers in your plans. White highlights and intensifies the other colors. Perhaps you have noticed how often white borders are used to set off secondary plantings of red, blue, yellow, or orange and a background planting of yet another color. The white border makes the entire bed stand out.

An outstanding combination planting I noted recently in Portland, Oregon, included a border of white alyssum followed successively by blue lobelia and yellow French marigolds. The planting was simple but effective and could be seen at least a block away.

Another interesting combination is white alyssum, yellow dwarf French marigolds, and tall-growing red salvia. Still another is a border of white alyssum, then blue ageratum, followed by red verbena or petunias. We have used the latter mixture in our own garden on several occasions. Actually, the possible combinations for an interesting display are endless.

Once you have decided on the color scheme, it should be carried throughout the entire landscape. This includes plantings in flower and shrub beds; container plantings for the patio, lanai, or entry area; and hanging baskets. By coordinating colors in this way, the overall display will complement your home, and the entire landscape will blend together.

Several years ago I used a combination of red salvia and yellow marigolds bordered with blue lobelia as a planting for a golf course. The hot yellow-and-red color combination could be seen for at least a quarter of a mile. A nearby planting included red petunias, yellow marigolds, and red verbena bordered with alyssum—a combination that provided a brilliant display in the garden.

At the Seattle Center one year, they achieved a dramatic display of plants by using various colors of celosia (a plumelike flower). These plants, in shades of red, crimson, bronze, and yellow, were used in both containers and open beds, carrying out a theme in one entire area of the center grounds.

At Minter Gardens in British Columbia, they have gone one step further in using hot colors. On one hillside, a beautiful rooster was planted in many multicolors; in another area, a rising sun. These plantings require large areas, but they can easily be scaled down to the average-size garden.

The special hillside planting at the Peace Arch at Blaine, Washington, always provides a beautiful combination of hot colors and cool colors also. Annuals are used in various colors and sizes to complete the floral picture.

TREES

Landscape trees are ideal for providing privacy, are valuable for furnishing shade during the summer months, and are an important part of any landscape. However, they can cause problems if they are planted in the wrong spot.

When large trees are planted too close to the sewer or septic tank lines, the young roots will occasionally penetrate the joints in the sewer tile and cause a blockage. It is often expensive to remove the roots or to hire someone to clear the lines. Sometimes it is necessary to either dig up the line and remove the roots or hire a special firm to come in and remove the roots by machine.

Are you having a problem with tree roots growing up in your lawn? If you are, simply go in and cut the roots out before they become a real nuisance. Try to begin this process when the roots first appear above the ground. Make your first cut at the end closest to the tree, then cut the root on the other end where it goes back into the ground. You may need to dig 4 or 5 inches into the lawn in order to remove the protruding root. If you carefully lift the sod around the root that is being removed, you can usually put the grass back in place, leaving only a very small bare spot that can easily be reseeded in the fall or early spring. Be careful not to remove too many of the roots around a single tree or you will weaken its support to the point where a strong wind might blow it over.

Tree roots can also become a problem by lifting sidewalks. Larger, quicker-growing trees are often the offenders in this case—especially ma-

ples—if they are planted within 10 feet of a walkway or driveway. Sometimes a very simple prevention technique will work wonders.

It is the surface roots that are generally responsible for lifting the pavement, so take a sharp shovel or spade and thrust it 6 to 12 inches into the soil along the edge of the pavement, cutting to the same depth along the entire length of the side that faces the tree. This way you remove the roots that have the potential to lift the pavement.

If you already have the problem, you can often pry up that section of the pavement, chop out the root with a hatchet or ax, then simply replace the concrete. However, if it is a large section of concrete, it may be necessary to install an entirely new section.

Before planting trees in your garden, be aware of some of the problems that can arise and take precautionary measures to prevent them.

If you have large trees on your property, you probably know how difficult it can be to grow plants under them. A rather common garden question is, What plants will grow under a tall tree? The answer is really quite simple. It isn't a matter of which types or varieties to grow but a matter of providing proper care for the plants so they can compete successfully with the robust root growth of a tall tree. So as you plan your landscaping, remember that it is possible to grow plants under tall trees if you follow certain basic rules.

One of the most important factors to keep in mind when selecting plants to be grown under tall trees is that the overspreading branches will provide a certain amount of shade. Therefore, you will need to select plants that grow and flower best in this type of environment. That is why you will so often see rhododendrons, camellias, azaleas, viburnum, and similar plants growing under tall trees.

Some of the finest plants to grow under tall trees are our natives, including such plants as salal, kinnikinnick, and mahonia. Other top-notch plants include hosta, ferns, skimmia, *Sarco cocca*, and many other broad-leaf evergreens. Some of the best ground covers to grow under tall trees are *Vinca minor*, ivy, salal, and kinnikinnick. In locations where sun reaches the plants under tall trees for several hours, the list of types that can be grown is almost unlimited.

The major problem in growing plants under tall trees is the encroachment of tree roots into the areas where the plants and shrubs are being grown. Since tree roots are so dominant, they tend to rob valuable nutrients and moisture from the smaller garden plants. Here are a few pointers to keep your plants healthy in such locations.

Special attention should be given to watering plants under tall trees. Large trees use voluminous amounts of water, so the soil under the trees tends to dry out quite rapidly. Plants will thus require more watering than those grown in the open garden. In fact, it may be necessary to provide extra water even during the winter months. The addition of peat moss, compost, and processed manure at planting time will greatly aid in holding moisture around shrubs and plants under tall trees.

It may also be necessary to feed the plants a little more frequently. The best time for fertilization of these plants is in late February and again in early June. If necessary, a third application could be made in early July. To make sure the tree roots don't steal it, you can apply a liquid fertilizer in a foliage application rather than applying the dry fertilizer on the soil. Fish fertilizer or other types of liquid fertilizers that can be safely applied to plant leaves can be used for these foliar feedings.

Another prime consideration in growing plants under tall trees is proper light exposure. Often it is a good practice to remove some of the lower-growing branches so the plants underneath will receive as much indirect light as possible. The pruning of these lower branches can be done at almost any time of the year, but it is best done during the winter dormant season from November until March.

Shrubs growing beneath tall trees often require more pruning attention than those grown in the open garden; because they necessarily receive less light and often inadequate water and food, they sometimes tend to grow straggly or uneven. A light pruning will bring them back into shape, helping to create a bushier, neater plant. Most broad-leaf evergreens are best pruned during the spring months of March, April, and May; deciduous plants can be pruned during the winter dormant season.

NATURAL LANDSCAPING

It is not unusual for the suburban homeowner to devote at least a part of his yard to native plants. The developers of suburban homes in recent years have often left at least a portion of the surrounding native terrain intact. In such instances, one can combine native plants with compatible garden shrubs and trees to create a low-maintenance, naturalized landscape setting.

Creating a pleasing naturalized setting in your garden requires basically the same consideration you would give to conventional landscaping: It is important to combine foliage textures, leaf colors, flower colors, various plant shapes, and fragrances whenever possible.

Sometimes you can get your greatest landscape ideas by just observing what Mother Nature has done in naturalized settings. A good example is the natural rock, tree, and shrub placement in the foothills and mountains of the Pacific Northwest. By copying Mother Nature's touch here and there, you can create an outstanding native, naturalized garden, especially if the surrounding trees, shrubs, and setting lend themselves to this type of landscaping.

If a part of your property has been left in its natural state, your landscape can be a natural extension of that area. This can be done quite simply and tastefully by including those same native plants in and around the portions of the landscape that were disturbed when your home was being built.

The following are just a few of the very basic native plants you might want to include in your naturalized garden.

Salal, *Mahonia nervosa*, kinnikinnick, and the evergreen huckleberry are excellent native plants to use as ground covers. Low-growing varieties of ferns and dogwood canadensis both make good seasonal ground covers. Pachysandra, myrtle, lingonberry, and wintergreen are a few of the garden shrubs that combine well with your natives as ground covers.

For taller-growing shrubs, it is hard to beat the beautiful Oregon grape, with its attractive spring flowers and fall berries. There are many other varieties of mahonias that blend well in the native setting. Of course, rhododendrons, camellias, and azaleas all lend themselves to naturalized plantings.

Many types of ferns blend nicely with other native plants in the shaded garden. Among the most popular are the sword fern, maidenhair fern, and deer fern—to mention just a few.

Bleeding hearts, trilliums, dogtooth violets, and primroses are colorful native perennials. Daffodils and narcissus are the most popular garden bulbs that blend well in native plantings.

The honeysuckle is probably one of the most colorful native vines. The flowers also have a pleasant fragrance and are bee attractants. Climbing hydrangea is also great as a garden vine in a naturalized setting.

The mock orange is one of the most colorful native deciduous shrubs. Chinese witch hazel, buddleia (better known as butterfly bush), quince, and forsythia are other deciduous garden shrubs that are attractive in the naturalized garden.

It is hard to beat the beautiful vine maple. This native tree has magnificent autumn leaf color and an interesting habit of growth. It is undoubtedly one of the most popular of the deciduous native trees for landscaping.

If you want to include some flowering trees in a native landscape setting, among the most popular are the open, spreading varieties of flowering cherries, dogwoods, flowering crab apple, and flowering plum. The white-flowering hawthorn is an excellent tree to use in the native garden, and its berries provide food for the birds.

Hemlock, madrona, shore pine, Douglas fir, and western cedar are among the popular evergreen trees to use in the native garden.

We all enjoy viewing the beautiful wildflowers that grow so abundantly on hillsides and in the meadows and forests of the Pacific Northwest. Fortunately, many of them can be grown in the garden, too. Lupines, sweet peas, columbine, bleeding heart, avalanche lilies, and trilliums are especially nice. Specialty nurseries often offer them for sale.

BONSAI

One type of landscaping that is becoming more popular each year is bonsai gardening. People define what this is in many different ways.

The art of bonsai includes shaping, pruning, training, and root-pruning plants, in conjunction with a regular schedule of watering and feeding. A bonsai arrangement cannot be created overnight. It takes time, patience, and some artistic ability.

Small arrangements generally planted in clay, ceramic, or stone containers are the ones most often associated with bonsai. It is not impossible to find such an arrangement that is several hundred years old, having been passed down from generation to generation.

A bonsai arrangement may consist of only a single plant that is upright, slanted, twisted, or cascade-shaped. It can also contain a group of miniature trees as in a grove. Such plantings are most often found in three styles: formal, informal upright, and cascading. To add interest, the roots are sometimes partially exposed. At other times they are shaped around a decorative stone.

Several styles of specially made containers are

available. They are usually very low and flat. Some are round or square; others are artistically shaped; still others are very plain. Usually they are made of ceramic or stone. Wooden ones are suitable in some instances. Sometimes the bonsai planting is built on a flat stone instead of using a container. This method is called "landscape bonsai" or *bonseki*.

If you want to try your hand at bonsai gardening, start looking for suitable plant material. You can use a plant with a weathered trunk, an exposed gnarled root system, a twisted or unusual shape, or you may find some other interesting oddity that particularly appeals to you. The selection of any plant for bonsai purposes should depend on your personal taste.

Once you have chosen the plant material and container, it is time to begin conditioning the plant. First of all, establish a fibrous root system. This can be done in several different ways, but probably the most effective way is to trim off at least one-third to one-half of the existing root system—even more if necessary. I have found that this is best done after the plant has been bare-rooted in a bucket of water containing a pinch of rooting hormone. Keep the roots moist while you are trimming them back. They should not be allowed to dry out at any time. When you have finished, place the specimen in a planting medium of fine bark.

Let new roots develop in the bark medium. Over the next few months, continue to bare-root the plant and root-prune until you have established a sturdy, prolific, confined root system. This continuous pruning will not be as severe as the first pruning.

After you have root-pruned two or three times and have developed a fibrous root system, the plant is ready to be placed in the chosen container. Should the plant tend to be top-heavy, place small pieces of bent wire shaped like hairpins over the sturdier roots to help anchor them in place until they become established.

Several types of potting soil are suitable. I have had excellent results using one-third each of peat moss or leaf mold, fresh-water sand, and sandy loam. From this point on, any pruning or top shaping that is done will be determined by the particular design you want to create. Beginners usually use the three-level style: heaven, man, and earth.

As you prune, be sure to remove any misshapen, weak, dead, or crisscrossing branches. Continually spread out the branches and study the plant so you can thin and shape for best artistic value. As the plant begins to develop, you may also find it necessary to do some tip pinching or pruning to maintain its shape or restrict its growth.

I have found rubber- or plastic-coated electrician's wire ideal for altering the growth of branches. Simply wrap the wire loosely around the branch and then bend the wired branch into the desired shape. You can also use the wire to tie or weight down a branch to obtain a particular shape. The wire probably will have to remain in place at least one year to permanently alter the shape of a branch. Remove it when it has accomplished what you wanted.

To add to the interest of your bonsai subject, it is a good idea to collect mosses growing on brick, in flower beds, or possibly on the roof of the house to cover the soil area at the base of the planting. Thyme, miniature mint, and baby tears are other plants used for this purpose.

The bonsai specimen will need to be protected from hot midday sun and wind. It should be placed in a sheltered spot until it has time to become established. Then it can gradually be moved to its permanent location.

Remember that bonsai containers are very small, so you will have to watch the watering carefully. In summertime, it may be necessary to water daily. During spring and fall, the rainfall will probably provide enough moisture.

During the summer growing season, from May through September, bonsai plants should be fed about once a month. A fish fertilizer or other well-balanced all-purpose liquid fertilizer is usually used for this purpose. Apply at half the recommended strength, using the full amount of water.

Probably the most common plants used for bonsai are pines and other conifers, junipers, and some broad-leaf evergreens. However, the list of possibilities is almost endless. As a beginner, consider mugho pine, Japanese red or black pine, lodgepole pine, azaleas, dwarf rhododendrons, junipers and conifers of all kinds, quince, maples, dogwood, and seedling birch. As you become more adept at bonsai gardening, you can experiment with many other types of plants.

Bonsai gardening will not appeal to everyone, but some gardeners really enjoy dwarfing and artistically shaping plants in containers. It can be a challenging hobby and add great interest to your landscape over a long period of time.

LANDSCAPING IDEAS

All of the foregoing are just possibilities for your landscaping that you may want to consider. For actual design ideas, you will find garden books, landscape books, and seed and garden catalogs to be very good sources of information. Look through some of them and see which ideas best suit the style and character you want to create.

Other excellent sources of landscape ideas are the established residential and commercial plantings in your area. Observe them and make notes about the ones you especially like. Often, as I said, you can add your own personal touch to something you have seen and create something entirely new. Some of the most interesting plantings I have seen were created in just this manner.

Perhaps you are planning a landscape around a mobile home. More and more people are choosing this way of living, and some of the landscaping in such areas is very creative. Colorful shrub plantings, containers, and even vegetable gardens are often combined in the overall design. Occasionally a small grassy area may be in evidence.

Planning is the key to any good landscape design, but it is particularly important when gardening around a mobile home. Several special circumstances should be taken into consideration. First of all, the light, shiny siding on the home will reflect considerable amounts of light and heat, which is damaging to some types of plants. Be especially careful to select plants that can withstand such reflected light and heat. Avoid such plants as rhododendrons, camellias, and azaleas, which would be likely to burn up in such locations.

Second, since the home is smaller in scale than a full-size house, the plants you select should be scaled down as well: Large fast-growing trees and shrubs will soon overpower the surroundings.

Third, people who choose to live in mobile homes often do not want to spend a lot of time gardening, so low-maintenance design is very important. A lawn can be eliminated completely. Instead, ground cover plantings, crushed rock, or coarse bark can be used between planting areas. They are all attractive and help cut down on the growth of weeds. A small deck or a concrete or asphalt patio is often incorporated into the plan as well.

You can even grow vegetables when you live in a mobile home—many have attractive leaves and are pleasing plants in the general landscape. They can also be grown in containers; in fact, some varieties seem to do better when their roots are confined in this way. Beans, corn, and peas can be included in the landscape beds. Tomatoes, pumpkins, squashes, and others can be grown in containers or in the garden area. Root crops can be grown along with annuals and perennials—a special area need not be set aside for edible roots. But be sure that toxic insecticides, herbicides, and other chemicals are not used where they are grown; use only products that are safe for vegetables.

If there is a mobile home in your future, rest assured that pleasing low-maintenance designs can be achieved if all the elements of good design are incorporated.

Landscaping a Home Near the Seaside

If you live on the coast or have a summer home anywhere along a saltwater beach, you will need to select landscape plants suited to that environment. Soil, exposure to salt spray, and weather will all be factors in determining which plants to use. However, in some of the sheltered areas, the range of plants one can use is even greater than in the average garden.

If you are landscaping a summer home or weekend cabin, you must also consider how much time will be necessary to maintain each plant. This is a major factor, because many of the plants will receive only weekend attention or possibly only seasonal care.

In protected areas near salt water, practically all plants will do well. In fact, the warmer temperatures often permit one to grow semitender plants that may not grow in the home garden. A good example of this is the magnificent eucalyptus tree that grows in gardens at Long Beach along the Washington coastline.

The major problem areas will be those spots where winter winds and resulting salt spray are factors. In such spots, only a few plants will survive. After a severe storm, salt spray can be washed off with a garden hose before it burns the leaves of exposed plants.

Another factor to consider in growing shrubs and trees near salt water is the soil, which often tends to be very sandy. To properly prepare it for planting, mix in generous quantities of peat moss, leaf mold, or processed manure, plus the correct amount of an all-purpose transplanting fertilizer.

Pruning and feeding schedules will vary with the different types of plants, so use good judgment when it comes to these projects.

Here are a few suggestions on the sturdier plants to use near salt water:

SCREENING SHRUBS AND TREES

Cypress. Many different types and growing heights are suitable as windbreaks or privacy screens.

Ceanothus. The attractive blue flowers of this evergreen make it a most interesting shrub to be used near the water. It likes a rather dry soil, and can be grown in a hedge or screen or used as a specimen plant for landscape purposes. The lower-growing variety of gloriosis is a good ground cover type.

Pines. Scotch and coast pines are good evergreen trees to use for privacy screens or as windbreaks. They can be allowed to grow naturally or can be trimmed and trained.

Firethorn pyracantha. White spring flower clusters and red berries in the fall and winter make this a showy plant for individual use or as a freestanding screen.

LANDSCAPE SHRUBS

Escallonia. This versatile plant is available in many different flowering varieties. Summer flowers cover the plants for a couple of months. Rosea, rubra, Alice, and apple blossom are good ones to use.

Mugho pines. These are well adapted to areas close to salt water. Their texture blends well with other evergreens.

Azalea mollis. Give it just a little protection from direct salt spray and this deciduous azalea really does well. The brilliant blooms come in shades of white, pastel pink, salmon, and rose to red and are very colorful in the springtime.

Arbutus unedo. Called "strawberry tree" because flowers are followed by decorative fruit that looks like strawberries. Broad evergreen leaves make it an attractive-textured plant in the landscape.

Broom (cytisus). Many varieties are available. The moonlight broom so often used along our freeways is especially attractive in the seaside garden. Soft yellow flowers appear in April and May. The only drawback is that it has a pungent smell.

GRAY-FOLIAGE PLANTS FOR CONTRAST

Senecio greyi. This is a fine gray-foliage plant that can easily be kept bushy and attractive by pinching or pruning. The yellow flowers distract from the leaf color and should be removed.

Dusty miller. The cut-leaf, gray foliage is showy. It needs to be pinched and pruned to keep it compact. Remove the yellow flowers as they appear.

The list could be much longer. The degree of exposure to wind and water will determine how selective you must be. For example, in many areas the rhododendrons and camellias will do very well if they do have limited protection. Likewise, evergreen azaleas can often be used.

Enjoy your garden near the salt water. Local established landscapes will undoubtedly give you additional ideas as to plants that you can use.

Getting Your Soil in Shape

Are you having mediocre results with your lawn, vegetable garden, flowers, or shrubs? If so, chances are you need to have your soil tested to know exactly what is needed to properly grow your plants. This should be done before you do any soil preparation or any planting.

If you want to test your own soil, you can easily do it with a soil test kit. Most garden outlets feature soil test kits such as the one sold by Sudbury Laboratory of Sudbury, Massachusetts. A good soil test is essential because it lets you know the specific nutrient needs of your garden so you do not waste money on the wrong fertilizers. The soil test will also let you know whether you need to raise or lower the pH of your soil. Soil pH determines whether or not plants are able to consume nutrients. If the pH is too high or too low, nutrients in the soil lock up and become unabsorbable by the plant; thus, fertilizer goes to waste while your plants literally starve to death. Careful soil testing and correction of the soil to the specific needs of your garden will assure that each crop gets exactly what it needs to grow and yield its fullest potential. The most important of these are nitrogen, phosphate, and potash.

Nitrogen. Adequate nitrogen produces luxuriant growth of stalks, stems, leaves, and grasses. Excessive nitrogen causes too rapid growth, softness of tissues, general plant weakness, and an abundance of green growth, which retards flower and seed formation. Plants suffering from nitrogen deficiency are more susceptible to disease, infestation, and injury.

Phosphate. Phosphate gives plants a rapid start, stimulates root formation, hastens maturity, and assists blooming and seed formation.

Potash (potassium). Proper amounts of potash stimulate early root or tuber formation, which is essential for all underground vegetables and tuberous flowers. Excessive potash reduces the plant's resistance to drought and frost injury and delays plant maturity.

To gather a soil sample, take it from 2 to 3 inches below the surface, using a clean instrument such as a soil sampler, trowel, or spoon. The test results are sensitive to external factors such as ashes, so never smoke while gathering and testing your soil, and avoid touching the sample with your hands.

Put samples in clean containers and label them according to the part of the garden from which they were gathered. Samples should be taken from various areas. There might be a variation of the soil in a particularly sunny spot, an area beneath a tree, a part of your garden that has been under cultivation, or a low-lying area that collects water. It is best to take samples from each corner and the center of the lawn in any case.

Soil should not be too wet. If it is not dry enough to walk on, allow it to dry naturally. Remove solids and debris such as stones and pieces of wood without touching the soil. Crumble soil as finely as possible. This is easily accomplished by putting the sample in a small plastic bag and going over it with a rolling pin. Your sample is now ready for testing.

Soil test kits include valuable charts listing the ideal pH for hundreds of flowering plants, vegetables, grasses, and trees. They also include charts illustrating how to determine exact nutritional needs after testing, instructions on how to raise and lower pH, and instructions on when and how to fertilize.

Soil Preparation

To have your soil ready when planting time arrives in the vegetable garden, it is especially important to mix fertilizer and lime into the soil in the winter. Of course, you will have to wait until the weather is suitable—you cannot work the soil when it is too wet or when the ground is frozen—but as soon as conditions are favorable, proceed.

First of all, remove weeds and old plant parts that may still remain from the fall. (They can be recycled by adding them to the compost pile.) Next, till or spade the soil, then level the garden area.

The method used to cultivate will depend largely on the size of the plot. Small areas can be worked with a spade, shovel, or spading fork. In larger areas, it is more convenient and less time-consuming to use a garden tiller. Tillers are very thorough and are a much more efficient way to mix additives into the soil. Whichever method is used, cultivation should be to a depth of about 8 to 10 inches.

The next step is to add fertilizer. You can use well-rotted barnyard manure, or a commercial fertilizer like 5-10-10, or an all-purpose vegetable garden type. Avoid using fresh manures, because they tend to burn the vegetable crops. (Fresh manure is best added in the fall so it has a chance to leach out during the winter rainy season.) Another excellent soil additive is compost humus if it is available. Many soils benefit from the addition of dolomite or agricultural lime, about 40 pounds per 1,000 square feet. Cultivate a second time to mix these additives into the soil.

Immediately after you have tilled or spaded, rake the entire area level so there is no chance of water gathering in low spots, which would keep the soil cool and damp, thus delaying planting time.

Peat Moss

When planting trees, shrubs, vegetables, and flowers, it is generally recommended that you mix sphagnum peat moss into the soil. Better water retention, improved aeration, and the ability of sphagnum peat moss to help bind soil particles are just a few of the major reasons why it is an effective soil conditioner.

The word "sphagnum" is often confusing to the home gardener because there are two types of sphagnum moss. Sphagnum peat moss is the decomposed form of sphagnum moss. It should not be confused with the fresh sphagnum moss that has been somewhat dried and is often used to line hanging baskets or as filler in flower arrangements. Sphagnum moss is a purely organic material that comes from a unique plant that grows from the top and has no root system. It is found in northern climates generally above the 42d parallel; during the frigid winter months, it dies off at the bottom to form peat. It is capable of retaining from twelve to twenty times its weight in water. Sphagnum peat moss is 95 percent organic. It has a predictable pH level of 3.5 to 4.5. It is free of chemicals and other foreign materials.

Sphagnum peat moss is especially beneficial in the soil of the Pacific Northwest because it loosens and aerates the soil, thus encouraging healthy root growth. When preparing clay soil for planting trees or shrubs, up to 25 percent of the soil mixture should be sphagnum peat moss for best aeration, water retention, and organic humus.

In sandy soil, water tends to drain away quickly, often taking valuable nutrients with it. Adding up to 25 percent peat moss to your sandy soil helps to bind the soil particles, thus retaining water and nutrients in the root zone.

In addition to sphagnum peat moss, there are reed and sedge peats, peat humus, and many others. One of the greatest advantages of sphagnum peat moss is that it decomposes at a much slower rate than the other peats; thus it continues to work in the soil much longer, has greater bulk, and is three to four times more water absorbent.

A mixture of one-third sphagnum peat moss, one-third garden loam, and one-third sand is generally recommended for containers and hanging baskets. This soil mix helps to retain moisture around plant roots, cuts down on the frequency of watering, and makes nutrients more easily available to the plants.

In vegetable and flower gardens, it is generally recommended that about 6 cubic feet of peat moss be used for every 150 square feet of garden area. However, if you have a heavy clay soil or exceptionally sandy soil, you should use about double that amount. The sphagnum peat moss should be spaded or tilled into the top 6 inches of the soil.

Another common use for sphagnum peat moss is as a top dressing for a new lawn. A light layer of approximately 1/16 inch of peat moss helps retain moisture over newly seeded lawns until the seeds germinate. The ability of peat moss to retain twelve to twenty times its weight in water helps cut down on the frequency of watering.

You can help get the plants off to a better start in all parts of your garden by mixing sphagnum peat moss with your soil at planting time.

Wood Ashes

The next time you clean out your fireplace or wood stove, save the wood ashes and keep them in a dry place so that you can use them in your garden as a soil additive. Wood ashes contain potassium, some phosphorus, and magnesium. Ashes from hardwoods such as maple, elm, oak, and beech contain a third more calcium plus more potash than the ashes from softwoods. In addition, wood ashes help neutralize acid soils.

They are thus especially beneficial in areas where you have deciduous plants—fruit trees, vegetables, root crops, bulbs, annuals, perennials, and deciduous vines. Avoid using wood ashes around acid-loving plants like rhododendrons, camellias, azaleas, junipers, and conifers.

I am often asked whether wood ashes can burn garden plants. Since the nutrient content of wood ash is rather low, there is little danger of burning as long as moderate amounts are used. Of course, the ashes must be allowed to cool before being used in the garden. It is also very important to keep wood ashes dry until they are used in the garden—rain leaches out the soluble chemicals.

It is estimated that about 60 pounds of wood ash will accumulate from each cord of burned hardwood. So unless you burn several cords of wood a year, there is not much likelihood that you will have enough ashes for your entire garden.

Christmas and Plants

TREES

One of the biggest decisions to make during the Christmas holiday season is whether to have a cut tree, a flocked tree (tree sprayed with artifi-cial snow), an artificial tree, or a living tree. Each type has its own advantages.

If you decide to buy a cut Christmas tree, here are a few things to look for. Remember, a good fresh tree will be less of a fire hazard in your home. By taking a little extra time and being aware of what to look for, you can select a tree that is fresh, looks good, and is less of a fire danger. A fresh tree naturally lasts longer, too.

We are fortunate here in the Pacific Northwest to have a wide range of cut Christmas trees. Probably the most popular, and the one we consider the typical Christmas tree, is the Douglas fir. However, there is also the noble fir—a neat, symmetrical, deep green needled tree—plus many varieties of pine, spruce, and fir. Most of the cut trees sold on local lots are grown in the Shelton area of Washington or on tree farms throughout western Washington, British Columbia, and Oregon. Since the trees are locally grown, you can generally count on their being of highest quality. Needle drop is seldom a problem unless the trees have been improperly handled.

Of course, the freshest cut trees are those that you yourself cut. There are numerous "you cut" farms throughout the Pacific Northwest, and it is also possible to obtain a permit and cut trees on some national park lands. Be sure to decide early enough if you want to do this, because some districts are on a lottery system. Tree-cutting permits are available for a fee at the district offices of the particular national forest or park where you wish to cut your tree. Under no circumstances should trees be cut down without prior authorization or without obtaining a permit.

The most popular way of obtaining a cut Christmas tree is by buying one at a Christmas tree lot, or at a nursery, garden center, or other established outlet. When selecting a cut tree at one of these places, there are a few things you can look for to be assured of getting a top-quality tree.

If you are selecting a Christmas tree from a cut-tree lot, you will need two people in order to do the job right: one person to turn the tree while the other judges its size, shape, and freshness. Once you have judged a particular tree, you should change roles to let the other person pass judgment on the tree as well.

In more than fifteen years of selling Christmas trees, I learned how to be reasonably sure that the trees I purchased were fresh. I also found that the biggest mistakes people make in selecting trees are waiting too long, looking too long, and selecting a tree at night. Most of the season's Christmas trees have been purchased by the middle of December, so if you wait too long you are going to make a selection from the leftovers. In other words, you are going to get a tree that someone else did not want.

If you look at Christmas trees too long, pretty soon they all begin to look the same. So after you have examined twenty to thirty trees, take a break. Go have a cup of coffee or do something different for ten or twenty minutes before continuing your search for just the right tree. Otherwise, you are apt to get very confused and disgusted and are bound to end up with an inferior tree just so you can get the job done.

If it is necessary to select a tree at night, follow these steps. Once you have found a tree of the size and shape you desire, be sure to thoroughly examine it under a light. You want to be certain that it is fresh, has good color, and is not dropping needles. If possible, take the tree into a building that has normal light conditions so you will know exactly what the tree will look like when you get it home. Too often poor-quality trees are selected at night; don't let this happen to you.

The price of a Christmas tree is usually based on the grade and type of tree, its freshness, shape, and sturdiness. You will find that prices do vary from one location to another, but when it comes to buying cut Christmas trees, you usually get what you pay for.

The first thing I look at when buying a Christmas tree is the number of needles on the ground. Ordinary handling of a tree will cause a few needles to fall to the ground, but large quantities of needles on the ground in the lot usually indicate that the trees either have been improperly handled or are of poor quality. Also check the color of the needles: Old, dried-up brown needles drop naturally from all trees, so they are really of no concern; but if the needles are green or yellowish in color, then you'll want to examine each tree closely. In fact, if there are too many needles on the ground, I would be tempted to turn around and go elsewhere.

Once you have selected a particular tree, check its freshness by lifting the tree upright about a foot off the ground, firmly hitting the trunk on the ground, and observing how many green or yellow needles drop.

Occasionally you will see cut trees being advertised as having been fertilized. This is important because research has proven that fertilized trees last about twice as long indoors.

When you get the tree home, cut an inch or two off its base before placing it in a Christmas tree stand that holds water. Cutting the base of the tree allows water to be taken up, which will help keep the tree fresher longer. Also, keep your Christmas tree away from the fireplace or any heating ducts. There are several types of Christmas tree perservatives that can be mixed with the water in the stand to help keep the tree fresh for a longer period of time.

Christmas trees used in commercial buildings must be treated with a fire retardant. Check with your local fire department for their recommendations on how the tree should be treated so it conforms with current fire regulations.

After Christmas, boughs can be cut from your tree and used as winter protection over chyrsanthemums, primroses, and other perennials and tender plants.

LIVING TREES

You might consider using a living tree instead of a cut tree for Christmas. It will require just a little special care, and after Christmas a living tree is worth just as much as it cost the day you purchased it. As a bonus, the living Christmas tree grows in value as it grows in size in your garden.

Living Christmas trees create less of a fire hazard in the home because the fresh, green needles are not as flammable. In addition, a living tree placed in the garden can often be used as an outdoor Christmas tree or as a source of holiday greens in years to come. A living Christmas tree can also be placed on the patio in a container and brought in at Christmas time each year, thus eliminating the cost of purchasing a tree annually.

We are fortunate here in the Pacific Northwest to have a wide selection of evergreens to choose from when purchasing a living Christmas tree. Just to give you an idea of the range of living trees, consider these:

Alberta spruce. It grows very slowly, remains small, and is ideal as an outdoor container plant on a patio, deck, or lanai. It makes a great living tree for the apartment dweller, mobile-home owner, or thrifty shopper.

Colorado blue spruce or *Moerheim* or *Koster's blue spruce.* The colorful bright blue foliage of these trees makes them excellent living Christmas trees.

Noble fir. The dark bluish green needles and symmetrical growth habit of this tree make it an outstanding living Christmas tree.

Douglas fir. This is another popular native tree that can be used as a living Christmas tree.

Norway spruce. A bushy, symmetrical tree that is probably the most popular of all to use as a living Christmas tree.

White fir. This is another fine choice, with attractive grayish green needles and a uniform growth habit.

Several varieties of pines also make nice living Christmas trees. Their one drawback is that they are hard to decorate, but, their nicely scented needles make up for it by providing a fresh aroma in the home during the holidays.

Avoid using soft-needle trees like hemlock, *Cedrus deodora,* and *Cedrus atlantica,* because their branches are too light to support ornaments or lights. They also have a tendency to drop their needles when exposed to the hot, dry air in most homes.

The key factors in keeping your living Christmas tree alive are how long you keep it indoors, its care while it is in the house, and the care you give the tree immediately after Christmas. The following are a few of the basic points to observe in properly caring for living trees during the holidays.

If the roots are balled and burlapped, the tree should be placed in a container before being taken into the house. Be sure to line the container with waterproof foil or polyethylene so that water does not drain out onto your floor or carpeting. You can use soil, peat moss, vermiculite, bark, or sawdust as the medium around the rootball in the container. When possible, it is best to use soil, because it helps to keep the tree in an upright position and does a better job of retaining moisture than any of the other planting mediums. Today, many living trees are already in containers.

It is a good idea to check your tree daily to see if it needs watering. The frequency and amount of water needed will depend on temperature, tree size, and location in the home. The tree should never lack for water; keep the soil continually moist but never wet.

A living Christmas tree should be kept in the home for only seven to ten days. If it is kept indoors longer, it is apt to force tender new growth that is likely to freeze when the tree is placed outdoors after Christmas. If possible, keep the evening temperatures a little cooler than normal while the living tree is in the house.

Commercial Christmas tree paint or "snow" should not be used on the branches of your living tree. One of my readers suggested the use of shaving cream to achieve the look of snow on a living tree. I found this not only costly but not really effective in appearance.

Place the living tree in an area where it is away from heating ducts or the fireplace. And be sure to use low-watt Christmas tree lights—the larger, standard Christmas tree lights often tend to burn the needles.

Weather permitting, the tree should be placed in the landscape immediately after it is used in the home. However, if a tree is taken from warm indoor conditions and placed in the garden when the weather is exceptionally cold, you take a great chance of losing it. It is best to keep the tree in a cool place like a basement or garage until the weather moderates, then get it planted outdoors.

Follow recognized basic planting procedures when planting a living Christmas tree in the garden. It will provide excellent screening, privacy, or hedging. Many types of living trees also make good specimen landscape shrubs. Placed in a strategic location, a tree can also serve as an outdoor Christmas tree and be decorated each year.

EVERGREEN BOUGHS

If you want to add some holiday decoration, it is possible to use evergreen boughs from your trees. Pine, spruce, and cedar branches are the best ones for holiday decorating. You can also use cut branches from many evergreen shrubs for holiday arrangements. Wreaths and swags are popular as door decorations. They also make beautiful centerpieces, wall hangings, window ornaments, or cemetery pieces.

If you do not have boughs of your own to make wreaths or swags, you can often purchase them at Christmas tree lots, nurseries, and floral shops; or you can purchase ready-made wreaths and swags. Almost all of them are commercially made right here in the Pacific Northwest and are generally quite fresh. Commercial wreaths are often made of noble fir, incense cedar, pine, and juniper, and some may contain a sprig or two of holly.

When possible, it is nice to share some of these evergreen boughs, wreaths, and swags with friends and relatives across the United States who do not have these evergreens to use. Holly, cedar, pine, and juniper are the best evergreens for shipping.

If you use evergreen boughs left over from fall windstorms, be sure to make a fresh cut and give the boughs a drink of water before using them or shipping them. Boughs that you purchase should be treated in the same manner. The stems of branches that you cut fresh from the garden should also be placed in water before being used in the home. Holly should be dipped in a preservative and given water before using. The best method of providing water for your cut greens or holly is to place them upright in a bucket that contains about 2 inches of water.

In addition to pine, juniper, cedar, spruce, fir, cypress, and Christmas holly, you may also find many other evergreen branches that will provide excellent greens. Among the best are viburnums, camellias, rhododendrons, azaleas, and heather. In fact, you will probably want to take a survey of your garden to determine which plants best suit your particular decorating needs. Avoid using any of the soft-needle plants like *Cedrus atlantica, Cedrus deodora*, and hemlock, because they drop their needles too quickly.

If you want to add some bright color to your Christmas arrangements, swags, or wreaths, you will find the variegated foliage of some of the junipers, cypress, and others a nice addition along with the evergreen boughs. The blue foliage of some junipers and spruces is nice. You can also spray a few of your evergreen boughs to add color to your Christmas arrangement, swag, or wreath.

You can use several coat hangers to make a holiday wreath frame layered with greens from your yard.

Evergreen boughs used in the home can be kept in a water solution whenever possible so that they will remain fresher and somewhat fire retardant for a longer period of time. In fact, wreaths, swags, or cut greens used in commercial buildings must be treated with a fire retardant according to current fire regulations.

If you want to make a Christmas wreath for your front door, simply take two or three coat hangers and make a circle by interlacing the wires. Wire the cut greens to the coat hanger, add a nice bright bow, and you have an attractive wreath to hang on your door.

GARDENING GIFT IDEAS

If Christmas is not too far away and you have someone on your gift list who has everything and is really difficult to select a gift for, here are a few last-minute gardening gift ideas. Gardening tools, houseplants, garden accessories, and bulbs are among the most popular gardening gifts, and you can choose whichever kind, size, or quantity fits your budget.

Some of the most popular garden tools are hand pruners, garden scissors, edgers, bulb planters, hand sprayers, and other small tools. You will also find a fine selection of hoes, shovels, rakes, and weeders. If your budget permits, some of the new battery-operated shearers, pruners, and edgers make great gifts for both men and women. Charged overnight, these battery-operated tools will do an average daytime project before needing to be recharged. If children are looking for gifts for grandparents, friends, or relatives, they will find small hand tools like trowels and rakes rather inexpensive.

Practically anyone, whether they live in an apartment, a mobile home, a rest home, or their own home, can use a water metering device. These handy implements range in price from seven to fifteen dollars and are excellent for helping to determine how much moisture your houseplants need. They are also handy for the outdoor gardener in determining moisture levels in flower and shrub beds, in containers, and in the lawn area.

You can always count on a living plant as an ideal last-minute gift idea. One of its greatest advantages is that as it increases in size each year, it also increases in sentimental value. A few of the most popular outdoor plants to give at Christmas are the winter-flowering plants like sasanqua camellias; laurestinus; winter-flowering heather; some of the berried plants like skimmia, holly, and cotoneasters; and plants that have colorful winter leaves. Over the years, probably two of the most popular living gifts have been Japanese lace leaf maples and blue spruce. Dogwoods, magnolias, rhododendrons, and azaleas also are ideal plants to give at Christmas.

Houseplants make an excellent last-minute choice. The most popular flowering potted plants during Christmastime include poinsettias, Christmas peppers, Christmas cacti, chrysanthemums, azaleas, African violets, and cyclamens. These also make excellent hostess gifts. Of the regular tropical houseplants, a few of the popular ones include the Norfolk Island pine, rubber plants, philodendrons, the various varieties of ferns, flowering pineapples, and grape ivy, to name just a few. Houseplant accessories like macramé hangers, decorative pots, and potting soil are other possible gift ideas.

There are quite a few different types of garden accessories that also make excellent gifts. For example, who would think of a soil test kit as a possible present? Rubberized knee pads would also make a neat and unusual Christmas gift. Measuring cups, misters, and humidity trays are a few more possibilities that the average homeowner could use and would appreciate as a Christmas gift.

Although December is not the best time of the year to select bulbs, there are a few that can be given at Christmastime. Probably the most popular is the large-flowering Dutch amaryllis. These are featured at many garden outlets in December, in some cases already in bud or beginning to flower. A few places also feature the spring-flowering tulips, daffodils, hyacinths, and crocuses during the holidays.

There are also some excellent garden books that would make good last-minute Christmas gifts. These books cover a variety of subjects—

vegetable gardening, pruning, garden construction, landscaping, houseplants, and greenhouse gardening.

Needless to say, these are only a few of the many possible gardening gift ideas. When you visit your local garden outlet or specialty firm, you will probably find dozens of other gardening gift possibilities.

Miscellaneous Winter Projects

When colder weather arrives, there are a few things that can be done inside to prepare for the spring season ahead.

The major project that can be accomplished is the cleaning of tools. Actually, tool cleanup should take place in the fall, but sometimes it is put off because of more pressing demands. At other times we simply forget about our tools until it is time to use them again. Both power and manual equipment should be checked. Take time to clean any dirty or rusty surfaces, lubricate all moving parts, and sharpen any cutting blades.

You can use a rag, brush, or putty knife to scrape off dirt, rust, or old debris. If there is a very heavy accumulation of rust or debris, a heavy steel brush is a good tool to use. Once you get the surfaces clean, rub them lightly with an oily rag.

If the mower needs to be sharpened, you would be wise to get it into the shop sometime during the winter, before they are swamped with early spring business. While your lawn mower is in the shop, have them check to see that the blades are sharp, check the spark plug, and drain and refill the crankcase. In fact, it's a good idea to have them give the mower an overall checkup, including any belts or chains. If you are mechanically inclined and like to work on your own power equipment, you are certainly aware that it is important to remove the spark plug first as a safety precaution, so that there is no chance of the machine starting accidentally.

It is essential that all moving parts of power equipment be oiled properly. If you do the oiling on your own, refer to the owner's manual. Be sure you don't overlook any part of the basic maintenance procedures.

All types of pruning shears also require some maintenance. Sharpen the blades and lightly oil all moving parts. If the blades are not coated with Teflon, they may need to be lightly buffed with steel wool or a light-grain sandpaper, after which they should be wiped down lightly with an oily rag to keep them from rusting.

Pruning shears should also be sterilized. Use a disinfectant containing 10 percent Clorox—ten teaspoons to one pint of water will give the right proportions. Simply dip the pruners in the solution.

Grass edgers and power grass whips should

also be cleaned, lubricated, buffed, tightened, or adjusted so they operate efficiently.

As long as you are cleaning your garden tools, take time to also buff and rub down the surfaces of your garden shovels and spades. Again you can use a light grade of sandpaper or steel wool for this job. Be sure to wipe them down with an oily cloth afterward. These implements should also be sharpened with a grinding wheel, stone, or file. Later in the season you may find it necessary to sharpen them again. A good sharp gardening implement makes it much easier to accomplish your gardening tasks. In the long run, it should save you a lot of time.

Your wheelbarrow or garden cart will probably also need attention. Be certain to lubricate the wheels and any other moving parts. Buff down any rusty spots and wipe them with an oily rag.

If you have a tendency to misplace some of your garden tools, now would be a good time to paint the handles in a bright color so you can easily spot them in the garden. Speaking of handles, take time to sand down any rough surfaces before you paint them. If you have any tools around the house that have weak or broken handles, they should be replaced now. You can usually find a fairly good supply of handles at local garden outlets or hardware stores. If for some reason they do not have the particular type of handle you need, they will usually special-order for you upon request.

If the connections on your garden hose are leaking or you have any leaks in the hose itself, winter is a good time to replace the old fittings and make any necessary repairs.

Tools that are kept in top working order will last longer and require very little maintenance over the years. It is time well spent to clean tools after each use.

Besides tool maintenance, there are greenhouse projects that are excellent for winter months. In December you can take cuttings of evergreens, including rhododendrons, camellias, azaleas, heather, junipers, and other flowering shrubs. Many houseplants can be started from seeds or cuttings. Houseplants looking less than their best due to winter dormancy can be moved into the greenhouse to help improve their appearance. January is an excellent month to take cuttings of geraniums, fuchsias, and evergreens. You can also start seeds of pansies, violas, and calendulas. February is an excellent month to begin cuttings of many evergreen trees and shrubs and start seeds for summer-flowering annuals.

The point of the leaf indicates the direction in which the flowers will face.

Glossary

Annual A plant that grows, flowers, goes to seed, and dies in one year.

Biennial A plant that grows the first year, flowers the second year, and then goes to seed. Many biennials will then reseed and continue this process on their own for many years.

Bolting The early flowering of a plant before it develops its crop. Cabbage, lettuce, radishes, and several other crops are subject to bolting. Often caused by rapid temperature changes, cool temperatures, and overfertilization with hot manures.

Bracts Leaves that develop just below the flowers on some plants. For example, poinsettia bracts, which most people think are the flowers because they turn red, pink, or white. On close inspection, however, you will discover the flowers singly or in clusters above.

Broadcast To simply scatter seed by hand over the area to be seeded, rather than sowing in rows.

Bud Union The point where a plant has been grafted. Usually indicated by a small knoblike growth on a tree, shrub, or rosebush.

Cambium Layer The green growth layer just next to the bark.

Candles (Pine) New growth that has an upright habit and looks similar to candles until it unfurls. The new growth on pines.

Cane Berries Types of berries that grow on canes (stocks) rather than vines.

Compost Decomposed garden waste such as grass clippings, fallen leaves, and other organic matter. Recycling of garden vegetable matter. Once decomposed, these materials are put back into the soil to enrich it.

Conifer A plant that bears cones or similar seed cases. Most are evergreen and have needlelike foliage.

Cultivate To remove weeds and debris and loosen the soil.

Deciduous Plants that naturally lose their leaves during the winter.

Drip Line The outer edge of a tree or shrub, the point where water would drip to the ground from the outer leaves of a plant. Often used as a reference point for feeding plants.

Evergreens Plants that maintain their leaves all twelve months of the year.

5-10-10 Standard commercial fertilizer used for vegetable gardening. All fertilizers have three numbers. The first is nitrogen, the second is phosphorus, and the third is potash. Canadians often use 4-10-10 instead.

Foliar Feeding Applying liquid solutions of fertilizer to the leaves of plants, where they are quickly absorbed.

Germination When seeds begin to sprout.

Girdling Usually refers to tying wire or rope too tightly around the branch or trunk of a plant; it disrupts and restricts growth, often killing the plant.

Herbicide, Preemergent A weed or grass killer that kills seeds before they begin to grow.

Herbs, Aromatic Plants used for seasoning, medicinal purposes, or garnishes. Aromatic herbs are the ones that have fragrant or smelly leaves or flowers.

Hybrid Often refers to a plant or variety that has been developed by interbreeding two or more varieties, species, or genera.

Irrigation Method Watering plants by letting the water run from the hose on the ground around the plant—puddling or soaking instead of sprinkling.

Leaching The process whereby a substance, such as fertilizer, dissolves and is carried away by rain water.

Leggy Growth New growth that is out of proportion to the rest of the plant.

Medium A soil or soilless mix used to start or replant houseplants, flowers, vegetables, and other plants.

Mottling of Leaves Discoloration or spotting of leaves.

Node The point where leaf growth begins.

Outcropping Landscape beds extending out beyond their surroundings. An extended shrub bed.

Perennial A plant that grows and flowers for many years. Some are evergreens; others may die back to the ground but will grow back again the following season.

Pinching Using your thumb and forefinger to remove (pinch off) the tip growth of plants to encourage a bushier growth habit.

Processed Manure Sterilized, dried, and bagged manure. Usually sold in 40- or 50-pound bags.

Raised Beds Planting areas that are mounded or boxed above ground level. Hilling soil is another method of raising the soil level. Soil dries out and warms up much more quickly permitting earlier planting and later harvesting.

Rank Foliage New foliage that has grown too large.

Rhizome A thickened stem with root below and growth above. The area where food energy may be stored, as in bearded iris.

Sandy Loam A combination of sandy soil and loam. Sand content provides good drainage. Loam contains more body and is a combination of silt, sand, and clay.

Spent Flowers Dead or dying flowers.

Spindly Growth Leggy, long, or flimsy new growth that has developed out of proportion to the rest of the plant.

Thatch A layer of dead grass that builds up between soil level and the blades of the grass. It keeps air, water, and fertilizer from reaching the soil below.

Twist Ties Short lengths of wire encased in a protective coating; they are less likely to damage or girdle branches, stems, and other parts of plants.

Vegetable Thinning Removing seedlings that are planted too closely together, so those remaining have sufficient space in which to properly mature.

Volatile Action An uncontrolled and unintended chemical reaction to certain conditions. For example, if temperatures are too warm, Casoron will vaporize and be lost into the air and/or is apt to burn foliage due to the vapors.

V-Shaped Furrow A planting trench made in the shape of the letter V. It is wide at the top and pointed at the bottom.

Index